AWAKEN MEGA HAPPINESS

Master the Eleven Proven Skills of Personal Excellence And Create Your Dream Life

Victoria Herocten

For information contact: address www.success-achiever.com

Edited by Red Pen Edits.
Published by Orla Kelly Publishing
ISBN: 978-0-9935923-4-8

First Edition: January 2017

Acknowledgements

I dedicate this book to all the people who have helped me whenever I needed them during my life. I would particularly like to thank Nick, Joakim Larsson, Dagmar, Mary O'Dwyer, Brenda Cloney, my granny Emma, my parents, my sister and my godmother.

I also would like to thank Anthony Robbins, Brian Tracy, Napoleon Hill, Mac Victor Hansen, Nathaniel Branden, Tadeusz Niwiński, Stephen Covey, Wanda Loskot and Peter Majewski for their wisdom which has helped me to become the person I am today.

Thanks to all the other individuals who have contributed to my life in any way; those I have ever met, have talked to, have read about or have listened to. I also would like to thank and forgive those who have hurt me and have caused me much pain. These lessons were hard, but I am stronger now thanks to them.

I dedicate this book to all the people who suffer from long-term illnesses; physical or mental and moreover, those living with epilepsy. Let the wisdom of this book help you to overcome your challenges and find strength.

Introdution

Have you ever dreamed of being a happy person? I am sure you have. And what is the level of your happiness now? Are you satisfied with your achievements, wealth, health and relationships? If you are not, I have good news for you:

You can become a happy and fulfilled person.

The only thing you need to do is to master some happiness skills and you will change your life for good. Are you ready? You can be a total novice in personal development or you can know nearly everything about that subject – my book will satisfy the needs of all readers. This book may solve at least one of your problems. I will be writing about:

- How to set and achieve your goals.
- How to design your life.
- How to take charge of your life.
- How to tackle problems and obstacles on your way to happiness and fulfilment.
- How to handle negative emotions.
- How to change negative thoughts and self-limiting beliefs.
- How to change your language to be more positive.

- How to overcome procrastination.
- How to handle an illness.
- How to stop making excuses.

The system of skills you are about to learn will change your life. This book contains a unique synthesis of ideas, methods and techniques brought together in one place. At the end of the book you will find appendices – blank worksheets which will help you to work on the skills you will learn. I would also recommend that you start using a transformation diary; the journal in which you will write your personal discoveries and where you will do some of the exercises described in this book.

The individual components of the system are not new, but I present them in a way which is easy to apply in everyday life. Each skill contains condensed tips which you can use instantly when reading this book and doing the recommended exercises described in it. They will bring you results of a greater proportion than the effort you put in. You will propel your whole life onto a road of happiness and fulfilment, greater than you have ever known. By integrating these tips into your daily life, you will become happier, healthier more self-confident and more fulfilled in your personal life. You will experience a greater sense of power, be more confident and more focused. You will be able to achieve more and get along better with people.

It does not matter if you are young or old, male or female, black or white, healthy or ill. It does not matter if you were born with a silver spoon in your mouth or if you came from a deprived background. Nature is neutral. You can become a happy and successful person no matter where you come from. I know many people who have dramatically changed their lives – and you can do the same.

It took me over 20 years of testing the happiness habits in my life. I have read plenty of books, attended many seminars and met some successful people at them; people from the USA, Poland and Ireland. I have been living in Ireland for the last ten years. Here I have started an entirely new life, one which began with long-term illness and having no friends.

I was a teacher of English and am now the member of Wexford Toastmasters – where I can polish my public speaking and leadership skills. I write articles in English and have written two e-books about domestic abuse. I am also the co-author of **The Gratitude Book** which is a bestseller and has many positive reviews on Amazon.

But before I reached today's greatness, I was an entirely different person. My father is an alcoholic; my mother is overprotective and my sister is bossy. I had been living with them for many years and was not able to grow up before I arrived in Ireland. I have had epilepsy since I was two years old, so it has been a big challenge, starting a totally new life, in a new country. Therefore, I want to show you in this book that you CAN change your life – especially those of you who are struggling with illness. Despite limits, you can be happy, achieve your goals and be successful in both your personal life and in relationships.

This book is about personal excellence, how to be happy as an individual. I mentioned relationships and describing the challenges that you can face in your life, but first, you should be happy with yourself, love yourself and forgive yourself. Without that, others will never like you in the way that you deserve.

To become a happy person, you should get to know yourself first. Nathaniel Branden in his book *The 6 Pillars of High Self-Esteem* mentioned that self-awareness is the foundation of self-esteem. You need to know your values, the roles which you play in your life, your life mission and life purpose before you start setting goals or changing your life. You will learn how to use these happiness skills in Chapter One.

Self-acceptance is the second pillar described in Branden's book. I would like you to focus on accepting your limits, such as the lack of competencies in some areas of your life and long-term illness. You will learn some powerful techniques which will help you to gain peace of mind and happiness. You will learn all of that from Chapter Two. In Chapter Three you will learn how to take responsibility for your life, how to make smart decisions and prepare to take action.

The next step is to change your beliefs – if they impede your happiness. You will learn what negative beliefs you might have and what tools to use to transform these beliefs. Chapter Four will show you how to start a new, happy life when you master the skill of changing your beliefs.

Your thoughts shape your reality. Many self-development masters confirm that truth and to be happy, you will need to transform them. I will give you some examples of positive and negative thoughts and some powerful tools which you can use to change the negative thoughts. Chapter Five will help you to create the happiness way of thinking in your life.

We express our thoughts and beliefs by saying them. Therefore, what kind of language you are using is important. Do the words spoken by you boost your enthusiasm, encourage you to take even more action to work on your goals and be happy? Or do you become angrier, more depressed and guilty after saying something? You can also accelerate the happiness of your language by using even more powerful words or metaphors. You will master your language while reading Chapter Six.

How do you handle your emotions, especially the negative ones? If you are struggling here, I will demonstrate some proven tools which will help you to master your emotions and show you how to use them to create a happy life. Chapter Seven will help you to achieve this goal.

To become a happy person, you need to train some happiness habits and eradicate the language that is making you unhappy. You will learn some proven tools which will help you to transform your life into happiness. All that wisdom will be found in Chapter Eight.

Life without goals, which you set and achieve, is never a happy life. Thus, I will show you how to master your goals. You will learn some tools which you rarely find in most of the self-help books, such as setting emergency goals and how to monitor the progress on your way to your goals' achievement. Chapter Nine is designed for all who want to set and achieve remarkable goals.

I am aware that your life transformation and your journey to happiness might not be easy. There will be problems, challenges which may impede your motivation and performance. In Chapter Ten I will show you some powerful techniques which will help you to tackle any problem.

Time management is the last, but not the least important skill you will learn in this book. You will be able to overcome procrastination and perfectionism and be able to use some powerful tools which will help you to find more time for creating a happy life. Chapter Eleven will give you answers to the question: "How to create an extra hour each day?"

Are you ready to master these happiness skills? Before you start reading, check your attitude. This book is not for someone who:

- is not committed to mastering the happiness skills presented here.
- does not believe that these skills work.
- does not believe that his or her life can be happier.
- is not ready to take the challenge of mastering the happiness skills.
- is not willing to pay the price of becoming a happier person.

Let me explain. Firstly, I am aware that some issues described in this book might overwhelm you, or you are just not at this stage of personal development yet. Don't worry. Any skill that you will master will bring you nearer to happiness and self-fulfilment. Just changing your thinking will help you to attract happy people into your life. Secondly, there will be more than one tip presented in the chapters about changing beliefs, thoughts and language. Use one of them at a time, practice each one until you master the technique. Even if you might think that you are not ready for taking charge of your life and learning the happiness skills, don't forget that you can find other people who might benefit from reading this book. Give it to your spouse or relative, or even a friend as a gift. In this way, you may spread happiness all over the world.

You need to read this book more than once as every time you read it, you will find something new and inspiring. Some issues described in here need reflection and digestion before you apply them. Don't rush. Your growth will take some time. If you start monitoring your progress daily, you will reap the crops from the seeds you have sown while working with this book.

The strategies I am sharing with you are not a quick fix. They will not help all your problems to disappear after one reading – even worse, scanning it. Of course, you can choose one tool at a time and I would recommend that you work separately on your thoughts, beliefs and language. Also, if you read this book without doing the exercises described in it, your happiness level will not increase as theory without practice is not enough for achieving success.

However, if you take small steps and regularly monitor your progress, each day will bring you closer to ultra-happiness. Remember that it took you some time to learn how to walk, write, read or even how to use a computer. The same applies to happiness. By developing some good habits, you will gain peace of mind which is one of the ingredients of happiness.

This book is about personal development, focusing on your individual growth. I am writing another book and in it you will find useful tips on how to be happy around people. First you start by improving your life as an individual. You cannot love other people until you learn to love yourself. You will not tolerate flaws in other people until you accept your own. You will be critical of others because you criticise all your own achievements. As Brian Tracy said, your outer world will reflect your inner one. Changing your beliefs, thinking and language will instantly transform your relationships with other people. You will be more positive and people will want to spend more time with you.

Each chapter starts with an episode of my friend Tina, who has also struggled with the challenges we will tackle in this book. I met her at a training event in Dublin. Then I started working with her and I show you Tina's story as proof that you can also transform your life to become a happier person.

Tina is living with her boyfriend Tom, her parents and her sister. She is thirty years old. Her father Ted is an alcoholic and her mother Donna is domineering. She is working as a manager in one of the well-known multi-national companies in Cork City. Also, her boyfriend is sometimes aggressive.

Tina did not seem to be happy when I met her. She had hit a wall; she didn't seem to have any chance for promotion in her job and did not know how to deal with her family or her boyfriend. She also could not accept her recent weight gain and often felt helpless. I have since helped her to accept her life by making some changes, which in turn helped her to become a much happier person.

However, she did like working on computers and was interested in e-business. She had become involved in some affiliates, yet Tina was not sure which things she was doing right and which wrong. Having worked with me on her goals, she has since started her own business and is now working as a self-employed person, having given up her job in the company. You too can also change your professional life. How do you accomplish it? Read my book and master the happiness skills described there.

Because of working in the office and sitting for many hours, Tina became overweight and started to worry about her attractiveness. Tina had never set herself goals, she had finished her MBA degree and by chance she had found that job. She had been stuck in that job until we started working on her life. She had never given any thought to whether her goals were hers, whether she had really wanted them. She studied for the MBA because her mother was a successful businesswoman running a big pub in Dublin. Her mother wanted Tina to take over the business. How did Tina master setting and achieving her awesome goals? (I will give you the answer later in this book.)

When I met Tina, she was a shy woman, using the language of a victim and finding excuses for everything I suggested her to try. She had many self-limiting beliefs, for example that she will never be good at business. Therefore, Tina did not make much money from the affiliates she was involved in. Sometimes she was even losing 200 EUR per week on affiliate fees and had not considered changing her field of business.

Tina was a heavy smoker, smoking forty cigarettes per day. While working with me, she has given up her addiction and started exercising, running and callanetics.

However, Tina was a gifted speaker and often gave presentations within the company. Because she was a woman, it was harder for her to ask for a promotion and be noticed by the executives. Her negative thoughts and beliefs, together with an inability to cope with emotions, impaired her career.

During her MBA studies, she learned the basics of time management and some of them were applied in her job. Yet when she also tried to deal with affiliates, she had been lost and overloaded with all the tasks she had to do. Everything changed when I started to show her how to use the Pareto Principle, the four-quadrant formula according to which she is working now. She has improved her performance at work and started to make some money with the affiliates. How has she done that? You will find the answer in this book.

I would like you to treat the skills described in this book as if given to you by your best friend or your teacher. When you were at school, no one has taught you how to set life values or some awesome goals.

No one has told you that we often think negatively and use disempowering language. Now you can learn the skills which are necessary to become a happy person. Refer to the tips in this book at a time of doubt or lack of motivation. I am keeping my fingers crossed for your transformation and the creation of your happy, fulfilled life.

Victoria Herocten

Disclaimer

This book is not intended to provide and does not constitute medical advice. The content in *Awaken Mega Happiness* is designed to support, not replace, medical or psychiatric treatment. Please seek professional care if you believe you may have a condition.

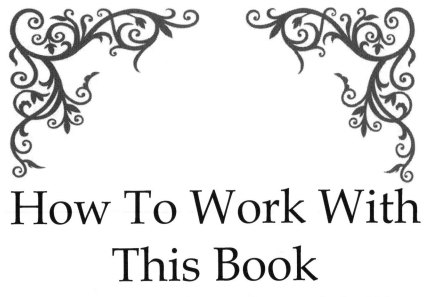

How To Work With This Book

In the past, I was a teacher. I have tested many methods which were efficient in learning a foreign language by my students. Changing your life and reaching happiness is also like learning a foreign language and one of my chapters will teach you how to use the happiness language.

You have been programmed by your parents, teachers, religion and the media. You often do not know what is right and what is wrong. Then out of the blue, you notice that your life can be different with new values, beliefs, taking responsibility and constantly working on your goals.

Our subconscious mind is a great learner. You have learned how to speak, write and calculate, but also you have learned how to think. And because you can learn everything, you can change your life and become a happy person by learning new, uplifting thinking, beliefs and change your values.

You can also unlearn things in your life, by not using them. Think of the foreign language which you have learned at school, but have had no opportunity to speak. You must practice it to be fluent again.

There is good and bad news about it. The good news is that when you abandon your negative beliefs, thinking and language, you will be able to hear the happiness ones. However, the bad news is that the old thoughts, beliefs and habits will never disappear. So, use the new skills regularly.

How do you work with this book?

1. You need the notebook called your transformation diary in this book, to define life values, setting your goals or changing your beliefs. In this way, you will be able to reflect on them and write the new ones, if necessary. In the case of setting and evaluating the progress of your goals, writing is a must. The same applies to questioning negative beliefs or thoughts. I started my work in 2003, by doing Nathaniel Branden's 30-week training from the book *6 Pillars of the High Self-Esteem*. Each week, for five days I ended some sentences by writing quick answers. Then on the sixth day, I analysed these answers and wrote conclusions. When I checked my notes a year later, I was surprised how much had changed in my life. This fact illustrates only one example where writing is helpful to transform the life.

    Print the blank worksheets from this book or draw tables to match them in your transformation diary. I suggest that you file and bind your printed sheets, in order not to lose them. After a month, ninety days and in one year, check your written recordings and make conclusions. What has changed in your life to become a happy person? Optionally, you can do all your transformation log on your computer or typing notes on your phone. However, by traditional writing, you will master the new skills faster.

2. You can also use a Dictaphone to record positive affirmations or your goals and then listen to them daily. But goals must be written down too. I will write more about using this technique in one of the chapters of this book.

3. Dedicate some time to working on your happiness – listening to uplifting audio, reading inspiring books and analysing your achievements and challenges.

4. In the case of problems, always refer to Chapter Nine and ask the ten powerful questions there. They will help you to overcome the lack of motivation and discouragement. Good luck on your way to your ultimate happiness.

Contents

Chapter 1
Discover Your Life Compass

When Tina started work with me, she had no idea what happiness it. Like most of her friends she thought that a good job, having a boyfriend and her own house was everything she needed to achieve peace of mind. However, she had never thought what role she is performing in her life and what is her life's purpose. This chapter will show you how to define happiness. You will learn how to:

- Define happiness.
- Know what is necessary to feel happy.
- Know what skills are needed to create long-term happiness.
- Identify important things in life.
- Define the values in life.
- Transform your values into the happiness ones.
- Determine what roles you act in your life.
- Define your identity.
- Define your life mission.
- Define the vision of your ideal life.
- Define the direction of your life.
- Measure what progress you make on your life path.

Happiness

What is happiness?

According to Wikipedia: "Happiness is a mental or emotional state of well-being defined by positive or pleasant emotions ranging from contentment to intense joy. A variety of biological, psychological, religious and philosophical approaches have striven to define happiness and identify its sources. Various research groups, including positive psychology, are employing the scientific method to research questions about what happiness is, and how it might be attained."

Happiness can be defined differently in various religions. In Judaism, the biblical verse "worship The Lord with gladness; come before him with joyful songs," stresses joy in the service of God. In Catholicism, "the ultimate end of human existence consists infelicity, blessed happiness. In Buddhism, ultimate happiness is only achieved by overcoming craving in all forms."

How happy are you?

Tina had no idea if she was happy or not. She was doing well at her job but was unable to handle her family in a way that gave her peace of mind. Sometimes their relationships were beautiful and then she had the illusion of happiness, yet in most cases, there were conflicts and uneasiness.

At first, fill in the questionnaire below. Choose one option for each of the statements:

	Always	Often	Some times	Rarely	Never	Score
I like and respect myself.						
I am optimistic.						
I know how to have fun						
I have a good work/life balance.						
I enjoy good relationships with others.						
I make time what gives me more pleasure.						
I know my strengths and qualities.						
I am positive and motivated.						
I have personal boundaries.						
I believe that I deserve the best that life has to offer.						
TOTAL SCORE						

Calculate your score. Mark the number of points for each statement using the scale:

always – 5 points, often – 4 points, sometimes – 3 points, rarely – 2 points, never – 1 point.

Then add up all the points.

10-25 Your happiness needs improvement. You do not know what it means to be happy. Most likely your parents have not shown you how to be happy, and your later experiences only affirmed that. You need to read this book and follow all the steps to improve your happiness skills.

26-40 You manifest an average happiness. Most people belong to this category. You have ups and downs, sometimes you can enjoy pleasure and sometimes not. This book will help you to improve your happiness skills.

41-50 Congratulation, you belong to the small group of happy people. However, if you are reading this book, there is still something to improve. Check the next chapters and work on the area found in the next questionnaire.

Now I want you to do another test. This time, you will evaluate how well you master the happiness skills which I will describe in this book.

Happiness Skills Test

These are the skills which will enable you to enjoy the long-term mega happiness. If you improve at least one of them, the chances are that your level of happiness will grow dramatically. Look at the table below. Fill it in, ticking one of the answers: yes, a bit, or no.

	Yes	Some-what	No
I have defined my life values.			
I have established my life path.			
I know my beliefs.			
I have set my long-term goals.			
I have set my 90-days goals.			
I have set my monthly goals.			
I know my definition of happiness.			
I've taken responsibility for my life.			
I am ready for change.			
I can make decisions easily.			
I can face the challenges of my life.			
I accept my limits and illnesses.			
I practice gratitude.			
I can handle negative emotions.			
I can destroy negative thoughts and do it on daily basis.			
I have destroyed self-limiting beliefs.			
I can overcome procrastination.			
I can motivate myself to take action.			
I can overcome addictions and bad habits.			
I can manage stress.			
I can manage the time effectively.			
I use the language of happiness.			

Now count the score for each skill:

yes – 3 points for yes, a bit – 1 point, no – 0 points.

List all of the happiness skills. To make things easier for you, choose three items. They are your biggest challenges and need immediate work. The next chapters will show you how to train these happiness skills effectively.

....

....

....

If there are more skills which scored 0. List them all in your transformation diary and choose three which you think impair your happiness the most.

....

....

....

Now list three habits which are partially mastered (i.e. which have 1 point). They will be your secondary challenges.

....

....

....

Now you know the starting point for your happiness level. You can read every chapter thoroughly or choose the happiness skills which need attention and work on them. I assume that you will need to read this book more than once as you might not be ready to implement all the habits during the first reading. Some skills are more complex and contain more issues to work through. Therefore, each skill includes the most common questions. I am giving you the solution and will show you how to master happiness skills.

Life Values and Roles

How to Define What is Important in Life

Knowing what is important in your life will help you to make better choices, and they will bring you more happiness. Let's do an experiment.

Take your transformation diary and write down all of the things you did during the last week. Be very precise – add hours or at least the length of time spent at these activities. Continue to record your activities for the next few days.

Now look at the list. What can you see? The map of your values. It shows you what is critical for you. The more time you spend dwelling on a given thing, the more important it is for you. Circle the activities which take up most of your day. Define why you spent so much time on any given thing. Choose the five of these activities which were the most time-consuming.

ACTIVITY   **WHY DID I DO IT**

....

....

....

....

....

You have just found your positive values. Then do the same exercise for the rest of the activities on your list. The next step is to list the things that you dislike doing and define why you avoid them. Doing this will help you to discover the negative values in your life.

ACTIVITY	WHY DID I AVOID IT
....	....
....	....
....	....
....	....
....	....

How to Define Life Values

The Move-Towards Values

According to Google: "Values are the basis for your behaviour and motivation. Values are hierarchical, abstract and dynamic concepts that mostly describe what we desire or seek to achieve. When I say you hold a value, it means that you aspire to something, or you feel that value is worth something to you. Values have a hierarchy, and there are some of them for which you would sacrifice your life."

If you have done the exercise from the previous question, you can easily find your values. However, or any relationship I will now show you a second way of defining your values.

Now make a list what is important for you – brainstorm, without thinking for too long.

List 10 things.

1. .... 6. ....
2. .... 7. ....
3. .... 8. ....
4. .... 9. ....
5. .... 10. ....

Define what each value means for you. Love or work can have different meanings to you and your friend. For example, love can mean taking care of the other person or it can mean passionate sex. Now it is your turn to define what the most important things in your life mean to you. Then number the values from the most to the least important:

VALUE   **DEFINITION**

....
                                         ....
....
                                         ....
....
                                         ....
....
                                         ....
....
                                         ....

If you have no idea what values to choose, here are some examples:

home, family, fun, health, beauty, challenge, honesty, flexibility, my spouse/partner, achievement, comfort, creativity, dignity, equality, environment, excellence, integrity, fairness, fitness, forgiveness, freedom, ambition, character, friendship, generosity, cheerfulness, courage, gratitude, growth, happiness, communication, adventure, honour, children, education, admiration, wealth

The Move-Away-From Values

After having defined the move-towards values, time has come to find out what repels you. Follow the steps described below:

1. Make a similar list with the values which repel you – because there are some things which are important, but you avoid them, or you are ashamed of them. What are yours?

List three of them below:

1. …......................................
2. …......................................
3. …......................................

If you are not sure, choose examples from the box below:

uncertainty, manipulation, anger, distress, humiliation, guilt, illness, corruption, deception, emptiness, frustration, fear, aggression, hate, loneliness, rage, depression, remorse, anxiety, pain, self-criticism, hostility, self-pity, failure, shyness and debt.

2. Now define each move-away-from value

VALUE	DEFINITION
....	....
	....
....	....
	....
....	....
	....
....	....

3. Number the values from the most to the least important. In this way, you will learn what the thing you move away from the most is. This value may stop you from taking a reasonable risk and leaving your comfort zone.

4. In each group (the moved-towards and the moved-away-from values), circle the three values. The positive values are so important for you that you sacrifice your life to keep them. The negative values are so painful that you do everything to avoid them. These six values are critical as they will always have an impact on your decisions – unless you transform the negative values into some positive ones.

How to Create the List of Happiness Values

What do you think looking at the lists of values? Are you sure these values will bring you plenty of happiness? I can tell you – probably not. What's more, your negative values make you unhappy when you focus on them.

Many unhappy people focus on the things that they want to avoid and attracting more of that. How to change it? You can transform the negative values into positive ones. Aiming for the positive values will make you happy. Here are some examples of transformation:

aggression to peacefulness	hostility to friendship	depression to joy
anger to excitement	manipulation to fair play	emptiness to love and warmth
anxiety to gratitude	loneliness to giving away	humiliation to admiration
illness to growth	uncertainty to hope	self-criticism to self-love

frustration to determination	remorse to self-confidence	guilt to self-confidence
helplessness to practicality		

How to Define the Roles of Life

Defining the roles of your life is another brick of your happiness foundation. List who you are in your family (e.g. the spouse, children, parents, siblings, relatives) and in your job (e.g. manager, the boss).

WHO I AM IN MY FAMILY   **WHO I AM AT WORK**

....

....

....

Here are some more examples:

home-maker, husband, instructor, manager, salesperson, sister, mother, adult child, therapist, teacher, coach, employee, business man/woman, godmother, care taker, grandma, breadwinner, uncle, volunteer, lover, friend, any occupation you do at work (i.e. accountant, lawyer, doctor, musician, writer etc.)

Now define each of the roles – what they mean to you:

WHO I AM IN MY FAMILY   **DEFINITION**

....
                              ....
....

....

....

....

....

....

....

....

....

....

....

....

WHO I AM AT WORK   **DEFINITION**

....

....

....

....

....

....

....

....

....

....

....

....

....

....

Now you know what you are doing in your life. For example, consider whether you are really happy being a lawyer. If not, you can learn a new profession. Some roles are life-lasting, like being a mother or a daughter, yet they change over time. If you are a mother, you will treat your child differently when they are twenty-five than when they were five.

How to Define Your Identity

Your identity is usually defined by the environment – parents, religion, society. But have you ever thought that you could determine your identity yourself? I will show you how to do it.

Victoria Herocten

"Unlike a drop of water which loses its identity when it joins the ocean, man does not lose his being in the society in which he lives. Man's life is independent. He is born not for the development of the society alone, but for the development of his self."
- B. R. Ambedkar

Think for a while. Do you like the name and surname that has been given to you at birth? If not, you can always change it, even without getting married. Remember that identity is what distinguishes you from everyone else.

Learn about your name in the dictionary. Discover if your name would be described in just three words, or would your narrative consume a page or even a volume of its own?

Victoria does not only apply to the famous British Queen or the posh (for example, Victoria Beckham), but also to a Swedish princess. You can find the following description of Victoria on **www. behindthename.com**: "Means 'victory' in Latin, being borne by the Roman goddess of victory. It is also a feminine form of VICTORIUS. This name was borne by a 4th century saint and martyr from North Africa. Though in use elsewhere in Europe. The name was very rare in the English-speaking world until the 19th century, when Queen Victoria began her long rule of Britain. She was named after her mother, who was of German royalty. Many geographic areas are named after the queen, including an Australian state and a Canadian city."

Right now, write down the definition you would find if you were to look up your name in a dictionary.

....

Now create your ID card. It will represent who you truly are. What would be on it? Will you include a picture or not? What about your vital statistics? Will you list your physical description, your accomplishments, your emotions, your beliefs, your motto or your abilities? Take a moment to describe what would be on this identity card.

....

My Personal ID

My name's definition (e.g. in the dictionary, in the media, by religion)

....

....

Who I am according to my own judgement

....

....

....

....

....

Establish Your Life Path

Knowing your purpose will help you to be happy and fulfilled. You will have lots of enthusiasm and motivation to work on your goals and to act the roles of your life.

"Awake, arise, and assert yourself, you dreamers of the world. Your star is now in the ascendancy."
- Napoleon Hill, Think and Grow Rich

How to Define the Vision of Life – The Ideal Life

"To create an extraordinary quality of life, you must create a vision that's not only obtainable, but that is sustainable." - Anthony Robbins

Enthusiasm for life and passion are the traits that all successful and happy people cultivate. You need a compelling vision for your life, the vision that is so powerful that you are driven to do whatever it takes to achieve it.

You find fulfilment and joy when you pursue something greater than the current moment. The ultimate vision flows from knowing that you have had a special and unique purpose on this planet. Use the 5-step formula to use to create your ultimate vision. Here is what to do:

1. Go to the place that inspires you and where you won't be interrupted. It might be the beach, a park, an art museum. Take this book and the transformation diary with you. Turn off your mobile phone.

2. Answer the questions below in writing. Take your time and think on each of the questions. However, when you are writing, don't think too much about the answer, don't evaluate it, be spontaneous:

• What do you want to create for your life?

• What would your life be about?

• What do you want to contribute to your life and the lives of others?

• What do you want to give?

• What do you want to feel?

• What do you want to share?

- Who do you want to be?
- What would get you up early and keep you up late at night?
- If you had no fear about moving forward, what would you do in your life?
- What challenges might you be excited to overcome?

After doing this exercise, I realised that I wanted to be a writer, to teach people how to be happy, how to overcome their challenges and how to awaken their ultimate potential. What about you?

3. Check if your vision is emotionally charged. Your vision should have the power to move you to action and provide a consistent focus and continually remind you what it is you are committed to creating in your life, career or business.

4. Create your ideal life in great detail. Stop concerning yourself with the process of getting from where you are to where you go. This advice will help you assess where you are versus where you want to be. Write for 20 minutes without interruption.

5. Create a collage. Try drawing or cutting out pictures of things that inspire you or that describe your vision. You can also choose a song that becomes the theme song for your life. Get creative, as there is no right or wrong way to describe your ultimate vision.

How to Define a Personal Mission Statement

According to Stephen Covey: "a personal mission statement is based on habit 2 of *The 7 Habits of Highly Effective People* and it is called 'begin with the end in mind'." The most efficient way to start is to develop a mission statement with the end in mind. This statement does not only focus on what you want to be character-wise, but also on what you want to do about your contribution of achievements. Writing a mission statement is one of the most important foundations of happiness and leading a fulfilled life.

"Successful people are always looking for opportunities to help others. Unsuccessful people are always asking, What's in it for me?" - Brian Tracy

What is a mission statement? It is like a personal constitution, the basis for making significant, life-directing and daily decisions, amid the circumstances and emotions that affect your life.

Why should you create a mission statement of your own and choose to live by it? Because then you can flow with changes and you don't need prejudgement's or prejudices to figure out everything else in your life.

You will not create your mission statement overnight. It takes deep introspection, careful analysis and often many rewrites to produce it in its final form. You may need several weeks before you feel comfortable with your mission statement, until you feel it is complete and that it manifests your deepest values and directions. Review it regularly and make minor changes as the years bring additional insights or developments. Do it in writing. Spend 30 minutes every day, writing your mission until you are happy with it.

Collect notes, quotes and ideas you may want to use as a resource before you start writing your personal mission statement. Take a pen and the transformation diary which you have used in the previous exercise. Find a place where no one will interrupt you; it can be a quiet room, a park, a river bank. Turn off your cell phone.

A personal mission consists of three parts. Each of them is the answer to the three questions below:
- What do I want to do?
- Who do I want to help?
- What is the result? What value will I create?

Now write down the answers to these questions. Write the first thing that pops into your head without editing. Give yourself less than 60 seconds a question. Remember to be honest. Alternatively, you can use the questions requiring more detailed answers.

- What were your favourite things to do in the past? What about now?
- Who inspires you most?
- Which qualities in these people inspire you?
- What are you good at? (your skills)
- What do people ask you for help with?
- If you had to teach something, what would you teach?
- What causes do you firmly believe in?
- What were some challenges, difficulties and hardships you've overcome or are in the process of overcoming? How did you do it?

Now time has come for the last, but not least important question:

You are now 90 years old, sitting in a rocking chair on your porch. You are blissful and happy and are pleased with the wonderful life you have been blessed with. **While looking back at your life and all that you have achieved and acquired, all the relationships you have developed – what matters to you most?** List it.

....

....

....

....

"Writing or reviewing a mission statement changes you because it forces you to think through your priorities deeply, carefully, and to align your behaviour with your beliefs."
- Stephen Covey, '7 Habits of Highly Effective People'

If you are still struggling with writing your life mission, I will give you these tips:

Review your mission. List of action words you connect with. For example: accomplish, guide, educate, teach, understand, master, encourage, organise, empower, spread, improve, produce, give, inspire, nurture, integrate, motivate, promote, travel, share, satisfy, write.

List everything and everyone that you believe you can help. For example: people, organisations, causes, groups, the environment. How will the 'who' from your above answer benefit from what you 'do'? For example: educate people to be happy, to use a computer, etc. Combine all the information in one piece of writing.

For example:

"I am a committed recreational skater's advocate. I will do everything in my power to ensure that novices achieve the most positive first experience possible. This means encouraging them to buy the best equipment they can afford and to learn the basic skills, especially how to use the heel brake. To fight skate bans due to congested popular trails, I will help more experienced skaters build their speed and hill skills so they can train on a wider variety of trails without the risk of alienating other users. I will continue to encourage all skaters to improve their skills so they can adopt a well-rounded online lifestyle. "- Lizz Miller

My mission statement

....

....

....

....

I am aware that you might not be happy with your mission statement at the moment. Spend 30 minutes every day writing your mission statement, then review it after a week, and rewrite if necessary. Do this for as long as you need to, until you have the ideal mission statement.

How to Define the Direction of My Life

Tina said: "Okay, I know my life mission and vision. But how do I implement it?" To answer this question, you need to define your life direction.

"All successful people men and women are big dreamers. They imagine what their future could be, ideal in every respect, and then they work every day toward their distant vision, that goal or purpose." — Brian Tracy

Life direction is the sequence of goals which belong to one of your life categories.

For example, you can be good at history, study history on the third level and do research in history, work in a museum or heritage centre. In this case, history is your direction.

The same may apply to your job; you have studied marketing and management, have become a junior clerk, then the junior manager and a senior manager. In this case, control determines your career. Finding someone, getting married, having children and follow their growth, then having grandchildren describes the "family and relationships" life category. How to find a life direction?

1. Write down what goals you have achieved during your life. Refer to the life categories: physical health, mental health, finance, relationships, career, spiritual life, personal development. For example: what school you have graduated from, what job(s) you have found, where you have lived, what was your income, how did it change during your life, what partners did you have.

2. Find similarities. For example: you could choose the same kind of boyfriend or your spouse is like your father. You could have rented three flats so far, all similar. You could work in a company, being promoted in time, but within the same department.

3. Name the direction of each life category. For example: rented houses, abusive boyfriends, teaching people, taking care of family members. Define if you are happy with that. If not, what would you like to change?

4. Determine what goals you can set for the future in the direction you want to follow. If you are not sure how to do it now, read Chapter Nine and follow the tips described there.

How to Measure Progress on Your Life's Path

To answer this question, you need to look at your life from a few perspectives: in the past, now and in the future. You will reach the moment of truth, but also pride when you notice how much you have achieved within such an extended period. Let's analyse the last 5-year period of your life. Take the transformation diary and think for a while: Where were you in your career, relationships, health and fun five years ago? Don't evaluate, just write the answers down. Then mark how satisfied you are with your achievements now. Use the one to ten scale, where one means 'total disaster' and 10 'extremely happy'.

5 years ago

The Area of Life	Satisfaction 1-10	Comments
Physical health (weight, fitness)	....	....
Mental health (mood, fears)	....	....
Relationships (family, networks)	....	....
Career (job, business)	....	....
Finance (living conditions assets, salary/profit)	....	....
Spiritual Life	....	....
Personal development (goals, thinking, beliefs)	....	....

Fun	....	....
		....
		....

Now time has come to define your starting point in the major areas of your life. This exercise is very important as you will use the conclusions in Chapter Nine when setting your short-term and long-term goals.

Fill in the same table, but this time describe today, the moment you are doing this exercise:

Today

The Area of Life	Satisfaction 1-10	Comments
Physical health (weight, fitness)	....	....
		....
		....
Mental health (mood, fears)	....	....
		....
		....
Relationships (family, networks)	....	....
		....
		....
Career (job, business)	....	....
		....
		....

Finance
(living conditions
assets, salary/profit)   ….........   …....................
                                                    …....................
                                                    …....................

Spiritual Life   ….........   …....................
                                                    …....................
                                                    …....................

Personal development
(goals, thinking, beliefs)   ….........   …....................
                                                    …....................
                                                    …....................

Fun   ….........   …....................
                                                    …....................
                                                    …....................

Again, evaluate your achievements. Use the same scale from one to ten, where 1 means 'total disaster' and 10 'extremely satisfied'.

Tina became proud after doing these two exercises because she noticed enormous progress within the last five years. The only challenge was her health; taking medication and her weight. I told her that she could change it, by defining what to achieve in the future.

Now look what you have written in the table referring to the past and in the other one referring to the present. What conclusions can you make? Are you happy with your achievements? Write your comments in the space provided and in your transformation diary:

…..

…..

…..

Even if you are not happy with your discoveries now, don't worry. The next chapters will help you to tackle these challenges. The first thing you need to do is to accept the reality. The next chapter will help you with this.

Now think about the future. What kind of life would you like to have in 5 years' time? Your health, career, relationship? Reflect on that and fill in the table below. You can use your life vision as a helping guide.

Future (5 years' time)

The Area of Life	Satisfaction 1-10	Comments
Physical health (weight, fitness)	....	....
Mental health (mood, fears)	....	....
Relationships (family, networks)	....	....
Career (job, business)	....	....

Finance
living conditions,
assets, salary/profit)   …..……..   …..……………..
                                                            ………………….
                                                            …..……………..

Spiritual Life   …..……..   …..……………..
                                                            ………………….
                                                            …..……………..

Personal development
(goals, thinking, beliefs)   …..……..   …..……………..
                                                            ………………….
                                                            …..……………..

Fun   …..……..   …..……………..
                                                            ………………….
                                                            …..……………..

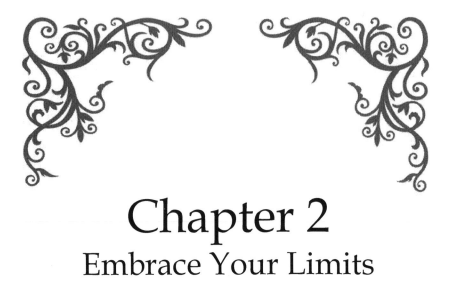

Chapter 2
Embrace Your Limits

Now you have much greater knowledge about your life and where you are at the moment. Regardless of whether or not you are happy with your discoveries right now, do not worry. The next chapters are written to help tackle the challenges in your life. But first thing you need to accept the reality. This chapter will help you deal with this.

Tina had a big problem with accepting herself. She hated her fear of failure and had a general anxiety disorder. Being on medication, she has put on weight and has started to feel uncomfortable going to bed with her boyfriend.

I have shown her how to accept her shortcomings and long-term illness. Tina has learned that having a mental illness is not a stigma, that this is the same kind of sickness as diabetes or epilepsy.

I also would like to help you to accept your limits and flaws so that you can enjoy more happiness. In this chapter, you will learn:

- What self-acceptance is.
- How to accept your limits.
- How to handle self-criticism.
- How to apply compassion in life.
- How to stop comparing to others.

- How to accept your illness or disability.

Self-acceptance

At the moment, you do not need to think about whether the future described in the table is real or not. You will validate this in Chapter Nine.

How many times did you tell yourself: "I hate my looks, my little achievements, my health limits?" Doing so you manifest a lack of self-acceptance which makes you unhappy. And you want to be happy. This chapter will help you to accept your limits and health problems.

So, what is self-acceptance? It is loving and being happy with who you are now. It's agreement with yourself to appreciate, validate, accept and support who you are at this moment.

Self-acceptance leads to a new life with new possibilities. You may have trouble accepting yourself because of a lack of motivation or have the misconception that if you are happy with yourself you won't change things about yourself.

Why Is It Important to Accept Limits and Long-Term Illnesses?

You might ask: "Why should I accept my limits and long-term health problems? I have the right to be angry! Why should I suffer when other people are illness-free and enjoy a better life?" I will tell you why. Because even if you have an illness, are short, slower than other people – you still have lots to offer to the world. Here is why it is advisable to practice self-acceptance.

You gain peace of mind. It is much better to start to focus on something that you have than on the things you lack. How to do this? I will teach you later in this chapter. You will also gain peace of mind because of being authentic: you are aware of your pros and cons, acknowledge them and use your strengths to live a full life.

You will think positive. The universal law of focus states that what you focus on grows. If you only think about how miserable you are because of your limits and how unfair the life is, the chances are that you will notice only these things in life – which confirms your expectation. On the other hand, if you focus on your strengths and how you can make other people happy, you will notice that you can help many people, who in turn can help you.

How to Accept Life Limits?

1. Be kind to yourself. You may be hesitant to show even a shred of self-kindness because you see it as selfish. However, the key to self-compassion is "to understand that weakness and frailty are part of the human experience," according to Deborah Serani. She adds: "Coming to accept who you are involves loving yourself because of your flaws, not despite them."

2. Celebrate your strengths. According to Ryan Howes, Ph.D.: "We are much better collectors of our shortcomings than our strengths." When you start focusing on your strengths, then your limits will not be so critical and they will stop bothering you. The feeling that you are in control and can do something about the challenge will make you happy. Write down five of your strengths now. Then copy the list to your calendar or somewhere where it is easily seen. Read this list daily after waking up and before going to bed.

1. ....
2. ....
3. ....
4. ....
5. ....

Examples: I'm a kind person, I'm compassionate, conscientious, hard-working, witty, flexible, a good listener. Howes suggests making another list. This time write down ten accomplishments: the hardships you've overcome, all the goals you've achieved, all the connections you've made. And again, keep this list nearby to read it in the times of doubt and low mood.

1. ....
2. ....
3. ....
4. ....
5. ....
6. ....
7. ....
8. ....
9. ....
10. ....

3. Set an intention. According to psychotherapist Jeffrey Sumber, MA: "Self-acceptance begins with intention. It is vital that we set an intention for ourselves that we are willing to shift paradigms from a world of blame, doubt and shame to a world of allowance, tolerance, acceptance and trust."

Therefore, right now, set an intention of living your life with self-acceptance. Make a commitment to accept your life, body and limits as they are.

Today ....(date) I .... (your name), decide to live a happy life, accepting my body, health limits and the past. In particular, I accept this list of five things that I dislike about myself and my life at this moment:

1. ....
2. ....
3. ....
4. ....
5. ....

Your signature _____

4. Quiet your inner critic. Many people equate their inner critic with a voice of reason. You may think that your inner critic is only speaking the truth, this is not always the case. To shut down your inner critic, you can choose a realistic mantra. For example, you could use this one: "I am only a human being, I am doing the best that I can. That is all I can do." Write your own mantra below:

....

....

5. Forgive yourself. Past regrets can prevent you from practicing self-acceptance. Thus, forgive yourself and move on.

"Whether it's about something you've done or a personality quirk that resulted in a social faux pas, it's important to learn from the mistake, make efforts to grow, and accept that you can't change the past." - Howes

When the twinges of remorse resurface, remember these words:
"I made the best decision with the information I had at the time. The behaviour or decision might not seem correct in hindsight, but at the time it seemed like the best choice."

Write down the three things which you want to forgive yourself:

I _____ (your name), forgive myself:

1. ....
2. ....
3. ....

Signed ....

6. With whom do you spend the most time? Are they nurturing you or do they disempower and criticise you? Make a list of the six people who you spend the most time with:

1. ....
2. ....
3. ....
4. ....
5. ....
6. ....

Now answer the questions:
- Which of them speaks negatively to me?
- Who reinforces my negative self-talk?
- Why do I allow such people to hurt me?

This last question is crucial because it is you who chooses the people to spend the time with. Instead of wasting your precious time in your life with the negative people focus on the connections with those who support and empower you.

7. Create a support system. Now make a list of all the people who could support you. They can be your family neighbours, friends, co-workers or just somebody you have met during your holiday travelling. Choose six people:

1. ....
2. ....
3. ....
4. ....
5. ....
6. ....

Answer the question:

• What specific support can I receive from them?

....

....

8. Grieve the loss of unrealised dreams. Howes says that many of our problems with self-acceptance come from our inability to reconcile who we are with the idealised dreams of our youth. So, you need to mourn these dreams, admit that you have lost something and that it causes you pain.

However, while having lost something, you have achieved something else instead. Write down 10 things which you have accomplished in your life:

1. .... 6. ....
2. .... 7. ....
3. .... 8. ....
4. .... 9. ....
5. .... 10. ....

9. Perform charitable acts. Contributing to the lives of other people can help you to feel needed and fulfilled. This kind of taking action, in turn, will make you happy. Instead of thinking about what you cannot stand in your life, think how many people are satisfied because of your help. List the people you have helped here:

……………………………………   ……………………………………
……………………………………   ……………………………………
……………………………………   ……………………………………

10. Speak to your Higher Self. Susan Jeffers describes your empowering voice as the Higher Self while your inner critic is the Lower Self. Now you can practice how to develop your Higher Self.

Visualise that your Higher Self lies deep within you. Imagine that your Higher Self is stepping outside of you and is looking at you in your current life circumstance or situation. Imagine what this highest or best self advises you to do. Write that down and take immediate action to implement this solution.

In this way, you can tap into the wisdom that already lies within you This exercise teaches you how to be your best self and demonstrate empathy, compassion and love towards yourself. Take a few minutes to meditate and practice this visualisation whenever you are in crisis or need some direction or some self-soothing.

11. Fake it 'til you make it. If you are unconvinced that you are a worthy person, keep the faith and keep at it. Keep practicing self-compassion. Do the exercises described in this chapter as if you believe you can do them. If you feel reluctant to accept yourself, do this as if you want to accept yourself. Create a habit of working regularly on your self-acceptance.

How to Handle Self-Criticism by Cognitive-Behavioural Therapy

Now the time has come to deal with your inner critic, the chatterbox of the Lower Self. You can use various strategies and tools. I will describe one in detail, the cognitive behavioural method.

You can use cognitive and behavioural strategies for reducing self-criticism. By doing so, you are improving self-confidence and self-esteem. However, people sometimes have difficulty following the rules of the cognitive method or become discouraged doing the behavioural experiments, and they then discount the whole approach. Instead of giving up altogether, I suggest you adapt your chosen strategy by using compassionate self-awareness.

To apply the cognitive behavioural your lack of acceptance method, you need to work on completing a chart daily for at least 30 days. Of the worldwide known therapeutic practices, Dr. Burns presents one example in the **Feeling Good** book. Susan Jeffers uses the tool called 'Risk of the Day,' in other words, to do a small deed to overcome the inner critic. I have decided to combine both tools as then you are not only aware of your critical thoughts, but also can do something about them and accept yourself more.

Every day you will be filling in a chart with the following information (found in the appendix):

Describe the situation (what happened). Focus on pure facts, without analysing. For example: "I have met an attractive member of the opposite sex and walked away instead of saying hello."

Define your self-critical thoughts. Write down what you thought of the situation described in the first column. Again, refrain from judgement, whether your thought is right or wrong. You could think; "I'm such an idiot. I will never find someone. I will always stay alone..."

Define the twists of your thoughts. Your thinking is based on your beliefs and opinions and often does not show the reality. For example, you can generalise the problem or see only the negative aspects of the situation, in black and white. If you have not said hello to a member of the opposite sex you met on the street, you may assume that you have poor social skills. However, I believe that there are, and certainly were, cases in your life when you could talk to a member of the opposite sex.

Now have a look at the types of twisted thinking. This is only one of many ways of classifying them. Remember one thought may have more than one twist.

All-or-nothing thinking. You look at things in a black-and-white way. It is a very common approach when you are self-critical. Mixed with discounting the positive, overgeneralisation and mental filter, this kind of twist may significantly impede your self-acceptance.

Overgeneralisation. You view a negative event as a never-ending pattern of defeat. Think of the words like: always, never, everybody, nobody. Any thought having any of these words classifies it as overgeneralisation.

Mental filter. You dwell on the negatives and ignore the positives. And the more you focus on the negatives, the fewer positives you will see.

Discounting the positives. You insist that your accomplishments or positive qualities don't count. This twist is similar to the 'mental filter' twist.

Jumping to conclusions. You conclude things are negative without any definite evidence. You can jump to conclusions in two ways: by mind-reading, such as if people are reacting negatively to you and by fortune-telling, such as prediction, that things will turn out badly.

This kind of twisted thinking is very common in the case of people suffering from social anxiety.

Magnification or minimisation. You marginalise things or make them more meaningful than they are. For example, you can minimise the fact that you are being abused by your violent partner, while you magnify the good deeds he has done for you.

Emotional reasoning. You reasoning based on how you feel: "I feel like an idiot, so I must be one." This is a very tricky kind of twisted thinking, yet manageable like all of them. You will learn it soon.

'Should' statements. You criticise yourself or other people with – must, ought, should, shouldn't and have-to. This kind of twisted thinking is very common in the case of the perfectionist, the people struggling with guilt and anyone who is doing the job of pleasing others, yearning for their approval.

Labelling. You tell yourself, "I'm a loser" or "I'm a jerk" instead of saying, "I made a mistake." Labelling is another kind of twisted thinking used during criticising yourself. You learn it from your parents, teachers, boss or spouse.

Blame. You criticise yourself for something you were not entirely responsible for, causing guilt. You can also blame other people and overlook ways that you contributed to a problem. I will write more about blaming in the next chapter when you commit to taking responsibility for your life.

I am aware that working on automatic thoughts is not easy. I agree with Dr. Burns that the best method to question automatic negative thoughts is through regular monitoring of them for at least 30 days.

But it is important to mention here that your inner criticism is the result of negative thinking and negative beliefs. Your critic communicates with you by generating thoughts based on your beliefs and then you can affirm them, practicing negative self-talk. Therefore, apart from the exercises presented in Chapter Four and Five, I encourage you to start working with your thoughts now. Any change made here to cut your negative thoughts and beliefs will magnify your happiness instantly.

Now I will give you some examples of negative thoughts and show you which twists they have. For a more thorough list, check Chapter Five.

I'm such a jerk. – labelling, blaming, discounting the positive, mental filter.

I can't do it because I'm frightened. – emotional reasoning, all-or-nothing.

I always forget his name. – overgeneralisation, all-or-nothing.

If I say "Hello" to her I will faint. – fortune-telling, all-or-nothing, discounting the positive.

If I say "Hello" to her she will mock me. – mind-reading, discounting the positive, all-or-nothing.

I should have said "Hello" to her. – should statement, blaming.

To practice finding the twists in your thoughts, imagine something which causes you fear. Write down the five automatic negative thoughts which come to your mind. Then identify the twists:

Thoughts	Twists
....	....
....	....
....	....
....	....
....	....

For the next week, record all your critical thoughts and identify their twists. Do it in your transformation diary. You will be surprised how many times your thinking does not reflect the reality.

Describe the consequences (feelings and behaviours) of your critical thinking. What will be the result of thinking/behaving in any given way? For example, if you are afraid to talk to new people, the consequences might be your discomfort (tension) and lack of friends.

Now take one situation to which you have listed negative thoughts and their twists. Describe all the negative consequences of your critical thinking:

Situation:

....
....

Negative critical thoughts and their twists

Thoughts	Twists
....	....
....	....
....	....
....	....
....	....

The consequences of critical thinking:

....

....

Write down alternative thoughts. These are some more positive statements. For example, if you say "I can't do it," the more rational response will be "At this moment I need some help with other people and new skills to win this challenge." Take the thoughts from the previous exercises and write down the alternative thoughts.

My negative critical thought	Alternative thoughts
....	....
	....
....	....
	....
....	....
	....
....	....
	....
....	....

You can also use the questions to disarm the critical thoughts. More techniques are described in Chapter Five:

- When is it not true?
- Who said that and is he/she an expert in this field?
- Will it matter in 10 years' time?
- What would my friend say in this situation?

Practice disarming your critical thought. Take one of these listed in the previous exercise and answer the questions listed above:

My thought:

....

When is it not true?

....

Who said that and is he/she an expert in this field?

....

Will it matter in 10 years' time?

....

What would my friend say in this situation?

....

The Risk of the Day – define an activity which you can do to overcome the problem which appeared in the situation you described in the first column (e.g. in the case of meeting the person of the opposite sex and running away – it may be social anxiety, lack of communication skills or inability to handle stress). Then think what small steps you could take to improve the lacking skills.

For example, if you met a beautiful man/woman and hadn't said hello because of your anxiety, your task might be saying hello first to the mirror and then to five people daily starting with those of the same sex. What counts here is your effort, the number of individuals approached counts, not whether they said hello back or ignored you. When you become comfortable with that, then you can say hello to members of the opposite sex. Then you can try to start a longer conversation.

Now define what your inner criticism concerns:

....

Having done that, you can plan what kind of action to take every day to improve the issue which your inner critic attacks, such as skills, financial status, health, the quality of your relationships. You will learn how to set goals in Chapter Nine, but even now you can set a mini-goal on which you can work. The first goal you could pursue is to eliminate the negative thoughts and beliefs generated by your inner critic. Use the tips described in Chapter Four and Five.

The whole table used for cognitive-behavioural techniques for coping with self-critical thoughts and beliefs looks like this:

Situation	Automatic Thoughts	Types of Twisted Thinking	Effects of Negative Thinking	Alternative Thought	Risk of the Day

By repeatedly completing the cognitive-behavioural log and taking action (small steps), you will be able to diminish self-criticism. Always remember that you will need patience with yourself. At first, it can take time to even realise that your thoughts of "that's just the way I am" (e.g. I'm an idiot) are self-critical. When you do realise this, more rational alternatives might not come to mind easily. Just practice, be patient and give yourself some time so the new thinking will be established in your subconscious mind.

How to Apply Compassion in Life

There is a simple method which can be used to help you to practice compassion, towards yourself and other people. You can achieve a positive result taking the following steps:

1. Understand your behaviour. Mathew McKay suggests that the first thing you need to do to become compassionate is to learn more about what you are doing, thinking and what you believe in. Therefore, answer the questions listed below. Do it in your transformational diary now.

- What beliefs or awareness influenced the behaviour?
- What need was he/she/I trying to meet with that behaviour?
- What pain, hurt or other feelings influenced the behaviour?

Analysing your behaviour, can help you focus on your reactions or other people's, therefore, the questions above contain the third person.

Let me give you some example answers to these questions. Avoiding saying hello to someone new you meet on the street may result from the belief "I'm not worthy" or "I'm not wanted" which generates more specific beliefs like "he/she will not like me." Avoiding talking to people may be an attempt to protect yourself from pain caused by social interactions. On the other hand, someone who bullies you will probably want to be noticed. Answering the third question, in case of impaired social skills, saying hello to a new person may cause discomfort or even a panic attack.

Choose one aspect of your life of which you are not happy now. It might be your physical appearance, illness, a lack of some skills or personality traits. Answer the three questions listed above. I will present them once again here:

- What beliefs or awareness influenced the behaviour?
- What need was (he, she, I) trying to meet with that behaviour?
- What pain, hurt or other feelings influenced the behaviour?

....

....

....

For example, your lack of acceptance of your poor social skills may come from the core belief "I am unworthy" and you when you realise this you add why: "Because my parents criticised my achievements at school." Therefore, you are trying to satisfy the need for approval here. Lack of support causes your lack of acceptance.

2. Accept yourself or someone else without blame or judgement, no matter how unfortunate the choices that have been made. Filling in the sentences listed below in writing will significantly improve your mood and you will gain peace of mind.

- I wish …... hadn't happened, but it was merely an attempt to meet my/other people's needs.
- I accept (the person who has done the thing x) without judgement for that attempt.
- No matter how unfortunate my/other people's decision was, I accept the person who did it, as they are trying to survive.

Let me give you an example first. Suppose that I have bullied my friend. I may feel guilty. Instead, I say:

I wish I hadn't bullied you, but it was merely an attempt to meet my need of being noticed. I accept myself without judgement or feelings of wrongness for that attempt. No matter how unfortunate my decision was, I accept myself as someone who is trying to survive.

Now choose a situation where you have done something wrong or someone has hurt you. Fill in the three sentences to which I have given you an example:

....
....
....
....

3. Forgive and let it go. This is the last but not the least important stage of compassionate response:

- It's over. I can let go of it.
- Nothing is owed for this mistake.

Rewrite the sentences from step 2 again and add one of the above conclusions. Then read all the piece of writing aloud, until your mood improves:

....
....
....
....
....

4. Learn this sequence by heart. Here are the questions and unfinished sentences from the first three steps.

Step one

- What beliefs or awareness influenced the behaviour?
- What need was he/she/I trying to meet with that behaviour?
- What pain, hurt or other feelings influenced the behaviour?

Step two

- I wish .... hadn't happened, but it was merely an attempt to meet my/other people's needs.

- I accept (the person who has done the thing x) without judgement for that attempt.

No matter how unfortunate my/other people's decision was, I accept the person who did it, as they are trying to survive.

Step three

- It's over. I can let go of it.
- Nothing is owed for this mistake.

You might need that formula more often than you think. In the case of ferociously negative thoughts of your inner critic, this formula will do wonders. You can first practice it in front of the mirror, taking a hypothetical challenge. It is also advisable to record it and listen repeatedly. Your voice will soothe your mind.

How to Stop Comparing Yourself to Other People

I mean negative comparison to others here. It occurs when you compare yourself to someone who has gotten something which you haven't. In this case minority complex, frustration and anger appear. How can you handle negative comparisons?

1. Identify your comparative behaviours. This kind of behaviour happens when you compare yourself to other people. You might feel superior or inferior while comparing to others. In some cases, social comparisons can be helpful, but negative comparative behaviours can damage your self-esteem. List the five cases when you compare yourself to other people.

1. ....
2. ....
3. ....
4. ....
5. ....

2. Use some short statements which will help you to stop negative thinking, which is labelling and personalisation.

- Assume nothing!
- Hold it! No comparisons!
- Check it out.
- Don't be so paranoid about standards.
- I can describe myself accurately, without reference to others.
- Everybody is different, with different strong and weak points.
- I am just me, without comparisons.
- Most of the universe has nothing to do with me.

Learn them off by heart and use them any time you notice that you start comparing yourself to other people. To practice this skill, choose one comparison. It can be your child, your work or wealth. Question it with one of the statements in writing. Fill in one full page rewriting this statement (e.g. "Hold it! No comparisons!").

3. Focus on your own achievements. You have everything you need to accomplish awesome goals in your little section of the world. And focus on that part. You may say "But is it necessary for other people?" For some, it may be not, but you will find the people who will be grateful for what you are doing. And that is your success. With that opportunity squarely in front of you, become aware of your past successes. Whether you are a doctor, writer, musician, mother or student, you have a unique perspective backed by unique experiences and unique gifts. You have the capacity to love, serve and contribute. Find motivation in them to pursue more. Now describe your talents. List five of them below.

1. ....
2. ....
3. ....

4. ....

5. ....

List ten achievements in your fields of life (family, work, finance, health)

1. ....

2. ....

3. ....

4. ....

5. ....

6. ....

7. ....

8. ....

9. ....

10. ....

You also have higher pursuits, which have no measurement. They are your great treasures, such as love, humility, empathy, selflessness and generosity. Desire them above everything else and remove yourself entirely from society's definition of success.

4. Compete less. Appreciate more. Competition is appropriate in some cases. However, life is not one of them. You have all been thrown together at this exact moment on this exact planet. The sooner you stop competing against others to win,' the faster you can start working together to figure it out. The first step in overcoming the habit of competition is to appreciate routinely and compliment the contribution of others.

5. Practice gratitude. It is not the first time I mention the importance of gratitude. You will learn how to practice at the end of this chapter. Gratitude always forces you to recognise the good things you already have in your world. In the meantime, list the five things that you are grateful for today.

1. ....
2. ....
3. ....
4. ....
5. ....

6. Remind yourself nobody is perfect. Focusing on the negatives is rarely as helpful as an emphasis on the positives. What might help you here is to remember that nobody is perfect, and nobody is living a painless life? It is said that to succeed you need to face obstacles. And everybody is suffering through their own, whether you are close enough to know it or not.

7. Take a walk. Next time you are comparing yourself to others, get up and change your surroundings. Go for a walk, even if only to the other side of the room. Allow the change in your surroundings to prompt a change in your thinking.

8. Find inspiration without comparison. It is foolish to compare your life to others. However, finding inspiration and learning from others is much wiser. Work hard to learn the difference by humbly asking questions of the people you admire or whose biographies you read for inspiration. Remember that the great people of today have also started somewhere and been struggling with similar challenges to you.

9. Be kind to yourself. When you are kinder and less harsh with yourself, you will encourage yourself to go the extra mile and to try harder. Understand that you are in control of your life. I am aware that it is tough to resist comparing yourself to others. But you make the choices to lead your life in a particular way. You make decisions that are best for you, not for anybody else. Remember that it is not important what other people do or have. You are the one that matters in the course of your life as they cannot live for you, breathe with your lungs or walk with your legs.

10. If you need to compare, compare to yourself. Remember this sentence anytime when the negative thoughts of comparison come to your mind. You are a unique individual; it will never be fair to compare you to someone else.

You need to strive to be the best possible version of yourself, not only for yourself but for the benefit and contribution that you can offer to others. Work hard to take care of yourself physically, emotionally and spiritually. Commit to growing a little bit each day. And learn to celebrate the small achievements you are making without comparing them to others.

If you have done the exercise of comparing what you achieved five years ago to where you are now, the chances are that you can notice your progress and in this way, celebrate your success.

However, you can compare yourself to someone with qualities you admire. Rather than just envy this person for his good qualities, you strive to make yourself a better salesman. Then their better performance is not an obstacle; it motivates you to put in more effort. This is a positive comparison.

How to Remove or Replace Comparative Thoughts

Have you ever thought "He is smarter than me" or "My sister always dresses more attractively than me" or "I will never be as brilliant as them?" These are the examples of comparative thoughts. Your inner critic, which you have met earlier in this chapter, will also generate comparative thoughts. To deal with them, you can use the same strategies described in Chapter Five. However, you can also us these tips:

1. Replace negative thoughts with positive ones. You may find that your compare yourself with others negatively. If you do have negative self-thoughts, change those thoughts to something that you are proud of yourself for doing. How does it work? This is just simple reasoning. However, sometimes you need to use more drastic tools; they are described in Chapter Five of this book.

Let's say your partner earns more money than you. You can either focus on what you don't have or list all the things which you have and he has not. Think that it is your merit that you have found this job or started your business. Believe that your wealth is the reward you reap for your hard, conscientious work.

Let's look at another example: if you know someone else who is great at maths and statistics, instead of envying their talents, think about yours. Tell yourself, "I may not be the best writer, but I can calculate awesome figures. Besides, if I want to improve in statistics, I can work towards this goal for myself instead of envying others for their talent." Now think of one thing that others are better than you. Write it down and then list three things at which you are good.

1. ....
2. ....
3. ....

2. Avoid the media that show ideal images. Have you ever thought how much damage you do to yourself by reading fashion magazines, watching reality television shows, certain movies and music? If not, just think who your idol is, think of his other fans.

This is very common in the case of music bands and sports teams. Therefore, you can be envious that other fans have more badges, new T-shirts every season and have seen the stars more often than you have. For the same reason, avoid some friends on Facebook, those who boast their achievements, placing photos from every gig or match, bought a ticket, etc.

Let's take an example: Imagine that you envy the perfect relationship that a friend has with her spouse. However, remember how difficult it was for her to find that partner and the challenges she may have faced. Empathy will replace jealousy then.

If you see someone with the car, body or life you want, think of actions you can take to increase the probability that these goals will be achieved. Now think of one thing you are jealous of and find the three ways to start working on that:

I am jealous of ....

Things to do to work on my jealousy:
1.   ....
2.   ....
3.   ....

3. Focus on your talents and achievements. Then you will not have the time to bother with the things you are longing for. Let's start by listing your achievements. I assuming that you have got your transformation diary in front of you. Now list as many achievements as your age. If you are forty, you need to be able to list at least forty results. Think of your grades at school, A-level, university degree, kids, your job and investments, skills which you have learned, projects completed, works written etc.

How to Accept an Illness or Disability

This part of Chapter Two will be special because I, the author of this book, am also struggling with a long-term illness and would like to share some of my experiences with you. They will help you to cope with your illness or disability.

What would you do if you were diagnosed with diabetes, cancer, schizophrenia or epilepsy? This is the one of hardest times, you would naturally be down about it. However, with a few changes, you might still be able to live your life to the full.

1. Allow yourself time to understand your illness. I understand fully how you feel. The whole world is upside down. Now you are in the middle of it, believing that life will never be the same for you again because of being miserable, fighting your illness or disability. You are afraid of losing your friends because you will not be able to socialise as you used to anymore.

However, this is also the time to find out who your real friends are. You will see that your true friends will be there to support you and do anything that is within their strength to help you. However, they will not feel sorry for you forever. You will soon find out that if the only topic of conversation is your illness, then even your kind-hearted friends will lose interest. Also, remember to judge whether your friends are honest with you.

Be careful as some of your friends could be taking advantage of you and drain you emotionally – even if it might not be obvious to you. Beware of emotional blackmail and emotional abuse. You are more vulnerable now.

2. Allow yourself time to let go of all the negative emotions.
Accepting an illness or disability might take time. It is always good
news to know that there are people to whom you can talk. At this
time, you might need counselling, life coaching.

I find the help of a life coach especially helpful at the stages of my
life when I am ill. I was always very ambitious and performed very
well at school. However, I have had epilepsy since I was two years
old. Everyone thought highly of me and believed I would do very
well in my life. My friends and family were always supportive. I
remember people were shocked when I chose not to go to university
and go abroad. But I did it and now I am happily living in Ireland.

I found it tough to accept the fact that I am not driving and because
of this some luxury jobs were unattainable. I even had thoughts that
life was not worth living. I felt frustrated because I was not getting
better; my illness was staying forever. I must take tablets for the rest
of my life. I kept asking myself why did this have to happen to me?
Why is life so cruel?

I could not find a good job, so I started searching for some alternative
solutions. I attended some training and started a business. Now I can
work from home, helping other people who struggle with illness and
other challenges, about which I know only too well.

When I moved to Ireland, I switched from living with my parents to
living with totally strange people. In many cases I had been used to
help these people with their English, but when I needed some help
they very rarely gave it.

Then I moved to another town and started seeing my life coach. She
and some other good friends told me that I needed to start thinking
differently. It is just the way life is and there is no point in trying to
find an answer as to why.

But there is one important point to realise – illness is not a punishment
for something you have done wrong. Seeing the life coach also taught
me to enjoy and appreciate the good things in my life. Because I still
have good things in my life. I always remember that because I have

many great things to enjoy in my life, things which help me to forget the harsh side of life.

3. Accept your illness. It can take a long time to accept an illness or disability. You can feel depressed – if you are enjoying it. However, you will soon realise that feeling sorry for yourself will get you nowhere. You still have a life that you can enjoy. What is even more, you can review what your strengths are and what you still can do. The time has come, not to dwell in the past, but to concentrate on the things you can still do in the future. Right now, list five of your strengths.

1. ....
2. ....
3. ....
4. ....
5. ....

Consider all your strengths. List the qualifications you have and ask a career adviser for help to you find a suitable job or start a business. In this way, you might still be able to work, bearing in mind your limitations.

Now list the three things which you can do in the future, making the most of your illness.

1. ....
2. ....
3. ....

For example, you can join the groups of people who face the same challenges and share your story, inspiring them.

4. Join support groups. Make the most of all help and support groups. Sometimes I take an older lady from the neighbourhood shopping with me. Like me, she has health problems. I enjoy talking to her.

If you are in a support group, you can complain to other people about your problems. You can learn from them how to deal with your ailments and what remedies alleviate your symptoms or which alternative therapies are helpful. You share a common problem, and I know that other members of the group will not be bored. You can put yourself into their shoes quickly.

Joining groups is a good option because the challenge is you might want to share your problems with your friends, yet you do not want to bore them with it. Instead of being self-centred, just listening to your friends will do the trick as people love to talk and be listened to and will appreciate that you are a good listener. You will soon learn that when you start telling your friends how unjustified your life is, they will only tell you how much more unjustified their life is.

Join support groups and be there for each other, learn from your strength. Sometimes you can meet people who complain of not seeing any point in such groups because at the end of the day these people still have to come home to their homes, and have to cope on their own. Support groups will not solve all of people's problems, yet they can help people overcome their challenges.

Therefore, always appreciate the help of the professionals who organise these support groups and put individuals in contact with each other. Remember that you can either ignore them or make the most of them. The choice is yours.

You might decide not join the group because family members sometimes disapprove of that. They might feel that you will just become more absorbed with your illness as you might think of nothing else and make yourself even sicker by analysing all the symptoms and your diagnosis.

Never look for your relatives' approval. Instead, decide what works best for you. Never go to extremes and enjoy the support of your like-minded friends but only to enrich your life. Beware of not complaining about your misfortune all the time. Surround yourself with people with whom you feel great and avoid individuals who are distracting you from achieving your goal.

5. Take care of yourself. Let me ask you a question: Who is the most precious person in your life, who do you value most? Think of this person as you read on. Is it your partner, your child or perhaps your parent?

However, there might be times when even the people who are the most precious can let you down. The only person you can always trust is yourself because you will always be in your company and can either cheer yourself up or make yourself miserable.

Therefore, firstly, you need to take care of yourself. Always make sure that you can keep yourself as healthy as possible. You cannot cure your illness or disability, but you can learn how to live your life to the best of your ability. You still can do so much to help yourself feel better. Everybody is a unique person; therefore, some remedies will work for you, but not for others. I know this myself. I have tried various medications for epilepsy – some made me drowsy, others induced weight gain. It took me more than ten years to find the optimal medication for me, and now I am happy with that.

The same applies to self-development tools. Some people might write down affirmations; others prefer reading books and doing the exercises described there or meditating while listening to a motivational audio. This book will give you plenty of tools to become a happier person, and you will be able to choose which works best for you. If you are not sure, contact me and we can discuss the issue.

You might say that you tried so many remedies or therapies and nothing ever worked. Sometimes you need to be patient and wait a bit for results. Some treatments take longer to start working. Monitor the changes, which are happening to your body.

6. Use visualisation. You can use this powerful tool for many purposes (i.e. working with your negative emotions, setting and achieving your goals, changing your habits).

Now let's try a simple technique. Think of the time when you felt guilty, frustrated and angry because of your illness or disability. Imagine that you throw all your negative thoughts and all your pain into the bin and getting rid of them. They might be anything you wish.

Now, after having gotten rid of the rubbish, relax. Think of yourself lying on the beach. The sun's energy travelling into each part of your body, which is making you feel warm and energised.

Then imagine yourself as a powerful, capable person. For example, imagine yourself being healthy, as a leader, as someone who can make it to the top of the mountain. While you imagine it, you can get all the benefits of it happening in real life.

7. Find something that you enjoy. Develop an interest or a hobby. What about reading a good story or just have a cup of tea on your own? Doing so, you will stop you from focusing on other peoples' approval. When you have an illness, it may be harder accepting that because of your illness nobody will say well done for something you really wanted to achieve but could not. As nobody else will praise you for coping with your illness, you are responsible for providing approval yourself.

For the next thirty days, every day write on page one of your transformation diary:

Well done for coping so well.

Praise yourself for anything in the day, no matter how small. Every time you are in the bathroom or pass the mirror, look at it and say aloud:

Well done for coping so well.

You can train yourself to make this a new habit. Every time you are having a meal or starting watching TV, say to yourself:

Well done for coping so well.

8. Do exercises. It may be challenging at first because you experience too much pain, stiffness or a lack of energy. It is often exercising that helps to alleviate stiffness or muscular pain.

Find the right exercise for you. In general, some gentle exercises are more appropriate than anything vigorous. Do little workouts and do them often. Now think of the activities that you could do, starting from today. Make a plan of your workouts and take massive action right now. Be persistent. After some time, you will look slimmer and will be fitter. Doing exercises is especially important if you suffer depression or any other mental illness as the medications used to treat them cause weight gain.

9. Eat healthy. It is important to eat regularly. Eat small portions more often, rather than big pieces less frequently. Include all the food groups (carbohydrates, fats and proteins) in your diet. Note that diets, which only involve one of the food groups, can be very dangerous for your health. And always consult your GP if you want to embark on any new diet plan.

To lose weight you should certainly not be going on any drastic diets. Some of the diets can cause havoc to your health because you are at risk of gaining your weight back, which is more dangerous to your health than maintaining the same weight at all times, as the body has to deal with the skin continually expanding and shrinking when you lose and gain weight too often.

10. Consider alternative therapies. Find out as much as you can about your health problem. You can try alternative therapies which are a great way of harmonising your energy, yet you will not be able to do everything. For example, the practitioners of acupuncture study and practice years before they master the skills in their field, which means that you would certainly not be able to apply any of the techniques on your own.

Nevertheless, you can, learn about acupressure or reflexology points and use them regularly yourself. Find out about which point corresponds to which organ in your body and which points you could press, how frequently and in which sequences. If you are not familiar with acupressure or reflexology, find the information in a bookshop, the library or on the Internet.

If you do not like pressing reflexology points on your feet, try walking without your shoes on grass, on the sandy or pebbly beach. In the past when people did not wear shoes and with no hard surfaces, their feet were always massaged in the same way that the principles of reflexology healing work. Stepping over small stones is very beneficial because you activate and rub all the reflexology points at the same time.

11. Concentrate on the present. You must stop dwelling on the past or worrying about the future. When you have an illness, it is natural that you analyse the family medical history. You make yourself feel guilty and put yourself under tremendous pressure when you are saying, "If this did not happen I would not get myself in the state I am in. I should have done things differently." Your assumption may be true, but also it may not be true.

You might be experiencing pain because someone has hurt you in the past. For your sake, let go of these ill feelings. This will naturally not be easy, and you might need to seek the help of a psychiatrist or a counsellor.

While experiencing disturbing thoughts from the past, you can keep saying to yourself:

What happened in the past has happened. I let it go. I let it go. I let it go.

Better than that, write down this affirmation until you fill in the whole page of your transformation diary. Continue this process every day for at least 30 days.

12. Practice mindfulness. Remember that the present is the most important part of your life. Take a moment to reflect on how you feel. Experience the here and now. Sit down for five minutes to be in a calm state concentrating on taking deep breaths, without any thoughts spreading to your mind. You might find this exercise difficult. However, meditation techniques are very beneficial because they help you discover more about who you are.

Today find 10 minutes (later extend it to 20 minutes) to sit down in a quiet place, where you will not be disturbed. Focus only on your breathing, your muscle tension. Let your thoughts go. They will be flowing fast, and you will be tempted to ruminate on them. When you notice such a thought, let it go and continue to focus on your breathing.

Practice this technique every day for at least one week.

Dr. Kabbat-Zinn recommends eight weeks of intense meditating which can help with many illnesses because people start to focus on more positive aspects of life.

The more advanced exercises include conscious walking, where you concentrate on every step you take or scan your body while meditating.

I have accepted that I shall never drive, I must ask other people to help me and I will always have to pay for a taxi. However, instead of ruminating, I would rather concentrate on what blessings I have and how I can help other people.

Although your life seems to you to be much harder than anybody else's, stop imagining it to be harder. You often follow what your mind tells you to do. Make sure you give it positive commands.

Stop worrying about the future. Sure, you want to plan for the future and see where you are going. It is only positive to have a dream or a challenge for your future. Your goal can only be achieved if you set yourself little challenges which you meet day by day.

13. Try to eliminate stress from your life

As you all know stress contributes significantly to many illnesses. When your body senses danger, it prepares to flee in which case your heart rate increases. If you experience such states too often, your health will suffer as a result.

Scientists proved that the slower your heart rate is, the longer your life is. Breathing exercises can help you calm down and can influence your heart in a positive way. Here are some techniques which will help you to cope with stress:

Relax. Are you breathing properly? Let's check. Stand in front of a mirror. Then take one deep breath and watch yourself. If your shoulders move up, then you are not breathing properly as you are breathing through your chest and not through your abdomen. Put your hand on your abdomen and take some more breaths. Feel your hand move up and down. Then you are breathing correctly. You will learn how to do so by doing this exercise:

Lie down or sit and put your hand on your abdomen. Take a slow deep breath through your nose until you feel it in your stomach. Count to three. Then hold the breath for 2 seconds and exhale – for another 5 seconds. Do this exercise daily for a month, for at least 5 minutes. Then continue for another month, but for 10 minutes. You will see the results after two weeks.

In case you find it difficult to sleep, then deep breathing can also help you to relax and go to sleep. Going to bed and getting up at the same time each day ensuring that you have at least eight hours' sleep is another rule of thumb.

Program your mind for positivity. Before falling asleep, let worry and anger go. Relax the hour before going to bed listening to gentle music or a book and stop watching television just before going to bed. If it is at all possible, have your bedroom television free.

Just think how parents put their small children to bed – they pamper them with a bath, then when they are nice and cosy in bed, they read them a bedtime story or sing a lullaby. Do the same for yourself now. Instead of singing a song, listen to uplifting affirmations which will program your mind.

Visualise your high points. Do this while lying in bed, before falling asleep. Remember to turn off the phone or TV. Think of at least one skill which you could use today to achieve your goals or to help the other people. Magnify it and perceive with all the senses. What can you see, hear, touch, feel?

Laugh and smile. This is a very powerful tool for alleviating stress. Even if you only force yourself to smile, your brain will start to secrete positive hormones as your mimics has such a powerful effect. Start from smiling when you are looking at the mirror in the bathroom; then you can do it as often as possible. It is one of the habits which you can train. How to do it? I will show you in Chapter Eight of this book.

Get on well with other people. Live harmoniously with everybody else. You know that this might not always be easy. You might be living around nosy and noisy neighbours who drive you mad.

Imagine that because of your illness you cannot work anymore and are on disability allowance. The neighbours may be malicious and intolerant, just because they have to go to work every day. They can judge and make you guilty. You may start feeling like a useless member of society.

Living with toxic people is just a reason to start focusing on your life, as their opinion is not something that should control your life. It is much better not to get involved in arguments with neighbours, but to learn how to deal with them constructively.

While being angry with somebody, take a few deep breaths. Then explain calmly to the person why you are angry and what you would like the person to do instead. Never swear at anybody or accuse them of being an idiot. The response you will get may be less hostile.

Write down in your transformation diary – something similar to the following quote:

I can express my anger, irritability or rage politely and effectively. It does not matter who with or what the issue is. I let it go whenever it appears.

Remember that if you can't do so, it is likely that you are always increasing your blood pressure which is not healthy for your heart.

You create the quality of your life. You might be thinking that it is not in your power to improve your life in any way right now. The truth is that even if you think you have little left, there are still some assets which you have and which I will help you to discover.

Start small by setting goals which are manageable each day. Break your tasks into smaller chunks if your challenge is larger than you can handle. In this way, you will be able to enjoy satisfaction because you will have achieved your goal, no matter how small it was.

It is important to take one step at a time. Let's say that it is an effort for you just to get out of bed and make breakfast. Then this could be challenge number one for the rest of the week to get up by a certain time. Slowly and gradually add a few extra challenges as you go along. At the end of each day or week make a review of what you managed to achieve that previously you could not do. If you struggle with an illness, check Chapter Two once again and set weekly goals which will help you to manage your illness. I will teach you how to set goals in Chapter Nine and how to create happiness habits in Chapter Eight.

Avoid perfectionism. It does not matter whether the house is not 100% clean. No one is 100% perfect. We are humans and have the right to make mistakes. Instead of thinking how much you lack for the job to be perfect, treat each task as a new version of software – like Microsoft does with Windows. Today everything is upgraded which means that your job can be right to some standard, let's say 60% of the ideal, but you can upgrade again. Focus on the progress rather than perfection. Chapter Eleven will help you to tackle perfectionism.

14. Find a job or start a business. You can find a job that will be enjoyable, suits you and will give you satisfaction. In this way, you will stop to stop thinking as an ill or disabled person who cannot contribute to society as much as others. Unfortunately, companies are often discouraged from employing people with disabilities because they fear that such people will be absent regularly. They are also afraid that ill or disabled people will not be as efficient as others workers because of their illness or disability, even though by law employers must not discriminate against employees with a disability.

What can you do? There are organisations that will help find a suitable job for you. There are also opportunities to take training for an appropriate job. Reduced alternative therapy treatments or start-up money packages are another option available for you while starting your business.

Volunteering is the other option. For example, I am the member of Wexford Toastmasters which is a non-profit organisation. Ask your counsellor or the people from support groups to find some information about volunteering options in your area.

15. Think like the victor. In the case of epilepsy working from home is a great option. You can help people online. And I will also teach you how to get rid of excuses, not only those about illness.

Remember to only go at a pace you are comfortable with. You are doing all the right things that will help you to achieve your goal one day in the future when you are patient.

Without inner strength, people with illness or disability would have no life at all. I know a person who is blind and develops all her other senses much better than we do. Otherwise, she would have to live in total darkness and isolation. The same applies to the deaf and those who are in wheelchairs.

I have a friend at Toastmasters, who is blind but musically gifted and prepares marvellous speeches. She is the president of the club for this term. I can learn from her how to develop my keen skills to compensate my illness. I just wanted to show you that this incredible strength is in you, and you have the capacity to use it to improve your life and the life of those around you.

Release the Negativity

Take your transformation diary and divide one page into two columns. Write down all the negative aspects of your life on the left, and the positive ones on the right. Do it now.

**POSITIVE ASPECTS
OF MY LIFE**

**NEGATIVE ASPECTS
OF MY LIFE**

Now weigh them all up. You probably wrote more negative things quickly while the positive stuff came up very slowly. This is all about appreciating the entire positive side of your life now. The negative parts are hard, but cross out the negative column. As you do so, imagine all these problems are erased now. Then cut the page in half and shred or burn the crossed negative things in your life. Read aloud the remaining positive things.

Every time you face negativity in your life, do this exercise again. In this way, you will program your subconscious mind to focus on the positive aspects of life.

Now let's concentrate on the positivity now. It may happen that you only managed to write down very little. Then let me help you to think of some more. Start with gratitude. You will read about it later in this chapter, but now just list the five things for which you are grateful.

1. ……………………..
2. ……………………..
3. ……………………..
4. ……………………..
5. ……………………..

Is it still difficult? Answer these questions in writing:

- Do you have a supportive family and circle of friends?
- Can you read, write?
- Do you have access to the Internet?
- Can you walk or have you enough strength to push yourself in a wheelchair?
- Can you afford to buy books?

Having some of these, you will be able to achieve your goals. Perhaps you can join like-minded people on the Internet; you can write about your problems and share your experience with others, or you can study something you enjoy.

And if you buy my book, you can become even stronger, applying all the strategies which you will learn in the next chapters.

I always felt people with health challenges were so much closer to God and artistically gifted because they have the time to notice little things that busy people cannot. You have probably heard of artists who paint with their legs, or their mouth and their paintings are truly marvellous. Saint Valentine was an epileptic.

If they did not have their disability they would probably have gotten on with their everyday lives, and they would never have discovered their special gift. Discover your gift and make good use of it. It does not matter that you cannot continue in your current job or achieve your original career ambitions. Instead, help those around you who will appreciate your input or expertise. You can also assist those who are facing similar problems as you. Find at least one person like that, joining groups on the Internet or in your community.

Sticking with your realistic goal, you will pursue it. Also, do not always listen to the predictions that have been forecast by doctors for the development of your illness. The same illness can behave differently in your case to your friends who are also struggling.

Let's say that the doctor told you that it would probably be three years at which time you will be in a wheelchair. Never fix this picture it in your mind. Instead, try to be positive and keep walking as much and as regularly as you can, as the longer you keep it up, the longer you can do it.

I have heard of people who were told by their doctors that their illness was not curable, yet they adopted a different approach to treatment than suggested by their doctor and have cured their disease. It happened even though their doctor has given them only a few years of life. Gratitude is another level of responsible adult life.

How to Practice Gratitude

What is gratitude? According to Wikipedia: "gratitude is a feeling or attitude in acknowledgement of a benefit that one has received or will receive. The experience of gratitude has historically been a focus of several world religions has been considered extensively by moral philosophers such as Lee Clement."

1. Commit to be grateful. Gratitude is a spiritual practice that gains momentum over time and with practice. This does not seem to come as easy, and you will likely resist this exercise. However, before you give up the idea of gratitude, list all the advantages of doing so. I will mention some of them:

- Firstly, you start to focus on what you have got and feel good about that instead of being unhappy because you do not have something. I cannot drive, but I can write an article or a book which can help many people to be happy.

- Secondly, practicing gratitude will switch your focus from yourself to others. You will want to reciprocate the good things that you have received and suddenly find some ideas how to do so.

- Thirdly, gratitude will help you to release negativity – thoughts, beliefs and emotions. How can you be angry, thinking of someone who loves you and visited you in the hospital when you were ill? And when you are sick, thinking of all the supportive people will bring your focus to positivity, instead of being unhappy because of your illness or you miss something that other people have.

Now fill in your gratitude commitment declaration:

I, _____ commit to practice gratitude on everyday basis for at least 30 days. I will write down some good things that I am grateful for and some people who were helpful. I will read this list after getting up and before going to bed.

2. Notice your day-to-day world from a point of gratitude. You will be amazed at all the goodness we take for granted. Start right now. Observe and make notes of all the beautiful things that happen to you. As an exercise, list the five good things that have happened to you today. Use all the five senses to describe it What could you see? How did you feel? What could you hear? What did you taste?

1. ....
2. ....
3. ....
4. ....
5. ....

And now list the five people who support you or who at least have done something good for you lately

1. ....
2. ....
3. ....
4. ....
5. ....

3. Keep a gratitude journal. You are aware of the good things in your life. Now create a habit of gratitude. For the next 30 days write down the three things you are grateful for and the three people who contributed to your life in a positive way. Answer the following questions:

- *Who or what inspired me today?*
- *What brought me comfort and deep peace today?*
- *What brought me happiness today?*

You can do it on your calendar, on a Word document or even in the notepad on your phone. You will notice a tremendous change in your attitude to life. You will become more humble, less focused on what other people have and what you don't have. Finally, you will also contribute more to society.

Read your journal aloud. You can even record your list on CD or mp3 and listen to it while driving your car. This will instantly make you happy and traffic jams will stop bothering you. Both writing and reading aloud program your mind to happiness and all that is positive.

Take a gratitude walk. This is a particularly useful exercise when you are feeling down or filled with stress and worry. Walk through a park, in your neighbourhood, around your office or somewhere else in nature for 20 minutes or more.

While walking, consider the many things for which you are grateful: loving relationships, the mind that allows you to understand yourself, the body that lets you experience the world, material comforts and your essential spiritual nature. Also, be grateful for the air that is filling your lungs and making your life possible.

While walking, you can also listen to the audio with your gratitude list which you can record reading the journal aloud.

4. Always seek the positive. I believe that even the worst events or people have something positive —you can at least learn from them. If you identify something or someone with a negative trait (let's say it is a rude person), switch it in your mind to an active character (he or she is nicely dressed). Now list one thing and one person who irritated you last week. Find and write at least one positive trait for each of them.

SITUATION/ PERSON	NEGATIVE TRAIT	POSITIVE TRAIT

5. Give at least one compliment daily. Think of all the people who support you. There is probably at least one thing in each of them which you like. When you see your helpers, give them a compliment.

6. Share your gratitude. Find someone else who will practice gratitude with you. In this way, you will keep each other going. Moreover, the sense of obligation to another person will push you to write your list on those days when it just seems too hard.

Reading what the other person has written helps you to access your gratitude more easily, and it is fun to watch your appreciation email grow longer and longer and longer! You can see your progress.

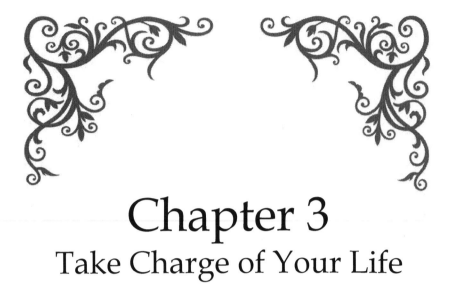

Chapter 3
Take Charge of Your Life

Tina has learned to accept her limits and decided to become a happier person. I have explained that it is not possible without commitment. For the next few sessions, Tina was fighting with her unwillingness to take responsibility. She had plenty of excuses and was paralysed by fear, which was the effect of her negative beliefs and thoughts.

I suggested her to start with a small step to take control in this area of life. She started by getting rid of her excuses. She has also learned how to make smart decisions. You can also learn how to take responsibility for your life. This chapter will show you:

- What it means to be responsible for your life.
- Why it is useful to commit to become a happy and successful person.
- What you are responsible in your life.
- For what you are not responsible in your life.
- Why taking responsibility for your life is difficult.
- How to take responsibility for your life.
- What are the most common excuses.
- How to stop making excuses.

- What you can change in your life.
- What stops you from change.
- What kills changes.
- Why you need to expand your comfort zone.
- How to leave comfort zone.
- How to plan risk of the day.
- How pleasure and pain impacts your life.
- How to use pleasure and pain to change your life.
- How to associate pleasure and pain with taking action.
- How to learn making better decisions.
- How to make a good decision.
- How to write commitment declaration.

To a happy person, you must commit to taking action which will make you happy and to avoid everything that decreases your happiness. Brian Tracy defines responsibility as experiencing only positive emotions and keeping negativity at bay. I can add that taking responsibility is equal to commitment and happiness. And this means no blame or no excuses, but continuous growth. Assume responsibility for your life and happiness has many benefits:

1. You build higher self-esteem.

Feeling that you have control over something is the quickest way to boost your self-confidence. You feel more competent and therefore happier. You act like a winner who takes action and makes decisions instead of blaming and finding excuses.

2. You stop relying on approval from other people to feel good about yourself.

Instead, you start building a sort of inner spring that fuels your life with positive emotions no matter what other people say or do around you.

"When we have begun to take charge of our lives, to own ourselves, there is no longer any need to ask permission of someone." - George O'Neil

3. Taking action becomes natural.

Your thoughts become your actions. However, without taking responsibility for your life those ideas often just stay on that mental stage and aren't translated into action. Then you work on other people's goals and are flooded with negativity. These thoughts attract unhappiness to you.

When you take responsibility for your life, you add that extra ingredient that makes taking action more of a natural thing. You become proactive instead of passive, taking control of your decisions, emotions, words and thoughts.

4. You become the better version of yourself.

You do it by learning from mistakes and learning from life lessons. Responsibility means constant growth, facing the brutal truth about yourself. You start taking action even if you dislike it. You stop procrastinating or being a perfectionist.

5. You give yourself the permission to live the life you want.

When you stop making excuses no one will stop you from working on your goals; which means living the life that you always wanted to live.

"Peak performance begins with your taking complete responsibility for your life and everything that happens to you." - Brian Tracy

Responsibility cannot be split. You and only you can take charge of your life. If you decide to resign from taking responsibility for your life, other people will control you.

6. You gain freedom.

When you accept personal responsibility, you gain the freedom to create your life any way you want it.

"Freedom is the will to be responsible to ourselves." - Friedrich Nietzsche

You immediately recognise how much control you have while admitting to yourself that you are solely responsible for your life. It is also true that external circumstances don't control your life, and any goal that you want to achieve is within your control.

7. You gain trust and respect from other people.

You learn lots of respect when you take responsibility for your actions. Let's say you make a mistake while working on a project at school. If you admit your mistake, people are more likely to believe you about other things you do. So, your word has more meaning to other people when you take responsibility.

Developing a reputation for being the guy who accepts responsibility for his actions, you will notice that people will often simply ignore the fact that you made a mistake altogether.

8. You experience fewer negative emotions.

It is just because responsibility excludes negativity. You may feel a negative emotion or have a negative thought, but you quickly tackle them and return to the track of happiness again.

"Read it with sorrow and you will feel hate.
Read it with anger and you will feel vengeful.
Read it with paranoia and you will feel confusion.
Read it with empathy and you will feel compassion.
Read it with love and you will feel flattery.
Read it with hope and you will feel positive.
Read it with humour and you will feel joy.
Read it with God and you will feel the truth.
Read it without bias and you will feel peace.
Don't read it at all and you will not feel a thing."
- Shannon L. Alder

9.You feel in control.

According to the Universal Law of Control, you feel happy with yourself to the degree you can control your life. You can quickly become depressed not having control over your life. The worst part about denying responsibility is an overall sense of powerlessness.

What Am I Responsible for In My Life

In short – for your thoughts, emotions, actions and language. However, to be more specific, you are not responsible for all in this world. According to Nathaniel Branden, these are the thirteen issues for which you are responsible:

1. The level of your consciousness. How well you know yourself, your beliefs, life mission, life goals? If you still have a vague idea about who you are, go back to Chapter One and do all the exercises which are there. There you will discover a vast amount of knowledge about it, even if you may not like some parts.

2. The quality of your life. That may sound brutal but is true. You decide what job to take, who to marry, where to live. Even if you may feel forced to make a give decision, the ultimate choice is always yours. The good news is that you can always change your decisions, even if sometimes the costs are high.

3. The quality of your communication and the language you are using. This means both communicating your ideas and listening to the other person. You must be aware of the differences –cultural, linguistic, sexual and environmental. Always ask if your partner understands a given message in the same way as you. Never read other people's minds.

4. Your choices. If you let someone else make the decision that you should take, chances are your life will be created on their terms, not yours. You will bear the consequences in both cases; making choices on your own or letting other people decide for you. Which would you prefer to carry? I know it is hard to make independent decisions and requires courage to make decisions on your own. However, the reward is massive.

5. Your happiness. What do you specifically do with your thoughts, language and behaviour? If you dwell on negativity and attract even more of this to your life, don't blame other people or circumstances. It was your choice. Happiness requires taking action and not letting negativity flood your life.

6. The quality of my relationships. In at least 50% of relationships work is needed, and I don't only mean in marriage, also relationships with friends, co-workers and parents. Even if your partner is abusive or not interested in contributing to the relationship, it is always your choice how you react to that situation and what you do; work on that or move on. It is brutally true that if one partner stops growing in a relationship, the relationship is over. Hence when you grow, you often change your friends or your spouse. Are you growing or have you fallen into your comfort zone?

7. The quality of your job. I don't mean "kind of profession" here, rather the quality of what you offer to the world, in whichever job. You can always give more the 100% of the quality required by others. This pays off in business and employment: you gain more loyal customers, recommendations and promotion. Giving less than expected puts you at risk of bankruptcy in business or losing your job. What can you do to commit 100% to the services you are rendering to others? This also applies in your relationships.

8. Your finance. Many people use excuses here: "I can't be richer because I will not find a better job. I have lots of expenses. I don't have the right skills." The truth is that you can always find a new job or changing the country if you have found few opportunities in your homeland. Gaining new qualifications, growing as a human being will help you to make the changes which will make you rich. Many people who are rich today started as poor and uneducated (I mean without the right skills, not a university diploma), came from poor and abusive families. But eventually, they have succeeded.

9. Time management. You have 24 hours her day, like everyone else. It is up to you how you use that period. I will show you how to manage your time more efficiently in Chapter Eleven of my book. The choice is yours to use the tips which you will learn there.

10. Your thinking. It is like taking care of your garden. Your sub-consciousness and other people will always sow the seeds of negative thoughts in your mind. It is your job to eliminate these seeds or weeds which have grown from them. Otherwise, you will lose your happiness and peace of mind. Instead, sow the seeds of your goals, dreams and positive statements about yourself.

11. Handling emotions. I can compare them to fire, to the lights which sparkle in your life. You can put them down to the environment where they are safe. But be careful of the fire, especially the fire of anger, guilt, worry, resentment and a few other disastrous emotions, if they are not handled in the right way. It does not mean to suppress your feelings for everything. I will show you in Chapter Three how to cope with them.

12. Your health. I think that it is self-evident. What about your diet, regular exercises and check-up? Doing so will improve your health. But you are also responsible how you handle your illness and disability. I have given you some tips how to do it in the last chapter.

13. Achievement of your goals. No one will kick your backside to get you to work on your goals. You have already made a plan and set the price that you must pay for the achievement of your goals. Now the time has come to take action. If it is still hard, I will help you to overcome this challenge in Chapter Three.

What You Are Not Responsible For

Now you may ask: "Are there any things for which I am not responsible?" Of course, there are. And what is more, you often put pressure on yourself putting them on your shoulders. You can do it yourself, or other people can manipulate you, making you responsible for their problems. I will write another book soon, and there will be many examples of how people can manipulate you and how to defend against it. At this moment, I will tell you what you are not responsible for:

1. Forgiveness given to you by other people: I mean the forgiveness given to you by other people. You cannot force anyone to forgive you. However, you are responsible for your resentment – when and if you forgive other people.

2. The reactions of others: Are they hurt by your rejection, assertiveness, clear communication? It is not your problem. If you think otherwise, beware – you may be the victim of emotional blackmail. They, the same as you, are responsible for what they do with their emotions, thoughts, decisions and what action they will take. If you hurt someone, you can always apologise.

3. Other people's decisions: Of course, if you have children under 18 you must be there for them and teach them responsibility. However, dealing with adults means that everybody is independent in making decisions. You can persuade someone to decide in accordance with your point of view – but never decide for him or her. Even if you are the manager

4. Other people's actions: Unless they are your children under 18 or subordinates in a corporation, you are responsible for your life. You cannot be responsible for somebody's vandalism because this person is angry or wants to be noticed.

5. Acts of force major: Tsunami, flood, earthquake, an impact of asteroids. You cannot stop them from happening. More than that, you cannot predict them in the long run. So, stop worrying in advance.

If they do happen, take some action, starting from keeping up your positive attitude

6. The government decisions: I mean that you have no control over them, unless you are living in the country where referenda and strikes can persuade the government not to impose things such as new taxes. As an EU citizen, you do have little control on the directives ordered by the European Commission.

Why Is Taking Responsibility So Difficult?

Many people develop this tendency to be unable to accept personal responsibility for their actions. Sometimes you can also feel that being responsible for your life is overwhelming. Learn why:

Taking action can be uncomfortable. I could also add that taking responsibility 's hard because people are lazy. The comfort zone has a significant impact on your decisions; it will be tempting you to choose something that is more pleasurable, even if it will not contribute to your happiness. You will always be facing temptations, just when you should work on productive tasks.

Responsibility requires humility and honesty. You must face your fears, limits, flaws and all other brutal truth about yourself. Then you can do something about it. However, it is easier to avoid discomfort, pain and other negative states of mind, and sometimes body. Therefore, you will find excuses and procrastinate. We are attracted to pleasure and avoid pain.

Prejudices can narrow your thoughts. Some of your beliefs and convictions may narrow your perception. If you have prejudices e.g. concerning the rich people, you will always see money as something wrong. This will stop you from meeting individuals who are wealthy and learning from them. You will not seek a better job or another option to increase your income.

Arrogance which makes you blind. You probably know this category of people who think that they are flawless. Lack of humility and ignorance are the most common reasons of arrogance. When you are arrogant, you cannot see other options for your choices.

Feelings of insecurity can paralyse you. High self-confidence and high self-esteem are crucial to take responsibility for your life. Otherwise, you may feel insecure. If you have been raised in a very chaotic environment, have constantly been put down, yelled at or emotionally abused, the chances are that at first it will be hard for you to take responsibility. You may also be tempted to blame your parents.

How to Take Responsibility for Your Life

1. Stop blaming. It is only you who has control over your thoughts, decisions, language and reactions. Even if someone hurt you, you are responsible for the way you will handle the pain.

There are three kinds of blame:

You can blame others for anything. But the truth is that it was you who took criticism personally or did not listen what other party has been speaking. Blaming others is easy. We blame the government, neighbours, parents… often for the things they cannot control.

You can blame the circumstances. Inclement weather, traffic jam, illness, lack of time, the past, personal limits are probably the most common excuses. However, the truth is that you did not want to move your backside to take some action. Bad weather can be a blessing if you use this condition in the right way.

You can blame yourself. In other words, you criticise yourself, cultivating guilt. Is it useful? No. Unfortunately, I know many people who beat themselves up. If you belong to that category, I will show you in the next chapters how to handle this challenge.

2. Stop complaining. Doing so you simply focus on the downside of life, which makes things seem worse than they are. It can also easily distract you from all the right things going on in your life. While complaining, you can create a habit and then you will always see things in a negative light. The more you complain, the easier you abandon personal responsibility.

3. Stop making excuses. In other words, stop blaming the circumstances for not taking or for taking the wrong actions. Setting new goals, you often have a sort of "backup excuse" in case you are to fail. Usually, this will be your biggest fear – of being weak, helpless, vulnerable. Making excuses is an unhealthy way of thinking. Failure or success in that goal is on you and no one else, regardless of external circumstances. By taking responsibility and recognising this, you are more likely to take the necessary actions to succeed.

4. Stop playing the victim. Playing the victim is the opposite of personal responsibility. It happens because the victim blames others or finds excuses. In fact, playing victim involves surrendering control of your life to external circumstances and other people. The victim is passive and reactive.

If you were brought up by your overprotective mother, then you have learned helplessness in order to receive what you wanted from your mother. Then it becomes very challenging to take personal responsibility.

Here is how Wikipedia defines "victim playing":

"Manipulators often play the victim role ("poor me") by portraying themselves as victims of circumstances or someone else's behaviour in order to gain pity or sympathy or to evoke compassion and thereby get something from another. Caring and conscientious people cannot stand to see anyone suffering, and the manipulator often finds it easy and rewarding to play on sympathy to get cooperation."

5. Learn life lessons. This means being honest with yourself and taking action. You know when you have not committed 100% to the task, avoiding the mistake, but did not want to change the way you acted. An honest approach to your flaws and mistakes will help you to take action to correct it.

6. Improve your self-esteem. Your self-perception and self-worth will be so high that there will be no need to avoid discomfort when you have such high self-esteem. You feel no sorrier for yourself or inferior. It is of great importance in the case of a long-term illness or disability. I have discussed this in Chapter Two.

7. Build your self-confidence. When you are confident in your abilities, you stop becoming defensive when you make a mistake. It becomes natural for you to own your contribution to a situation and take responsibility. How to build self-confidence? Stop comparing yourself to other people and change self-limiting beliefs.

8. Give of yourself in service to others. It teaches empathy and compassion. You gain more control and can be more proud of your influence on the world. You make a difference every time you make someone happy and see the delight in their eyes. Think for a while. What could you do today to make a difference and create more happiness in the world?

9. Learn ways to let go of fear. Fear can create insecurities and is the biggest obstacle in life. Especially the fear of rejection and the fear of failure. Changing negative beliefs and thoughts will help you to handle this emotion. You will learn these tips in Chapter Four and Chapter Five.

10. Accept yourself for who you are. Learn to love yourself unconditionally. Take your body, mental limits, your life choices and be kind to yourself. You have learned how to practice self-acceptance in Chapter Two. If you are still having doubts how to love yourself, read that chapter again and do all the exercises described there.

Excuses

Excuses are all the reasons you give to avoid taking responsibility, which may involve pain as you need to pay the price of the consequences for your decisions and actions. Excuses enable you to prevent the pain quickly.

Excuses are just our beliefs which automatically appear as negative thoughts when you face something causing discomfort. "I'm afraid of failure" is just the cover for "I won't handle this." Let's meet the most common excuses.

Think of your latest challenges – learning something new, starting a business, changing job, moving on from an abusive relationship or just clearing the clutter. What excuses come to your mind? Check if you agree (true) or disagree (false) with the reasons listed below.

EXCUSE	TRUE	FALSE
I have no appropriate skills.		
I have no team/ connections.		
I've got to pay bills.		

EXCUSE	TRUE	FALSE
I'm afraid of competition.		
I'm not educated enough.		
I'm not self-confident		
I'm not competent/good enough.		
I have no helpers.		
I can't drive.		
I'm married and have kids.		
I'm not as talkative/ persuasive etc. as others.		
I have nosy neighbours.		
I don't have the guts.		
Nobody will support me.		
I don't know how to do that.		
Too many people have already tried and failed.		
I'm too scared.		
It's too hard.		

Mark one point for each excuse which is true in your case. Count your score: ……………

0-6 points You are a responsible person, dealing excellently with your excuses. However, pay attention to the excuses with which you agree. You might use them frequently.

7-15 points Not good. You agree with half of excuses on the list. Read the tips below to question the excuses and start more responsible life.

16-18 points Alarm! You are flooded with excuses and use them nearly all the time. You will most definitely need to do the exercises from the next part of this chapter.

Now I will present you some challenges. Read them and write an automatic excuse that comes to your mind. You can use some from the list above.

Challenge: You are living with an abusive boyfriend/parents and know that this relationship does not make sense. It is time to leave.
Excuses:...

Challenge: Your friend hurt you and you need to tell him that in an assertive way.
Excuses:...

Challenge: You are supposed to clean your house and procrastinated about it for a month.
Excuses:...

Challenge: You are supposed to visit your grandmother.
Excuses:...

Challenge: Your job is low-paid and you make ends meet, will you change?
Excuses:...

Challenge: You consider starting a business.
Excuses:...

Challenge: You should go to the dentist/doctor for a check-up.
Excuses:...

Challenge: You are supposed to answer your sister's email.
Excuses:...

Challenge: You need to ask for something but won't because you're afraid the answer will be no.
Excuses:...

Challenge: You should quit an addiction.
Excuses:...

Now take one goal or task from your life. It will be something you don't like doing because of fear and self-limiting beliefs. Describe the goal or task below:

....

Having defined the case, list five automatic negative thoughts about it. For example: I can't do it. It's too difficult. etc. If you really do not like this task or goal, this exercise should be easy.

My excuses are…

1. ....
2. ....
3. ....
4. ....
5. ....

Now you are ready to face your excuses and overcome them. Do the exercises described below and you will soon notice how much energy and enthusiasm you have.

How to Stop Making Excuses?

1. Use the snippets. They are short statements which you can say when an excuse emerges. Use them when the excuses are strong, as an emergency tool. It is a brutal method. No discussion with the excuses is allowed, you just eliminate them. Here is a sample list:

• No buts!

• No excuses!

• Stop it!

• Stop excuses!

• B***s***t!

• I'm responsible!

- I'm in charge!
- I can do it!
- I will handle it!

Choose the snippet from the list above and learn it by heart. Then think of one of your challenges, the thing which you procrastinate about. Write it down again and add one automatic excuse you would use to justify your procrastination. Use the list which you have made before:

....

....

Now choose your snippet. Rewrite your excuse once and the snippet three times.

1. ....

2. ....

3. ....

For the next month, when you avoid taking action and generate excuses, use the snippet. You can also wear a rubber band on your wrist for the first week and pull it whenever you start making excuses. After 30 days check your progress and continue creating a new habit for the next 60 days, monitoring your progress on an app such as Habit Bull, an application for Android.

2. Question your excuses. This method is also good in case of changing negative beliefs. This tool can be used in less acute cases. Here are examples of questioning the most common excuses.

EXCUSE

I'm too old/ young.

QUESTIONS

- How true is that?
- What's the evidence that you are too old/young?
- What's the real problem with being old/young?
- How can you use your age to your advantage?
- Have you ever tried this thing before successfully?
- What does "too old/young" mean?

EXCUSE

I have no money.

QUESTIONS

- What does "not enough money" mean?
- Have you ever tried to make it?
- How true is that excuse?
- What can you do to make more money?
- What resources could you use to earn money?
- Who could help you to earn the money you need?

EXCUSE

I have no time.

QUESTIONS

- How could you manage your time to take action and do the thing?
- How can you be more productive?
- Are you sure that time is the real problem?
- What are you waiting for?

EXCUSE

I have no team/helpers.

QUESTIONS

- What can you do to find helpers?
- How true is it?
- What is the real challenge here and how can you overcome it?
- Who has already helped you and how could you ask them to do that again?
- What can you do right now to find the first person for your dream?

EXCUSE

I'm afraid of failure.

QUESTIONS

- What can you do right now to improve your skills?
- When was the last time you succeeded in this field?

EXCUSE

I'm not good/experienced/smart enough.

QUESTIONS

- What is the evidence that you are "not good enough"?
- What "not good enough" means?
- What are you waiting for?

Now take your excuses and answer the questions below. Do this exercise in your transformation diary.

My excuse

....

- What does _____ mean?
- How true is it?
- Does it make any sense?
- What is the worst-case scenario? How can you handle it?
- How probable is the worst-case scenario (%)?
- What resources do you already have?
- When was the last time you succeeded in a similar case?
- What are you waiting for?
- Why do you think so? What can you do about it?
- Are you really going to let this excuse stop you?

Answering the questions above, you will soon learn that your excuse is not true and the thing which you procrastinate about, is not so terrible to do.

What to Change in Your Life?

Many people have asked me what to change to become a happy person. The simplest answer could be anything that makes you unhappy. To make changes you need to take the following steps:

1. Expect more from yourself. This means leaving your comfort zone and setting ambitious goals. I have described an exercise in Chapter One in which you described your life five years ago, now and in five years' time. If you have not done it, do it now. Are you happy with what you have achieved within last five years? Now think what you could do to achieve more in each field of your life. At this moment think of one thing that you want to change in your life – right now. Write it down.

2. Change your limiting beliefs. You have already discovered the difference between uplifting and negative views. You have beliefs describing everything in your life: health, finance, relationships, the boss, your job, your parents, your appearance, the government, etc. Now the task is to change these beliefs which impede your happiness. You will learn how to transform your beliefs in Chapter Four.

3. Change your language. Words transform. How many times have you said to yourself "I'm an idiot?" You see, in this way you program yourself to being an idiot. What we say, we start believing in and then behave in that way. How to change your language? I will tell you in Chapter Six.

Exercise:

For the next three days note down what words you are using the most often, how you described yourself or your achievements. Then you will see how far from the happiness you are now.

My language: (the words, metaphors and questions used the most often – check Chapter Six for examples):

....

....

....

....

4. Change your thoughts. Your thoughts are like seeds planted in your subconscious mind. They program it. It is up to you if you think about positive things or dwell on negativity. In both cases, sooner or later you will reap what you have sown – by attracting the circumstances and people in harmony with your dominant thoughts. I will show you how to change the negative thoughts in Chapter

Three of this book. Now just take a while and describe what you are thinking the most during the day. This is your dominant thought:

My dominant thoughts:

…..

…..

…..

5. Change your behaviour. It will be obvious after you have changed your thoughts, words and beliefs. Your behaviour will also change. Do an experiment. From now on, start smiling at any person you meet on the street and see how people will respond differently.

We can say that what you do to other people, even what you think of them comes back multiplied, according to the universal Law of Boomerang. Therefore, any small change in your behaviour will dramatically change your life.

6. Change your strategy. It just means that if one way of working on your goals does not work, you can do it in a different one that you can choose.

You can also change your environment. It means that you can try to influence other people, their behaviours or thoughts. However, they will decide to change or not, and you cannot do anything about it. Changing the environment also means leaving the present one. If you are living around the toxic people, have a low-paid job, you can decide to move on. You can also change the circle of your friends as you grow.

What Stops You from Change?

You know that making changes is not easy. It requires courage, self-discipline and willingness to sacrifice something to become a happier and more fulfilled person. There are three conditions you need to meet to make any change. They are:

1. You need to take action. Nothing will change if you do nothing. Positive thinking, even for the day, will not bring you results if you do nothing. I know it is hard and the most difficult moment is to start doing something. For example, if you are supposed to wash up the big pile of dishes, picking up and removing the first one will be the hardest. The same applies to any task or goal that you are working on.

2. You need to leave your comfort zone. Changes mean facing discomfort and the unknown. But otherwise, nothing will change. One of the self-development gurus said that if you do the same things, in the same way, you obtain the same results.

3. You need to win the killers of change. I will describe them in a minute. Be aware that there will be many obstacles which will be stopping you from taking action or leaving your comfort zone. You will be tempted not to work on your goals many times. How you overcome the obstacles will determine if the process of changing your life is successful.

What Are the Obstacles to Change?

1. Fear. You may be afraid of the unknown, of failure or of not being good enough. All these concerns are summarised as the fear of change. How to deal with fear? I will tell you in Chapter Seven of this book.

2. Not having time is another reason. It is an excuse, the most frequent excuse by the way. When you do have to change, being forced by the external force, time does not count. For example, when the doctor tells you that if you don't stop smoking, you will die in a year's time. Then you will usually not postpone giving up the addiction. Chapter Eleven will teach you how to find more time.

3. Not wanting to be uncomfortable. You can see here how strong our comfort zone is and how we avoid pain. As I wrote earlier, leaving the comfort zone is a must if you want to change something. For example, finding a new job or meeting someone new always involves some stress. If we didn't expose ourselves to discomfort, we would not grow.

4. Perfectionism. In other words, the fear that you are not good enough – as a romantic partner, parent, child, worker or business person. But the truth is that we will never be perfect, and there always will be flaws and things to improve. Making changes mean making progress, growing, improving what you have already achieved.

5. Being overwhelmed with all that you should do. Overwhelming causes stress and then the last thing to do is to make changes. You have probably gone through that at least once. When you feel overwhelmed, you assume that change is impossible as you cannot tackle the current task. Then you need to learn how to deal with the feeling of being overwhelmed.

6. Not knowing how. At first glance, it may be the worst of all the obstacles. However, you can always find the solution on the Internet, in the books from the library or a bookshop, ask other people such as friends, counsellor, professional experts. Just define clearly what you want to change.

Why Leave Your Comfort Zone?

According to Wikipedia: "the comfort zone is a psychological state in which a person feels familiar, at ease, in control and experiences moderate anxiety and stress. In the zone a steady level of performance is possible."

Bardwick defines comfort zone as "a behavioural state where a person operates in an anxiety-neutral position." Brown describes it as: "Where our uncertainty, scarcity, and vulnerability are minimised — where we believe we'll have access to enough love, food, talent, time, admiration. Where we feel, we have some control."

To leave your comfort zone, you need to know the benefits of doing so.

1. Your comfort zone will grow. The more regularly you leave your comfort zone, the more you will increase the number of things you are comfortable with. Let's say that you dread public speaking and leadership. Practicing it regularly, if only in Toastmasters, will diminish your fear and make you more confident. When your comfort zone grows, you will also be able to enjoy more things in life since familiarity makes you more likely to experience something, even if it turned us off at first.

2. You will grow. This happens because expanding your current comfort zone means that you have more skills, can cope with more issues and that you are a stronger and more confident person.

3. You will be more productive. Comfort kills productivity. This happens as without the sense of unease that comes from having deadlines and expectations; you tend to do nothing and lose ambition to do more and learn new things. Pushing your personal boundaries can help you get more done, and find smarter ways to work.

4. You will find it easier to push your limits in the future. When you practice, it gets easier over time to step out of your comfort zone. As you leave your comfort zone, you will become accustomed to that state of optimal anxiety. Brené Brown calls it "productive discomfort." When it becomes more reasonable to you, you will be willing to push farther before your performance falls off. You will see that when you challenge yourself, your comfort zone adjusts, which means that what was anxiety-inducing becomes easier as you repeat it.

5. You will become more motivated. Paradoxically, novelty tends to increase levels of dopamine in the brain, which is part of the brain's reward centre. Dopamine motivates you to go looking for rewards, and novelty increases that urge.

6. You'll handle better new and unexpected challenges. Brené Brown explains that "one of the worst things we can do is pretend fear and uncertainty don't exist." Why? Because you can experience some of that change in a controlled, manageable environment. It happens when you take risks in a controlled fashion and challenge yourself to things you normally wouldn't do. Learning to live outside your comfort zone when you choose to, can prepare you for life changes that force you out of it.

How to Leave Your Comfort Zone

Now, when you know the benefits of stepping out of your comfort zone, there are four things that you must do.

1. Become comfortable with taking risks. Your comfort zone is comfortable because you know what to expect there. Leaving it can be scary because you might fail and lose something. However, you might also gain something. There are two things which you can do to become comfortable with taking risks:

(i) Practice acceptance. Acknowledge when things don't go your way, and they may not. Clinging to your comfort zone, you're hanging on to an idea that the world is supposed to be a safe and

predictable place. Accept that there will be challenges and that you will have to change your strategy or modify your goal.

(ii) Practice non-attachment. While deciding to do something, do it for its sake, not so that you can get a particular result. If you meet a nice person, don't assume straight away that it might be your boyfriend or even husband. If he does, perfect. Let go of your attachment to a particular outcome; instead, focus on the joy of doing whatever you're doing.

2. Plan the Risk of the Day. It is a small task when you expose yourself to discomfort. In a case of social anxiety, it will be staying around people, no matter what they say and if you say anything. What counts here is just the exposure for social situations.

3. Face your fears. There are the big fears, such as rejection, failure, criticism, but there are also many subtle scares you bow to every day, e.g. the fear of breaking a bone or falling. When you face your fears, you will instantly become more confident and stronger.

4. Enjoy the unknown. Recall the last time you felt excited about not knowing what was going to happen next? If you stay in your comfort zone deeply, it's probably been within a long period. Think how much you miss it; the mixture of anticipation and anxiety that makes your heart flutter at the same time? Bring that feeling back into your life.

Plan the Risk of The Day

Take a Risk of the Day – something small, uncomfortable, but will make you stronger. It may be learning new skills, improving social relationships, working on your weak points or overcoming them. Make the list of five things that you are afraid of doing right now.

1. ….......................................
2. ….......................................
3. ….......................................
4. ….......................................
5. ….......................................

Now plan what small thing you can do every day to expose yourself to discomfort and fear for the next week.

1. ….......................................
2. ….......................................
3. ….......................................
4. ….......................................
5. ….......................................

Impact of Pleasure and Pain On Life

It's human nature to move towards pleasure and to avoid pain. In other words, you will make most of your decisions based on avoiding pain and seeking pleasure. And you usually avoid pain more than want pleasure. It can work against the goals and objectives you are trying to achieve.

Be aware that every decision you make will lead to one or more of the following consequences: short-term pain, short-term pleasure, long-term pain, great pleasure.

Let's say that you are living around uninterested and unfriendly people. You are considering moving out. You see the joy and relief when you change the environment, but you also understand the stress of moving out. These are short-term pain and pleasure. You might prefer staying, despite the negative energy of the place, because fear and the unknown will be more painful. In the long run, however, you will experience more pain than pleasure.

In addition to this, the intensity of pain and pleasure will be ranging from low to high. There are two rules which you apply here: The higher the intensity of pain or pleasure, the bigger impact it will have on the decision you are about to make. On the contrary, the lower the intensity of the pain and pleasure, the less of an impact it will have on your decision-making process. So, the more you are fed up with your neighbours, the less uncomfortable it will be changing your accommodation.

Here's the fun thing. You make decisions based on what you think things will feel like in the future, not based on reality. It's all about our PERCEPTION of reality.

Do this next exercise which is described by Paul McKenna.

Let's say that you have been invited to a disco. You're still deciding whether you will go. Create the two images in your mind: Firstly, imagine standing awkwardly in a corner, surrounded by people you do not know and have nothing in common with. How much do you want to go to the disco, on a scale from 1 to 10, where ten means 'I want to go'?

Secondly, imagine yourself standing there comfortably, surrounded by people who are interested in spending time with you. How much do you want to go to the disco now?

You can do this exercise for any situation where you hesitate what decision to make. Choose one now:

…..

…..

Can I Use Pain and Pleasure to Change My Life?

A human being has three kinds of brain: the reptilian brain which is responsible for reflexes and instincts is referred to as the first brain, the mammalian brain which is responsible for emotions is referred to as the second brain, and the higher brain which is responsible for logical thinking is the third brain.

Whenever an older brain disagrees with a newer brain, the first brain always wins. So, you should not run away when you logically know there's nothing to be afraid of. However, your reptilian brain is seeing a danger and prepares the body to flee.

The reptilian brain recognises only two states: pain and pleasure. Each emotion can be classified to one of these states. For example, love and excitement are driven by pleasure while anger and guilt by pain.

By changing the pain and pleasure which you associate with some actions, your emotions will automatically drive you to take action. Here is how it works:

Let's choose the example of the toxic neighbours again. You can start thinking that your neighbours are even more nosy than it seemed before. Thinking so, you will decide to move out. Then you will take the action necessary to implement your decision. In this case, you are avoiding pain.

On the other hand, you are in a romantic relationship with a person you love. Being with them brings you a lot of pleasure. Therefore, you may be ready to move out to live with them in their house or flat, even if it means compromises and it is not yours.

Changing the pain and pleasure associations is incredibly easy, although may not be simple. You need to associate it with an action. Then your emotions will drive you to decide to do something about it. When your emotions work with your logical brain, what follow effortlessly is you stop sabotaging your actions. Just brainstorm how to put your association into reality.

Think of three areas of your life where you logically know what you want, but can't quite feel it emotionally. And write them down. It could be losing weight, getting the courage to approach someone or anything else that you want. All the scenarios mentioned above have one thing in common: taking action is too much of a hassle, so you end up doing nothing.

You say "Well, maybe I'd like to lose weight..." or "I would like to approach new people..." Using "maybe" or "would like to" means that you simply associate too much pain with change. When you transform your language into the more uplifting one, your words will be "let go of the rope and lose weight" or "I'm going to get this part of my life handled, no matter what!" The pain of staying in the same old routine is considerable, but the potential pleasure of change is so large that you just cannot wait to get started. This is an example of how changing your language can change your focus and attitude.

Just remember to associate pleasure with the desired outcome, and massive pain with sticking to the same old routine. In the case of nosy neighbours, moving out will bring you massive pleasure while staying in the old place brings only extreme pain, even if the former will also involve some stress.

You know that making changes is not easy. It requires courage, self-discipline and willingness to sacrifice something to become a happier and more fulfilled person. There are three conditions you need to meet to make any change. They are:

You need to take action. *Nothing will change if you do nothing.* Positive thinking, even for the day, will not bring you results if you don't do anything. I know it is hard and the most difficult moment is to start doing something. For example, if you are supposed to wash up the big pile of dishes, picking up and removing the first one will be the hardest. The same applies to any task or goal on which you are working.

This is a very powerful tool. Anthony Robbins shows how pain and pleasure work while changing neuro associations. Let's see how it operates in the case of abusive relationships. It may be your spouse, but also a co-worker or even your friend. You know about the abuse, but do not change your life. Let's see what you could do to be happier:

Think about the associations which you have right now. For example, if you're are living in an abusive relationship, you probably associate staying there with comfort and safety, at least a bit, even if he calls you names and even batters you. Leaving the abuser can be linked to the pain of breakup and uncertainty in your mind. In other words, you stick to what you're doing right now, because changing would mean pain.

Associate the pain with making no changes. Link pain to staying in the relationship. Notice how many times he has hit you, how many times you were bullied and how lonely you feel every day. Make sure you feel the pain. It's not about logical thinking. Feel the gut-level pain, and associate it with staying in an abusive relationship.

Next, associate pleasure to making changes. Imagine that you are moving on. What it would be like to be free and independent again, to find the people who will admire you. All the places you can visit without being controlled. And any other pleasure that relates to changing your life. At last, you can do what you could not dream about while living with your abusive partner. Find two other advantages to ending an abusive relationship.

Finally, make sure you can get any secondary pay-offs handled. In other words, the benefits you get from your current behaviour. Figure out how to get them in a different way. I will show you how to do it in Chapter Four. Now let's analyse the example with an abusive relationship.

Suppose that staying with the abuser gives you financial stability. This is your pay-off. What can you do? Start planning how you could be secure in yourself, without him. Maybe a new job?

The fear of loneliness is another pay-off. You don't want to go for coffee or a walk alone, not to mention a holiday. It is painful when you have no one to talk to, even if they may abuse you. However, think which is better: feeling happy on your own or unhappy with someone who undermines your happiness and self-esteem?

Let's take another example, concerning your self-responsibility for your life. If you decide that you want to eliminate blaming others from your life, just link pain to it and realise that it's not outside events that make you feel bad. It's your attitude towards them, like blame. Associate blame with feeling bad. Think of and imagine how people will enjoy being around you more if you stop blaming other people, and how much more fun you will have.

Another great technique is to ask yourself "Where will I be ten years from now if I keep doing this?" This question will show you how useless your pay-off is. Write your answers in your transformation diary.

You will learn how to change your beliefs, thoughts, language and how to transform your negative emotions in the next few chapters.

How to Learn to Make Better Decisions

You are not born with the license of making smart decisions. In many cases, you need to learn that skills by trial and error. Sometimes you might have a helper who will show you some options, like a business mentor. However, even then it is up to you what decision you will make.

Tony Robbins said, *"Not making a decision is also a decision."* Therefore, it is better to learn how to make them. Not making your own choices means that life or other people will decide for you, on their terms, not yours. So how can you learn to make better decisions?

1. Pay attention to your emotions. "Don't make permanent decisions based on temporary feelings", an old saying says. It rings true. Happy people recognise and understand their feelings so that they can look at decisions as objectively and rationally. Unfortunately, most people aren't good at managing or even recognising their emotions. Therefore, I have written Chapter Seven to show you how to handle your negative emotions.

2. Turn small decisions into routines. Decision-making works like a muscle. When you use it over the course of the day, it gets too exhausted to function effectively. Work around your decision fatigue to eliminate smaller decisions by turning them into routines. Doing so frees up your mental resources for more complex decisions.

3. Make big decisions in the morning. If you want to beat decision fatigue, save small decisions for after work (when decision fatigue is greatest) and to tackle complex judgements in the morning, when your mind is fresh. Facing a stream of important decisions, you wake up early and work on your most complicated tasks. Then, when you can face the bunch of distracting minor decisions like phones ringing, emails coming in, etc. You can also do some of the smaller things the night before, to get a head start on the next day. For example, lay out your outfit at night, so you don't even have to think about it when you wake up.

4. Evaluate your options objectively. When wrapped up in a decision, happy people weigh their options against a pre-determined set of criteria as they know that this makes decision-making easier and more efficient. Consider some helpful questions:
- How does this decision benefit me?
- How does it hurt me?
- Would I regret making this decision?
- How does this benefit …….. (someone or something)?
- How does it hurt ……….(someone or something)?
- Would I regret not making this decision?
- Do I make this decision by my values?

Exercise:

Imagine one of the challenges which you are facing right now. You are not sure what decision to make. Write your problem down.

……..………………………………………………………………………………………

Now take your transformation diary and answer the questions listed above in writing.

5. Sleep on it. Doing so, you ensure that you have clarity of thought when approaching it the next day. It also allows time for your emotions to run their course. Acting too quickly, you tend to react. However, when you give more focus and time to your decision, you expose important facets of it that you didn't see before.

6. Use physical exercise to recharge. The stress of a major decision produces cortisol, the chemical that triggers the fight-or-flight response. Cortisol impedes your ability to think clearly and rationally. Do some physical exercises when you find yourself stressing about a decision. 30 minutes are enough to produce a massive amount of endorphins and to regain a clear mind. Exercise also helps you to overcome that fight-or-flight state because cortisol is put to practical use. It has been proven by scientists that long-term exercise improves the overall functioning of the brain regions responsible for decision-making.

7. Always go back to your moral compass. Happy people know the importance of sticking to their morals when making an important decision. They use them as trusted guides when emotions are pulling happy people in a different direction. Your values are your moral compass.

8. Seek outside counsel. Approaching a decision, you may have a natural tendency to pick an alternative. Then you gather information to support that decision, instead of collecting information and then choosing a side. Research opinions and advice from people who bring different perspectives to your situation. Their views help you weigh your options more objectively and to spot your subjective or irrational tendencies.

How to Make Good Decisions

"Waiting hurts. Forgetting hurts. But not knowing which decision to take can sometimes be the most painful..."
— *José N. Harris, MI VIDA, A Story of Faith, Hope and Love*

According to Susan Jeffers, you can make 'no lose' and 'no win' decisions. Most people make the 'no win' decisions. Making the "no lose" decisions requires trust. You manifest it by affirming:

"I can't lose – regardless of the outcome of the decision. I look forward to the opportunities for learning and growing that either choice gives me."

'No win' decision assumes that if you make a wrong decision, it will ruin your life. This paralyses you with anxiety. You don't trust your impulses, but listen to what other people think. After the decision is made you create more anxiety by trying to control the outcome. Moreover, you convince yourself you've made the wrong decision. Now learn how you can make the decisions, in which you don't lose:

1. List the options for your choice. Think of one case which requires making a decision in the near future. Write down your options below.

…...

…...

…...

2. Define who could help you. Think of someone who you can talk to about the decision to be made. List three people.

1. ....

2. ....

3. ....

3. Think what you need to learn to make the decision. Apart from helpers, you need to know as much as you can about the options which you are considering. Answer the question:

 What must I learn about either choice? How can I learn as much as I can about each choice? Write the answers down.

OPTION 1   **OPTION 2**   **OPTION 3**

4. Pick one option. Not making a decision is also a decision and not taking action bears consequences of lost opportunities. The option which you will choose is not your final decision yet, so don't worry.

5. Check if your choice is consistent with your life values and life path. You already know them after reading Chapter One and doing all the exercises which are there. Look again at the three options which you have described above. Which choice meets your values and life path?

....

In case this option is not in your life values and life path, choose another because your decision will not be suitable for you. For example, if you value honesty, selling products using manipulative techniques will cause discomfort and sooner or later you will dump what you are doing.

6. Listen to your intuition. What do you feel? Excitement? Fear? The answer will help you to define whether the option is right. In the end, it will be your decision and even if others give you advice, you choose.

7. Make your decision. Trust fate. You have done all you could to increase the probability of success. You will not know if you succeeded by procrastinating. And remember that not making a decision is also your decision.

8. Check the effects of your decision. Having made your choice, monitor what is working and what is not. Adjust your behaviour until you achieve your goal. It may turn out that you need to make another choice because your decision is not working. But even then, remember that you did your best to learn all its pros and cons while making the decision.

9. Make another decision if necessary. There is no perfect solution, we are humans. It may turn out that you will have to make some decisions before you obtain the desired outcome. Don't be discouraged when after your first decision, you will not achieve the effect you want. Make another attempt until you are happy with the result.

How to Make a Commitment Declaration

Once you have learned what it means to take responsibility for your life, how to win excuses and leave a comfort zone, decide to commit to your life, to be happy and successful. How to do it? Write down your commitment statement. For example, Tina wrote it in this way:

I, Tina, declare here that I am making the decision to commit to creating a happy and fulfilled life. I commit to: change my negative thoughts, beliefs and language into the happiness ones and to manage my emotions wisely. I also commit to eliminating all excuses on the way to work on my fulfilment in life.

Now it is your turn. Write down your declaration of commitment to living a happy and fulfilled life. If you are not sure, use the template I will give you at the end of this book. Print it and hang it on the wall in a place where you can look at it on the daily basis while working and cooking.

It is even better when you read this commitment statement every day in the morning after getting up and at night before going to bed so you will create a habit and work on your life on autopilot.

Chapter 4
Transform Your Beliefs

"Beliefs have the power to create and the power to destroy. Human beings have the awesome ability to take any experience of their lives and create a meaning that disempowers them or one that can literally save their lives." – Tony Robbins

Tina had never thought whether her beliefs would have an impact on her life. During some sessions, I have shown her that she can become a much happier person changing some core beliefs. This chapter will show you how to do it. You will learn:

- What is a belief.
- How to define beliefs.
- What are examples of positive beliefs.
- How to recognise negative beliefs.
- How to identify core negative beliefs.
- How to define negative beliefs.
- When you are not ready to change your beliefs.
- What are the examples of negative core beliefs.
- What are the three core subconscious beliefs.

- Now to identify a negative belief.
- Whose beliefs you have inherited.
- How to change negative beliefs.

What Is a Belief?

There are some definitions of what 'belief' really means.

According to Wikipedia: "Belief is the state of mind in which a person thinks something to be the case, with or without there being empirical evidence to prove that something is the case with factual certainty. In other words, belief is when someone thinks something is a reality, real when they have no absolute verified foundation for their certainty of the truth or realness of something."

According to Cambridge Dictionary belief is "the feeling of being sure that something exists or is true: something that you believe."

You can have beliefs or convictions. The second ones are deeply entrenched beliefs, tough to change. They are like the dogma of your life. Convictions are used to protect you and are empowered by your sub-consciousness. You need a very sharp shift in your life to break a conviction. Phobias are based on convictions that the things you are afraid of are dangerous and can cause death.

This chapter will show you that you can transform both beliefs and convictions. How to do it?

Beliefs have an impact on your thinking and making decisions. But they also attract the things in which you believe because what you believe becomes your reality, according to one of the mental laws.

Beliefs also literally shape your map of reality, because they define what filter you are using to perceive information. Beliefs are those filters which determine why ten people can sit through the same experience and have ten different views (or realities) of what happened.

Define Beliefs

You have beliefs and convictions in each field of life. By discovering your beliefs, you can learn what your focus in life is.

If you want to meet the truth about what you believe in, take out your transformation diary. Finish each sentence, writing five answers as quickly as you can, without analysing if they are right. Just write. Let's take some important things in your life, based on your values:

Life is …......................... Love is …............................

People are …..................... I feel healthy when...........................

I feel happy when …............ I feel rich when...............................

Money is........................... I can …..................................

I can't …........................... I am …................................,...........

Sex is …........................... Work is …............................

I feel rejected when.............. I am afraid of …................................

I don't like........................... because …..

Now you know much more about yourself. At this stage, you don't know yet if your beliefs help you or not, i.e. are helpful or negative. First let's check what positive beliefs you could develop to become a happier person.

Examples of Positive Beliefs

Positive beliefs empower you. They help you to grow, to achieve your goals, to enjoy life and to be happy. They attract positive people and circumstances to your life. If you have no idea what positive beliefs you can apply, here is a list of twenty-eight of the best beliefs which you can have. I suggest you to print the pages with them and learn these beliefs by heart.

1. I am in charge of my life. Yes, you are. I will discuss it in more detail in Chapter Ten. In short, you are in charge, because you can choose how to react even on things which are beyond your control.

2. I can make tomorrow better. You can change your future by taking action today. Everything that you do is a seed which will bring some crops. It depends on you what kind of crops you will reap. But you can always sow better seeds than you have so far – by taking care of your thoughts, language, and beliefs.

3. There are a lot of opportunities around me. Happy people have their mind set on abundance and opportunity and not scarcity because this kind of attitude makes a world of a difference. Life, positivity, love, energy, opportunities, success and happiness are abundant and you can receive them – just change your focus.

4. I do not need the approval of others to succeed. You might find it difficult to believe. While looking for others' approval and consent you will not go very far and you will certainly not be self-empowered. You are chasing their standards, joining the race where there is no victory and losing your unique self. Happy people follow their heart even when others are sceptical, demean them or do not consent to their actions.

5. My intentions influence my reality. It does not mean that you should believe in magic where you can wish things into being. However, focused and strong intention is a powerful thing making a lot of things happen and certainly getting you to your destination faster.

6. People are catalysts, not obstacles, to succeed. You will leverage your efforts by a thousand-fold, networking with the right people. Even if there are people who want to destroy your success, you can always find someone who is helpful and supportive.

7. Positive thoughts are powerful and empowering. This happens because they attract positive things and happiness into your life. I will show you exactly what positive thoughts are worth to your intention to be happy.

8. Love is always available. Just choose to open your heart, even in the most difficult challenges and heart-wrenching tragedies. Love is not present when you close yourself off and shut down, when you restrict the flow of love into your lives. Love takes many shapes and sometimes can feel like grief, anger and sadness.

9. How can I use this situation? When you face a challenge, ask yourself: "How can I use this? What can I do right now to succeed?" When you ask these questions, your life will soon transform in a massive way because you will be seeking solutions instead of being overwhelmed by the challenge.

10. Hard work and perseverance are rewarded. As a rule of thumb, you may not receive the reward immediately, but it is paid off in the long run. However, always find the way to make your hard work a smart one.

11. My past can be reviewed and rewritten. You may be locked in your past or think that your past circumstances determine your future. You will not change the past but can reprogram wrong codes of your sub-consciousness. I will show you how to do it in Chapter Four of this book.

12.There are forces and energies, helping me if I'm conscious. You cannot perceive certain subtle energies but some happy people believe that positive and negative energy flows from things. People, just like ancient Chinese traditions, believe in the movement of the Chi (Qi) or life energy. You can make yourself aware of this although it takes practice.

13. I never take things personally. I stopped taking life circumstances personally. Otherwise, you will end up enslaved emotionally. Put all the rejections, criticisms, cold shoulders, etc. within an impersonal bracket. They are not rejecting or insulting you, but your automatic thoughts about them.

14. Everyone I meet is a teacher. Even your worst enemy or the person who humiliated you can be your teacher. They show you what you need to work on, what not to do and give you an opportunity to perform better the next time.

15. Bad patches are temporary. We all go through bad patches. These are the times when you are down, without motivation, struggling with many challenges. It's the cycle of life, like the seasons of the year. But you are always in charge and have the power to make decisions or to choose your reactions.

16. Everything will turn out all right at the end. I can assure you, it works. No matter how bad things might seem now, they will surely pass – as they always do. There is a lesson to be learned from every challenge, every crisis. Remember that within chaos and compost, opportunities and flowers bloom.

17. I can always be the better version of myself. You don't need to be perfect. You can always be better – as a person, at work, in your family. The progress is what counts. Your constant growth is the quickest way to be happy and fulfilled.

18. It is always okay to ask and to say no. When you learn to ask, you have a better chance to meet your needs the more you practice asking, the happier and more fulfilled you become. Ask for help or say 'no' to someone's request.

19. I am always developing and expanding new capabilities. Yes, you are. If you do not believe me – make a list of what you have learned and achieved within the last five years. Check the chapter where you defined your happiness in the major areas of your life.

20. By serving myself first, I can better serve the world. The truth is that the more you take care of yourself, the better you can take care of the others and give them more. Make a list of the things that you do for yourself. What else could you add to feel happier?

21. No one cares as much as I think. You do not realise that worrying about what others think about you is unnecessary because they are worrying about what you think about them. The next time when you become paranoid, think how anxious the person you are afraid of is.

22. The world changes, so never attach yourself to things. This is a Buddhist concept which the really successful have learned through experience. You might think that happy people are materialistic. However, the truth is that they are respecting the right of change and adjust to the new world. Can you?

23. Every 24 hours is the most important of my life. You have a choice: let this day, this moment be brand new, or ruminate the past and worry about the future. Make today a blessing instead of squandering it. New worlds will begin to open when you choose to act as if today is an incredible opportunity to give your gifts deeply and love fully.

24. Forget, forgive, rejoice. Never become stuck in resentment and grudges. The faster you let them go, the happier you will become.

25. I choose to die having done my best and having given everything. We will all die sooner or later. Would you rather die having given everything and loved to your depth or hold back? Every moment is a choice. Therefore, consider how your choice feels right now. Give your best right now.

26. I already have all I need to be happy and successful. The path to happiness is through self-discovery, not world conquest as you would believe. You don't need to chase money or fame just to be like the other people. And you have got enough to achieve your goals right now, even if you think that you haven't.

27. Life is a game to be played, not a problem to be fixed. It is a game, with some rules placed by the universe. It can be a rat race with fierce competition, teamwork contributing to the world or even the growth of an individual. Which option would you choose?

28. I can do it. Who knows, maybe the most powerful belief and affirmation. It is the antidote you your fear of failure and "should" statements. How often do you use it?

Positive Core Beliefs

Core beliefs are the very essence of how you see yourself, the world, other people, and the future. These core beliefs become 'activated' in some situations. Here's an example: Tina can challenge her thinking in most cases. Core beliefs usually start with 'I', defining your identity. Therefore, before we go any further, check your identity description from the first chapter to see if there are only positive core beliefs in this definition. Do it now.

My identity: ....
....

Some positive core beliefs will help you to become a happy person. Check if they are yours. Below there is the table with some core beliefs. Choose one option from the columns on the right – I agree, I agree somewhat and I disagree; mark your answer to each belief. This will be the map of your positive beliefs.

BELIEF	I AGREE	I AGREE SOME-WHAT	I DISAGREE
I'm patient. I listen well to others. I'm prosperous. I know how to relax. I trust myself. I love and approve of myself. I will handle what-ever happens.			
I attract the right friends and associates to me.			
I know what it is to be completely unconditionally loved.			

Now choose three beliefs from the lists above and start programming them. In Chapter Eight you will learn how to do it.

Recognising Self-Limiting Beliefs

To uncover your negative beliefs, pay attention to your daily thoughts. In a case of a negative thought, ask yourself why you think in such a negative way. This will uncover your belief.

Every opinion and thought are so because of your beliefs. You have some limiting belief about the thing which you don't like doing. If you repeat this negative thought all the time, you should realise that it is a belief that you have. In this way, you program your sub-consciousness and attract the things and people that are similar to your beliefs.

Some negative beliefs are hard to discover because they were formed at a very young age. They were taken from your parents, and these beliefs no longer serve you. However, they keep filtering your experiences their way because you fail to notice and eliminate them.

You can always eliminate a negative belief because everything can be unlearned. This rule works no matter how long you had the belief for. They can be hidden under innocent looking thoughts, but can be revealed by using the arrow technique.

There are techniques to identify unconscious beliefs. Let me mention the two most common of them. You can take a battery of psychological tests or tap into your inner wisdom via meditation. The techniques mentioned above can predict with 99% accuracy what your beliefs are.

Look around. Can you notice a problem repeating in one area of your life? Then you can be sure that you have a false or limiting belief in this field. This does not mean that just because you are in between relationships or jobs, you necessarily have a false belief. But if the problem continually reappears, then you can be 99% confident a false negative belief is involved.

Log your internal dialogue. Write down the thoughts that come to your mind. Then go back a couple of days later and read what you wrote. This is an even more effective process. Your thoughts may appear right, but false belief that is causing the reaction is behind the story. Illusions in the mind are revealed when you look at things from a different point of view.

Watch your self-talk. This one might sound silly. However, you might be surprised to notice the embedded agreements within your words. Many of the words you speak come out as an automatic reaction of your belief system. Being aware of your words can also reveal a great deal about your thinking. Chapter Six will help you to master the happiness language.

If you pay attention to the words that come out of our mouth, you find clues that will help you to identify beliefs. Seeing your thoughts and words as being true is a critical step if you are to make any progress.

Watch your emotions. Being aware of your emotions is a crucial element in solving the mystery of what you believe. When you identify an emotion, it is easier to see the specific belief. You will learn how to manage your emotions from reading Chapter Seven.

You will dissolve many negative emotions by identifying and changing the core beliefs in your mind. Being aware of them is the first and most critical step in this process.

Answer the three questions below. If there is at least one 'yes', the belief is self-limiting and needs changing.

- Is the belief unreal (impossible to be met)?
- Is the belief out of your control?
- Does the belief make you happy only for a while?

Let me explain the questions above in more detail:

Your belief is impossible to meet. For example, you cannot drive because of epilepsy or bad eyesight. Will you believe then that one day you will drive? No. The same applies to your height, eye colour, age. Having a belief that is not based on reality brings you frustration and puts you under pressure.

It is beyond your control. You may blame yourself for not being able to change the world where it is impossible, and this will make you unhappy. You, as the individual, will not replace the government, stop the banks from manipulating the market and charging you for foreign exchange transactions.

It makes you happy only a bit. You may believe that buying new clothes, toys or vacations will make you happy while it costs you a fortune and other people are jealous and therefore stingy. Another example is when you believe that a wealthy but abusive man, is better than none. What would you prefer, to be happy all the time even without some things or unhappy with a little bit, often being uncertain if you have it? Once again end each sentence. Now look at your beliefs. Define if they are positive or negative. Do this for each belief.

Life is ....

Love is ....

People are ....

I feel healthy when ....

I feel happy when ....

I feel rich when ....

Money is ....

I can ....

I can't ....

I am ....

Sex is ....

Work is ....

I feel rejected when ....

I am afraid of ....

I don't like ....because ....

Defining Core Negative Beliefs

A core negative belief is the main reason for your behaviour. It is the underlying answer for the more superficial beliefs. Let's do an exercise. Once again look at your beliefs which you have written before. Now let's define what is hidden underneath of your beliefs. Choose one belief and write it down. Then answer why you believe in that way. Then define what this belief means. Write another, deeper belief. Again, ask what it means. You will probably discover another belief, more hidden. Ask about the meaning again. Eventually, you will reach the real reason of your thought and even learn who has installed this belief in your mind.

I can't ....

because ....

because ....

because   ....   (core reason)

You can also use this sequence:

I can't ...... which means that ...... which means that ...... (core reason)

Do this exercise for three things which you believe you cannot do. Let me give you an example of how it works:

I can't start a business because I have no money.

I have no money because I am out of work.

I am out of work because I'm slow.

I'm slow because I'm not good enough.

*I'm not good enough because **I'm unworthy**.*

I can't start a business because if I try, I'll fail.

I'll fail because there is plenty of competition and they are better than me which means that I won't be able to make money which means that I'm not good enough to do business which means that **I'm unworthy and unwanted.**

The beliefs written in bold are the negative core beliefs. They may even be your convictions, negative subconscious beliefs about which I will write later in this chapter.

Many of these beliefs can be your convictions, something you strongly believe and which is hard to eradicate. Convictions usually protect you from feeling pain or death. They may be based on facts, often traumatic ones. However, even the worst conviction can be broken.

Fundamental Negative Core Beliefs

Most of the beliefs which you have are based on your conscious mind. However, there are three beliefs which are difficult to identify, yet have a massive negative impact on your life and are the roots of any negative beliefs. They are:

If I try, I'll fail. This belief means fear of failure. Thus, you are afraid to start a business or take any other risk.

I am not wanted. In this way, you are manifesting the fear of rejection, so you avoid asking for help.

I am not worthy. This belief reveals the fear of criticism or humiliation; therefore, you avoid social interactions or having an intimate relationship.

Look at the list of common core negative beliefs. Now I will add the subconscious core beliefs to them so you can see the relationship. Very often, more than one core subconscious belief can be applied.

I can't make …. work, because if I try, I'll fail.
I can't fix … because I'm not worthy, and if I try I'll fail.

I am not good enough at …. because I'm not worthy.

I am inferior because I'm unwanted and unworthy.

I am not interesting enough because I'm not worthy.

I am worthless – core subconscious belief.

I am invisible because I'm unwanted and unworthy.

I am unacceptable because I'm unwanted and unworthy.

I can't get it right because I'm not worthy.

I'm not understood, because I'm unwanted and not worthy.

I'm not valuable because I'm unworthy.

I am not special because I'm unwanted and unworthy.

I don't matter because I'm unworthy and unwanted.

I am unworthy – core subconscious belief.

I am insignificant because I'm unworthy.

I am plain and dull because I'm unworthy.

I can't understand because I'm not good enough =I'm unworthy.

I am nothing because I'm unworthy.

I am in the wrong place because I'm unwanted.

I am vulnerable I am in the wrong place because I'm unwanted. I'm not wanted and unworthy.

I am a mistake because I'm unwanted.

I am not lovable because I'm unwanted.

I am afraid because If I try I'll fail.

I am uncertain because If I try I'll fail.

I am unwanted – core subconscious belief.

I don't belong because I'm unwanted.

I am always wrong because I'm not wanted and unworthy.

I am alone because I'm not wanted.

I am no good because I'm unworthy.

I don't fit in anywhere because I'm unwanted.

I could never do that because If I try I'll fail.

I lack.... because I'm unworthy.

I don't exist because I'm unwanted.

I'm nothing because I'm unworthy.

I'm not safe because I'm unworthy.

I'm not anybody because I'm unworthy.

I am left out because I'm unwanted.

I am unsuitable because I'm unwanted.

I am fat = I'm unworthy.

I am uninteresting because I'm unworthy and unwanted.

I am helpless because I'm unworthy.

I don't matter because I am unwanted.

It's my fault because I'm unworthy.

I am guilty because I'm unworthy.

I am ugly because I'm unworthy.

I am not whole because I'm unworthy and unwanted.

I am awkward because I'm unworthy and unwanted.

I am unwelcome because I'm unwanted.

I am unattractive because I'm unworthy.

I am flawed because I'm unworthy.

I am stupid because I'm unworthy.

I am bad because I'm unworthy.

I am slow because I'm unworthy and unwanted.

I am unimportant because I'm unworthy and unwanted.

I am imperfect because I'm unworthy.

I'm dirty = I'm unworthy and unwanted.

I'm shameful because I'm unworthy and unwanted.

I lack sufficient formal education because I'm unworthy.

I have too many weaknesses because I'm unworthy.

I am unclean because I'm unworthy.

I am useless because I'm unworthy and unwanted.

I am crazy because I'm unworthy.

I have a mental problem because I'm unworthy and unwanted.

I make too many mistakes because I'm unworthy.

I can't pursue my dreams because if I try I'll fail, and I'm unworthy (I don't deserve them).

I am out of control because I'm unworthy.

I will fail (if I try) – subconscious core negative belief.

I am a failure because I'm unworthy and unwanted.

I can't stand up for myself v I'm unworthy (I don't deserve respect).

I finish last v I'm not worthy.

I don't deserve anything because I'm unworthy.

I am inadequate because I'm not wanted and unworthy.

I am a loser because I'm unworthy and unwanted.

I can't do it (because I'll fail).

I am unbalanced because I'm unworthy.

I am weak because I'm unworthy.

I am powerless because I'm unworthy.

I am a failure because I'm unworthy and unwanted.

I am ineffective because I'm unwanted (e.g. at work).

I don't deserve to be loved because I'm unworthy.

I don't have any choice because if I try, I'll fail.

I am less than... because I'm unworthy.

I am helpless because I'm unworthy and unwanted.

I am awkward because I'm unworthy.

There's something wrong with me because I'm unworthy.

I am always one below because I'm unworthy and unwanted.

I am always number two because I'm unwanted and unworthy.

I am inferior because I'm unworthy.

I don't deserve to be cared for because I'm unworthy.

I am a victim because I'm unworthy.

I can't say 'no' because I'm unworthy, and if I try I'll fail.

Now when you know what subconscious core beliefs lay underneath the conscious ones, check once again which of these negative core beliefs you might have. Define how much you believe in each of them. Choose one option from the columns on the right – Select Option 1 if you agree, Option 2 if you agree somewhat and Option 3 if you disagree. Mark your answer to each belief.

BELIEF	1	2	3
I can't make …. work.			
I can't fix …			
I am not good enough at ….			
I am unsuccessful.			
I am no good at ...			
I am inferior.			
I am not interesting enough.			
I am worthless.			
I am invisible.			
I am unacceptable.			
I can't get it right.			
I'm not understood.			
I'm not valuable.			
I am not special.			
I don't matter.			
I am unworthy.			

BELIEF   **1**   **2**   **3**

I am insignificant.

I am plain and dull.

I can't understand.

I am nothing.

I am in the wrong place.

I am vulnerable.

I am a mistake.

In danger or not safe.

I am not lovable.

I am afraid.

I am uncertain.

I am unwanted.

I don't belong.

I am always wrong.

I am alone.

I am no good.

I don't fit in anywhere.

I could never do that.

I lack....

I don't exist.

I'm nothing.

I'm not safe.

I'm not anybody.

I am left out.

I am unsuitable.

I am fat.

I am uninteresting.

I am helpless.

BELIEF   **1**   **2**   **3**

I don't matter.

It's my fault.

I'm not true.

I am guilty.

I am ugly.

I am not whole.

I am awkward.

I am unwelcome.

I am unattractive.

I am flawed.

I should not be here at all.

I am stupid.

I am bad.

I am slow.

I am unimportant.

I can't be me.

I am imperfect.

I'm dirty.

I'm shameful.

I lack sufficient formal education.

I have too many weaknesses.

I am unclean.

I am useless.

I am crazy.

I have a mental problem.

I make too many mistakes.

I can't pursue my dreams.

I am out of control.

BELIEF   **1**   **2**   **3**

I will fail.

I am a failure.

I can't stand up for myself.

I finish last.

I don't deserve anything.

I am inadequate.

I am a loser.

I can't do it.

I am unbalanced.

I am weak.

I am powerless.

I am a failure.

I am ineffective.

I don't deserve to be loved.

I don't have any choice.

I am less than.

I am helpless.

I am awkward.

There's something wrong with me.

I am always one below.

I am always number two.

I am inferior.

I don't deserve to be cared for.

I am a victim.

I can't say 'no'.

Choose five beliefs from the list above, those with which you agree. Then define the core belief for each of them, using the formula described above (your belief - e.g. I can't do... because.... - another deeper belief, because.... - another deeper belief, because.... – core subconscious belief). Do it in your transformation diary.

………………………………………………………………………………

………………………………………………………………………………

………………………………………………………………………………

………………………………………………………………………………

………………………………………………………………………………

There are examples of more precisely defined core negative beliefs below. Read them and mark if you agree with them or not. Select Option 1 if you agree, 'Option 2 if you agree somewhat and Option 3 if you disagree.

BELIEF   **1**   **2**   **3**

I am currently living a big lie.

I need to be right.

I have unresolved issues, problems, and difficulties in my life.

I am missing key, empowering relationships in my life.

I don't have anything better to do with my life right now.

My life is primarily about me and my problems.

I don't get how life works so well for other people but not for me.

My needs are not being met.

I am under a lot of stress.

I am not good at sex because I have erectile disorder/ I can't achieve orgasm.

I can't fix my life because I cannot find someone special.

I have not experienced very much in life yet. My life is boring.

I am always number two as my sister is more loved than me by my mother.

BELIEF	1	2	3

I am ugly because I have gotten a big belly.

I can't tell the truth because I may get judged…

I don't want to get close to this person lest my heart gets broken…

I don't want to ask for what I want because, what if I get rejected?

I can't trust people because I've been betrayed before…

I can't pursue my dreams because I don't know what I'd do if I fail…

I make too many mistakes when I try something new.

Taking risks always turns out bad for me.

I'm a failure because I cannot find a job

I'm a slow learner.

I'm not smart enough because....

I'm too old, too young, too fat etc. to do....

I'm not outgoing enough at........

I lack relevant experience.

I don't have the confidence to do that.

I don't have enough skills or talent.

I don't have what it takes to succeed.

I'm terrible at managing my time, money, etc.

I don't know what I want to do with the rest of my life.

I would fail for sure if I tried that.

I'm stupid when it comes to X.

Are You Ready to Change Your Limiting Beliefs?

We all know that we need to eliminate limiting beliefs and substitute them with more uplifting ones. However, first, check if you are ready to change your beliefs as there are five causes which will stop you from taking action.

1. The belief protects your health and life. Sometimes your view was created to protect your survival. As a child, you were totally dependent on your parents, so the fear of being abandoned forced you to create the beliefs which protected you. For example, you might learn that it is better to be submissive and avoid conflicts with your parents because they could leave you, which may happen if your mother or father blackmailed you this way. The fear may be adamant, yet what if you need a given belief to protect your health and life? In 99% most cases, it will not be necessary.

2. The belief is based on facts. In this case, you first need to question the facts. Let's say that you come from an abusive family, and it is the fact that your parents criticised you destructively or used emotional blackmail. What can you do? You will not change the past. However, you can always work out the emotions connected with the bad treatment by your parents. You can also find new evidence – this time, confirming that the belief is not true. And you will learn some other practical

ways how to eliminate this category of beliefs.

3. The belief helps you to achieve your goals (short- and long-term). Let's say that you are afraid of the opposite sex, and consider them as dangerous, aggressive and unpredictable. You yearn for peace of mind. This is your goal. What will you do to achieve it? Stay submissive and avoid any conflicts. You can also avoid contact with the opposite sex. Think whether this is the only efficient way of achieving your goals.

4. The belief helps you to avoid conflict with other people. The conflict involves emotional pain, sometimes aggression and tears. You probably would not like to experience all that drama. So, what do you do? Create a belief which will protect you from conflict. You might think that it is better to agree with everything, or to run away when you see the threat of confrontation. However, it will only work short-term. Remember that your unmet needs will cause negative emotions which might break out uncontrolled if you do not manage them on a daily basis. Instead of running away from conflict, learn how to work with your emotions.

5. The belief helps you to suppress unwanted feelings. Who wants to feel pain, disappointment, frustration? You'd rather avoid them. In many cases, anger is also suppressed and is dangerous for relationships. For example, you believe that it is embarrassing to show pain; for a man, crying. You then think that crying is something wrong. If you look around, you will find many cases of compassionate people.

The reasons listed above are the biggest pay-offs which can impair your ability to change negative beliefs. When you do the cost-benefits analysis described below, remember to mention some of these five reasons.

Meet the Origin of Your Beliefs

When you were born, you had no beliefs. As a young child, you even had less limiting beliefs than now. For example, you were unafraid. Later in life, you started to believe in being a failure or that risk is a danger.

What is even more, you probably rarely know whose beliefs you have. It is important who has installed the belief in you because then you can question the negative and self-limiting beliefs more easily.

Who installs your beliefs? Firstly, your parents and caretakers when you were a child. Then your teachers and life partners. Then according to your experience, you can create another set of beliefs, often based on the first core ones, installed in your childhood.

Now the time has come to question the importance of your negative beliefs. Each belief is established to meet a goal or even some of them. For example, to protect your life, in other words – for survival. As a child, you are entirely dependent on your parents. Therefore, you will do everything to gain their approval as you believe that when they leave you, you are at risk of death.

You can also hold onto a belief in order to avoid pain. Then your life is less stressful. You create the so-called safety behaviours which protect your ego. For example, you may avoid social interaction because 'people can hurt'.

However, now you are a self-reliant person and don't need your parents' approval anymore, even if you might be living with them or suffer from an illness. You are strong enough to take care of your needs and survive.

Let's define who has installed the negative beliefs in you. You have already made a list of such beliefs. Choose one now and write it down below or in your transformation diary.

…………………………………………………………………………………………

Then dig deeper, ending the sentence starting with 'because'. Do this until you find who has installed this belief in you.

because …………………………………………………………………………………

because …………………………………………………………………………………

because …………………………………………………………………………………

For example: "People are nasty because they make fun of me because I am ugly, because my sister told me so." In this case, you can see that your sister has installed this belief in you. Now when you know that, ask yourself the following questions:

- How important is my sister's approval to me?
- Do I want to hold a belief which is not mine?
- Is my sister such an expert in the field of relationships that she can define if I am ugly so that I need to believe her?

Take your next negative belief and do the same exercise in your transformation diary. You will learn more ways how to question your beliefs later in this chapter, so continue reading.

Change Negative Beliefs

Negative beliefs are the fruits of negative thinking; they are just thoughts which you consider to be true. Hence it is so important to question any negative thoughts so as not to become a negative belief. But what can you do to change the beliefs which are already installed like the software on your computer?

There is more than one way of changing negative beliefs. I have chosen the most useful ones, although you can probably find others, not listed in the book. I don't want to overwhelm you with the tools. You can choose one tool and practice it for a month, for example, or use more than one simultaneously.

Firstly, once again identify the belief, preferably the core one.

1. Determine the twist in your beliefs. Dr. Burns and a few other authors, have defined the ways of thinking which are twisted. You could already read about twists in Chapter Two. This set can also be used to uncover the distortions in your beliefs. Let me show you these twists once again, this time applied to your beliefs. There is usually more than one twist in a given belief, which I will show you in this chapter:

All-or-nothing beliefs You believe that things are black and white, absolute, with no shades of grey.

Jumping to conclusions You believe that something wrong will happen. You can mind-read (if people are reacting negatively to you) or tell the fortune (predicting that things will turn out badly).

Overgeneralisation Your belief is certain that bad things happen always or good things never happen.

Mental filter Your belief is based on the negatives and ignores the positives.

Discounting the positives You believe that your accomplishments or positive qualities don't count. So even if you are brilliant at public speaking, you might believe it will not help you to get promotion at work.

Magnification or minimisation You blow things way out of proportion, or you shrink their importance. For example, you can minimise the fact of being abused and magnify the good deeds the abuser has done for you.

Labelling Your beliefs contain negative labels. Instead of saying, "I have made a mistake", you tell yourself "I'm a jerk" or "I'm a loser."

Emotional reasoning You reason from how you feel: "I often feel like an idiot, so I must be one."

Blame You blame yourself for something you were not responsible for, or you blame other people and overlook ways that you contributed to a problem. For example: "It's my fault that my father left our family."

'Should' statements You criticise yourself or other people with should, shouldn't, must, ought and have-to.

Here are some examples of negative beliefs with their distortions:

Negative Belief

Children should be quiet and be submissive to their parents because otherwise they will be punished.

Twist

Should statement, all-or-nothing

Negative Belief

I should not be here at all.

Twist

Should statement, overgeneralisation

Negative Belief

I am stupid.

Twist

Labelling, blame, mental filter

Negative Belief

I am bad.

Twist

Labelling, blame, mental filter

Negative Belief

I am slow.

Twist

Labelling, blame, mental filter

Negative Belief

People are dangerous.

Twist

Overgeneralisation, mental filter

Negative Belief

I am bad at Maths.

Twist

Labelling, mental filter, overgeneralisation

Negative Belief

I feel like a jerk talking to strangers.

Twist

Emotional reasoning, discounting the positive

Negative Belief

I have to stay with my abusive boyfriend because no one will love me.

Twist

Minimisation (of his abusive behaviour), fortune-telling, should statement, all-or-nothing

Negative Belief

I have to be nicely dressed. Otherwise, they will have fun with me.

Twist

Should statement, mind-reading, all-or-nothing, magnification

Negative Belief

People will have fun with me if they learn the truth about myself.

Twist

Mind-reading, all-or-nothing

Negative Belief

Running a business is risky, and I may lose everything.

Twist

Mental filter, all-or-nothing, magnifying, overgeneralisation

Negative Belief

I don't like asking for help because then it is given out, like paying a debt.

Twist

All-or-nothing, emotional reasoning, mind-reading

Negative Belief

Living in a family is like living in the jungle, and it is the best school of manipulation, I can be used by the older members.

Twist

All-or-nothing, labelling, fortune-telling,overgeneralisation, Emotional reasoning, fortune-telling, magnifying, mental filter, all-or-nothing

Negative Belief

I don't like to show negative emotions (am afraid to be assertive) to men as they will become angry and hurt me even more.

Twist

All-or-nothing, mental filter, labelling

Negative Belief

Crying means weakness.

Twist

All-or-nothing, mental filter, labelling

Negative Belief

I can't tell the truth because I may get judged.

Twist

Fortune-telling, magnification, mental filter

Negative Belief

I don't want to become intimate with this person lest my heart gets broken…

Twist

Fortune-telling, mental filter, all-or-nothing

Negative Belief

I can't trust people because I've been cheated on before…

Twist

Emotional reasoning, mental filter, should statement

Negative Belief

I can't pursue my dreams because I am afraid that I will fail.

Fortune-telling, mental filter, magnification, all-or-nothing

Negative Belief

I can't do X because of Y...

Twist

All-or-nothing, mental filter, labelling

Negative Belief

I lack motivation.

Twist

Fortune-telling, mental filter, overgeneralisation

Negative Belief

I don't have enough resources.

Twist

All-or-nothing, mental filter, labelling

Negative Belief

It's too late to change.

Twist

All-or-nothing, overgeneralisation

Negative Belief

I have too many responsibilities.

All-or-nothing, magnifying

Negative Belief

I have no clue where to start.

Twist

All-or-nothing

Now look at the negative beliefs with which you have agreed. If you do not remember them, check the list above and choose three of the beliefs. Then identify the twists.

BELIEF	TWISTS
....	....
....	....
....	....
....	....
....	....

2. Weigh all the costs and benefits of the belief which you want to change. For example, if you believe that asking for help is like begging, think about what you lose by not asking people for help. It might be lost opportunities at work or in business, harder life, helplessness. What do you gain? The safety of your ego. Now think about the benefits of abandoning the belief: you will have more friends, you will learn to contribute better to society, you will be more self-fulfilled. And the costs? Just some discomfort. Choose one belief and list all its costs and benefits – sticking to that belief and dumping it.

My negative belief is…

....

Costs of using this belief　　　　**Benefits of using this belief (payoffs)**

Costs of dumping this belief	Benefits of dumping this belief

3. Question the pay-offs. You have already read about the pay-offs in Chapter Three and have learned the five pay-offs stopping you from changing your beliefs. Now the time has come to learn how to deal with them. Look at each of your pay-offs which you have written above. Erase them by answering the questions below: Write the answers down in your transformation diary.

- Do I protect myself from emotional or physical pain, holding this belief and behaving this way?
- Do I protect my health and life?
- Can I avoid conflict, abandonment, rejection, criticism?
- Can I change the past?
- Does this belief help me to achieve my goals and be self-fulfilled?

4. Create a leverage to overcome pay-offs. It may not be enough just to question the pay-offs of the negative belief. You need to find a leverage, associate as much pain as possible with the negative belief to abandon it. How to do it?

Choose the biggest pay-off as an example. If you believe that people will make fun of you when you show them the truth about themselves, the biggest pay-off is to avoid the pain of criticism and humiliation. Doing so, you will attract that kind of attention from other people

Victoria Herocten

and become paranoid. You will also lose some opportunities to meet decent people as you assume that they will hurt you.

Now choose the biggest pay-from your old belief and write it down.

....

Associate massive pain with holding on to the pay-offs. What will you feel, constantly being paranoid and suspicious, being more and more mocked by people? Imagine being paranoid more and more. You get crazy, are afraid to go out and talk to people, you develop a social phobia. Eventually, you will become a lonely person, and people do laugh at you or you will end up in the department of psychiatry, with a mental illness. Do I need to add more to this gloomy scenario? I can assure you; it will eventually happen if you stick to your negative beliefs.

Now define the biggest pain associated with your pay-off.

....

Visualise the pain if you stick to your pay-offs. Imagine being paranoid, afraid of even looking at the people, avoiding going to the café or the restaurant. Saying "Hello" is a nightmare and eye contact seems to cause you nausea. Then you come back home, alone, still being afraid of people. While being out, you noticed that someone is laughing behind your back, not even seeing you. You assume that you had done something wrong, and they were making fun of you. The next time you go out you will be even more sensitive to what people are saying or how they are looking at you.

Write down your worst scenario, what will happen if you don't stop following your negative belief. Use your transformation diary for this purpose.

— 148 —

5. Check the evidence. In most cases, you automatically assume that the belief is true. However, this is the result of the references you have associated with this belief. For example, if you think that family is a school of manipulation, someone has probably used you, made you feel guilty, used conditional love or criticised destructively. There were also moments when you were loved, they have helped you, and you felt happy. If you lived in an abusive family, you might stick to your negative belief. Even then, you can find some families who are healthy, and the members love each other. You can use them as a model. Now look at your belief again. List all the evidence – the facts confirming the righteousness of the belief and the arguments against it:

My belief is….

…..

EVIDENCE FOR THE NEGATIVE BELIEF

EVIDENCE AGAINST THE NEGATIVE BELIEF

6. Discuss the belief. Let me give you some examples of beliefs and questioning them.

BELIEF

I am stupid.

QUESTIONING

- What does 'stupid' mean?

- Who has told that you are stupid?

- Is this a person of authority to define your value?

- What are the fields in life where you are smart?

- When were you last smart?

- Even if you struggle in ...., when was the last time you have done it right?

- What are the facts supporting how smart you are?

BELIEF

People will make fun of me if they learn the truth about myself.

QUESTIONING

- What is the evidence that they will make fun of you?

- What does it mean exactly?

- How do you know that people will not like you?

- Who already likes you?

- What does 'people' mean, who in particular?

- Who told you that people would make fun of you? Is this person an authority for you, saying such things?

- When did people like you for what you are?

BELIEF

I always make mistakes.

Similar beliefs: I never remember names. I always burn my dinner.

QUESTIONING

- What in particular are these 'mistakes'?

- What is the worst consequence of making mistakes? Have you died?
- When were you last right?
- Who said you are making mistakes?
- What can you do to learn from your mistakes?

BELIEF

Running a business is risky and I may lose everything. Similar beliefs consist a fortune-telling distortion.

QUESTIONING

- Who said that running a business is risky? Can you show me some business people who achieved success taking a risk?
- What can you do to minimise the risk?
- What does it mean to 'lose everything'? Do you lose your sight, hands, legs, brain?
- How probable is it today that you will lose everything?

BELIEF

I don't like asking for help because when it is given out, they want it repaid – like repaying a debt.

QUESTIONING

- What do they want in return?
- Can I give that to them?

BELIEF

I can't do business because I cannot handle people.

QUESTIONING

- Who has said that you cannot handle with people? Are they masters of people skills?

- What does it mean, specifically, that you can't do business?
- Who has told you that you can't do business – are they an authority on you – do they run a successful business themselves?
- When was the last time you could handle people?
- What can you do to learn to handle with people?

BELIEF

I'm too old.

QUESTIONING

- Who has said that you are too old?
- What does 'too old' mean exactly?
- What can you do to take advantage of the situation despite your age?
- What other assets do you have, more important than your age?
- What great have you achieved at your age?
- What useful experience do you have? How can you use it now to compensate the age problem?

BELIEF

I don't have enough resources.

QUESTIONING

- Who has said that you don't have enough resources?
- What resources, specifically, do you lack?
- What can you do to obtain the lacking resources?
- Who can help you to obtain the lacking resources?
- When was the last time that you had enough resources?
- What resources do you have already?

BELIEF

I should be a perfect cook, otherwise my husband will not love me.

QUESTIONING

- How probable is it that he will not love you?
- What does it mean to be a perfect cook?
- What is the worst thing that will happen if your dinner is not perfect? Will he kill you?
- Is it worth being with someone who loves you conditionally?
- Who has told you that your husband will not like you? Is this person a reliable authority? Are they perfect cooks? Do they love their partners?

Here is the list of questions that you can ask while discussing your beliefs:

- What does _____ (e.g. idiot) mean specifically? (generalisations, labels)
- Who said that _____ (your belief)?
- Are they competent enough to give such judgement?
- Do you need their love and approval?
- What is the worst scenario and how can you handle that _____ (e.g. you will lose all)?
- How probable is your belief _____ (e.g. losing all)?
- What are the facts that you are _____ (the opposite to the belief, e.g. stupid, smart, make mistakes right)?
- What can you do to take advantage of _____ (being too old etc.)?
- When was it the last time you succeeded in _____ (when you believe that you are losing, making mistakes, etc.)?
- How probable is _____ (your assumption)?
- What would your true friend think about... (your belief)?

- What will happen if I don't to _____ (should statement)? Will I die?

Take your negative belief, analysed while reading this book. Discuss with it asking questions listed above and in the presented examples and writing down the answers.

YOUR BELIEF

QUESTIONS   **ANSWERS**

7. Eliminate the references supporting your negative belief. References are just the reasons why you believe in something. Anthony Robbins compares them to the legs supporting the table. Sometimes there may be facts, but in many cases the references uncover another hidden belief or opinion. You have already discovered some references working on your core beliefs. If you want to remove your negative belief from your mind, you need to question the references.

Let's do another exercise. Do it in your transformation diary for all your negative believes and for one here. Write down this belief and then list five reasons why you believe in it.

My belief ....

I follow this belief because:

1. ....
2. ....
3. ....
4. ....
5. ....

For example:

People are nasty...

...because someone on the street mocked me.

...because they don't say hello back when I say it to them.

...because my sister is nasty.

...because I was teased at school.

...because I don't get help when I am the most vulnerable.

Having listed all the references, question them. Use those listed in Step Six. You can also ask:

- Is it a fact or an opinion?
- How important is the opinion for me?
- How important will it be in 10 years' time?

8. Create an alternative belief. Now the time has come to find an alternative for your old, negative belief. You have already defined the costs and benefits of changing that belief. You have even questioned the hardest excuses for holding onto the old belief. You knew the evidence against the belief and questioned those supporting it. What will you do next?

You can write the new belief just contradicting the old belief. Let me give you some examples:

OLD NEGATIVE BELIEF

1. I'm a loser.
2. People will make fun of me if they meet the truth about me.
3. I always make mistakes in...
4. I don't like asking for help because when it is given out, it is like paying a debt.
5. I'm too old.
6. I don't have enough money.
7. I'm unworthy.
8. I'm unwanted.
9. If I try, I'll fail.

NEW BELIEF

1. I have achieved ...... in ...
2. Many people will admire and support me when they meet the truth about me.
3. There are times when I am excellent in...
4. I like asking for help as then I can reciprocate and always have a chance of getting that help, achieving more in life.
5. My age gives me a lot of opportunities to take, and I have many assets of which I can make the most of.
6. I have plenty of resources which I can materialise whenever I want, for myself or with the help of other people.
7. I'm divine and deserve respect, love, admiration, wealth, success and happiness.

8. My services/skills etc. are wanted, and I can help many people, making their lives full and happy.

9. If I try, I will succeed sooner or later, myself or with the help of other people.

Sometimes you may feel resistance writing just opposite statements. Then you need to add some clauses to the new belief. The formula looks like that:

Although .... (negative belief),
new belief .... plus, the evidence for it.

Now take your old, negative belief and create a new one, in accordance with the rule.

NEGATIVE BELIEF   **NEW UPLIFTING BELIEF**

Examples:

Although I was 40, and found it hard to find a job as a waiter, scientists proved that I had the excellent skills needed to start my own business and provide catering services because I have excellent sales skills. Although I had not enough money to launch the business at first, I learned how to make more money and gain help from investors. I have already done so and was successful.

Although sometimes people may give out or reject my request when I ask for help, I will gain more and be happier asking them, than doing nothing. Although I make mistakes while filling out the forms,

I am smart at reading maps, and there are situations when I can fill in the form correctly (mention when) …………

9. List all the benefits of your new belief. For example, "Although sometimes people may give out or reject my request when I ask for help, I will gain more and be happier asking them than doing nothing."

You can find the following advantages:

- You will be more successful in business.
- Your will get more things that you want.
- You will be more fulfilled and happier.
- You can achieve more.

Now take your new belief and list the advantages.

My new belief

…………………………………………………………………………………………

Benefits of my new belief

…………………………………………………………………………………………

…………………………………………………………………………………………

…………………………………………………………………………………………

…………………………………………………………………………………………

…………………………………………………………………………………………

10. Act according to your new belief. Use the principle 'fake it until you make it'. It may be challenging at first because your old belief is still installed in your subconscious mind. Yet if you eliminate the references supporting the negative belief, faking the new one will be easier. However, your new belief will only be installed if you condition your mind to start acting according to the new belief. Here are some techniques on how to do it:

11. Log the references for the new belief on a regular basis.

There might be facts already known to you or something which other people can share with you. Suppose that your new belief is 'people like me'. List all the reasons why you believe it is true. I am certain that you will find at least ten reasons right now. To practice finding references for the new belief, do this exercise. Write down one of your new beliefs:

....
....

List ten references for this belief.

1. ....
2. ....
3. ....
4. ....
5. ....
6. ....
7. ....
8. ....
9. ....
10. ....

For the next 30 days, record all new references for this new belief in your transformation diary.

12. Create an Affirmation

Write down the new belief several times, filling up all the page of your transformation diary. Then record all that you have written with a background of relaxing music. Listen to the recordings for at least

30 days, especially after waking up and before falling asleep. Let me give you an example, which you can use right now:

I believe that people will admire and understand me when they meet the truth about me.

I believe that people will admire and understand me when they meet the truth about me.

I believe that people will admire and understand me when they meet the truth about me.

I let the old belief go. I let the old belief go. I let the old belief go.

I love and approve of myself. I love and approve of myself.

I love and approve of myself. I love and approve of myself.

I love and approve of myself. I love and approve of myself.

I love myself no matter what. I love myself no matter what.

I love myself no matter what. I love myself no matter what.

I love myself no matter what. I love myself no matter what.

I believe that people will admire and understand me when they meet the truth about me.

I believe that people will admire and understand me when they meet the truth about me.

I believe that people will admire and understand me when they meet the truth about me.

I let the resistance go. I let the resistance go. I let the resistance go.

I let the old belief go. I let the old belief go. I let the old belief go.

I love and approve of myself. I love and approve of myself.

I love and approve of myself. I love and approve of myself.

I love and approve of myself. I love and approve of myself.

I love myself no matter what. I love myself no matter what.

I love myself no matter what. I love myself no matter what.

I love myself no matter what. I love myself no matter what.

I believe that people will admire and understand me when they meet the truth about me.

I believe that people will admire and understand me when they meet the truth about me.

I believe that people will admire and understand me when they meet the truth about me.

I let the old belief go. I let the old belief go. I let the old belief go.

I love and approve of myself. I love and approve of myself.

I love and approve of myself. I love and approve of myself.

I love and approve of myself. I love and approve of myself.

I love myself no matter what. I love myself no matter what.

I love myself no matter what. I love myself no matter what.

I love myself no matter what. I love myself no matter what.

13. Visualise Your New Behaviour According to Your New Belief

Write down the description of your new behaviour.

Let me give you an example:

Now I am not afraid of asking for help. Therefore, whenever I need advice or help while doing business, I can open my mouth, call the helper or write to him. I am also able to ask my spouse for help when I need it. I am ready to reciprocate the helpers, giving back something if they needed my help. (Now you can describe even more precise cases where you ask for help.)

You will learn more about using affirmations in the chapter about changing habits and addictions.

14. Reward Yourself for Acting According to The New Belief

Whenever you have done something according to your new belief, reward yourself. Now list five things which can be your rewards.

Victoria Herocten

1. …..

2. …..

3. …..

4. …..

5. …..

Chapter 5
Create Thoughts of Happiness

"Change your thoughts and you change your world."

Negative Thoughts

After having worked on some of her beliefs, Tina noticed that her life had become more balanced, and she coped better with her challenges. However, that was the only partial success. Tina still had many negative automatic thoughts which devastated her plans and impaired her commitment to become a happy person. This chapter will help you to handle negative thinking.

You will learn:

- How thoughts have an impact on the quality of your life.
- How to recognise a negative thought.
- The consequences of negative thinking.
- The most common examples of positive thoughts.
- The most negative thoughts and how to transform them into the positive ones.
- How to challenge negative thoughts with questions.
- Ten ways to change negative thoughts by taking action.

- How to change the most persistent negative thoughts.

How Thoughts Have an Impact on The Quality of Life

Every thought you have is creating your reality, opportunities. It is also affecting your relationships. It does not matter if the thought is conscious or subconscious. You must be willing to release your negative mental programming and step out of your comfort zone if you want to work on your subconscious thoughts. Then you will make room for a positive, healthy self-image and belief system.

Conscious thoughts are easily malleable. However, subconscious thoughts will usually manifest themselves as dense feelings or emotions.

Do you know how to identify what your subconscious is putting out? Just notice your feelings. If your subconscious thoughts are negative, you feel that you aren't good enough, or that things never go your way.

However, you can always reprogram your negative thinking. And that is the good news. Just identify the negative thoughts sent you by your subconscious mind and start working on them. I will show you how to do this.

Never try to resist the negative thought pattern, just redirect it. In this way, you will take the energy of the negative thought and re-channel it into a positive thought. Then visualise this positive thought, in detail. Use all your senses to amplify the positive thought – see it, hear it and feel it. Doing this will shift your energy and allow you to easily and efficiently attract the positive energy and experiences that you want in your life. Your mind will automatically flow into the linked positive thought when you condition your mind, whenever the negative thought occurs.

Did you know that your thoughts control what happens to you? There have been many books written on thought and how powerful it is. All the biggest self-help gurus confirm that changing your thoughts will change your reality. Thoughts do affect you. Whatever happens to you, good or bad, all of it is determined by our thoughts.

Thoughts create your emotional state and your health. They even influence what you do and say to people. No matter what the situation or circumstances, everything you do stems from thought, which then turns into feelings, then turns into actions and finally to results. There are three classes of thoughts you experience each day of your lives. These thoughts include positive, action and worry.

You might think each of these thoughts throughout the day. If you have gratitude for who you are and what you achieve, you have positive thoughts. Worry thoughts occur when you dwell on a future event that hasn't even happened. And, if you think about what you need to do for the day, like going to the store or shop for an object, then you have action thoughts.

Would you believe many of your thoughts are centred around worry? You are not even aware of it at times, yet you do it. When you worry about something you have no control over, what you have is fear turned inside and usually accompanied by some mental programming that tells you all the bad things that will happen before the event even started.

All kinds of worry are just learned behaviour acquired over time. Fortunately, any thoughts that are learned can be unlearned very quickly. You would be surprised that your health would improve drastically if you focus on positive thoughts instead of negative or worry ones. The reason for that is that positive thoughts create healing and produce joy in your life. They also reduce stress.

If you want to be productive in life, you must learn to control your thoughts, to use the right types of thoughts that enter your mind daily. Also, remember that not all thoughts produce actions that lead to results. Only those thoughts that you dwell on predominately are what will bring results for you.

Because your thoughts are powerful and can dictate what happens to you, so they must be controlled. When you start thinking negative thoughts, you start getting a lot of emotion for those thoughts. Your heart races. You begin to panic. You start thinking of imagined things that could happen. You become irrational, which happens to all of us occasionally. You may be in a very stressful situation and find that you are thinking the worst-case scenario instead of thinking positively.

What can you do in this situation? Just stop yourself. Remind yourself of the Law of Attraction, and get your thinking back on track. You will learn more tips in the further part of this chapter.

Thoughts are dangerous because they can lead you to get whatever you think. While thinking, you vibrate to the universe which receives your transmission and delivers. If you aren't careful, you may not like what you get back.

What Are the Consequences of Negative Thinking?

"Watch your thoughts, for they become words.
Watch your habits, for they become your character.
And watch your character, for it becomes your destiny."
- Margaret Thatcher

The most important reason you need to eliminate negative thoughts is that most of us are used to thinking of them habitually. Like any other habit, you barely notice you are doing it, and you do not realise just how destructive those thoughts can be in your life. They bring negative energy, people and situations into your life.

Negative language. How often do you talk to yourself or others in a negative way? These are just your thoughts, manifested by your words. Changing your language will help you to eliminate negativity from your life. I will teach you how to do it in one of the next chapters.

Negative feelings. The challenges described in this book are the result of negative thinking. If you worry, feel anxious or disappointed, the chances are that there are many negative thoughts in your mind.

Lack of action. Avoidance is the result of negative, anxious thoughts, mind-reading and particularly fortune-telling. All the things which you avoid are flooded with negative thoughts, which have become beliefs.

Negative action. Apart from avoiding things, you can also act in accordance with your thoughts. If you start thinking that someone says bad things about you, the chances are that you will become suspicious, and the conversation with this person will be impaired. Having angry thoughts can lead to conflicts and arguments. Worry will make you blind to opportunities.

Negative beliefs. After thinking about something, sometimes you start believing that it is true. In this way, your thought is saved in your mind, infecting it. You start seeing things through the negative filter.

Unhappy life. After you have formed your negative beliefs, you start producing an enormous number of negative thoughts, like on autopilot. At the same time, you act according to your thoughts, creating your reality. As these are negative thoughts, your life becomes inauspicious and you unhappy.

The Most Common Positive Thoughts

I'm responsible and in control of my life.

I can choose my attitude towards circumstances.

I am learning to love myself.

Every challenge is an opportunity to learn and grow.

I accept the ups and downs of life.

I love and accept myself the way I am.

I am improving one step at a time.

I deserve the right things in my life.

I am open to discovering new meaning in my life.

I am looking forward to the new freedom and opportunities I will have when I have fully recovered.

I respect and believe in myself regardless others' opinions.

I am healthy, strong and fully capable of recovering.

I am getting better every day.

I am committed to overcoming depression.

I can accept and learn from constructive criticism.

I can recover by taking small risks at my pace.

I am learning to be comfortable with myself.

If someone does not return my love, I let it go and move on.

I am learning to be myself around others.

Taking care of my needs is important.

I appreciate my achievements.

I am learning how to balance work and play in my life.

It's OK if I'm unable always to foresee everything.

The greatest success is living well.

I am satisfied doing the best I can.

I am a unique and capable person just as I am.

It's OK to make mistakes sometimes.

I'm OK if I don't always have a quick answer to every problem.

I am willing to accept my mistakes and learn from them.

I am willing to allow others to help me.

I do the best I can, and I'm satisfied with that.

I acknowledge my need for other people.

I am open to receiving support from others.

I am willing to let others assist me in solving my problems.

I am willing to take the risk of getting close to someone.

I am learning to relax and let go.

I am learning to accept those things I can't control.

I'm learning honesty with others, even when I'm not feeling pleasant or friendly.

It's OK to make time to rest and relax.

When I love and care for myself, I am best able to be generous to others.

I am doing the best I can as a.........

It's OK to be upset when things go wrong.

Instead of focusing on negativity in myself I will identify and develop the positive.

It's OK to be angry sometimes.

I am inherently worthy as a person.

I believe that I can change; I am willing to change.

I am learning to let go of guilt.

I will focus on myself more because I am important.

I believe that I am an attractive, intelligent, valuable person.

Worrying about a problem is the real issue.

I am willing to trust other people.

I will not let the negativity of others interfere with my attitude.

I am learning that it is OK to make mistakes.

I am willing to become self-sufficient.

I am learning to let go of worrying.

I will let my good attitude influence me as much as it influences others.

Nobody's perfect; I am learning to go easy on myself.

I can replace worry with constructive action.

My thoughts and feelings are important. I will not let others discount them or me.

I will not let my fear of failing lead me to procrastinate.

I accept myself just the way I am.

I will be satisfied with my actions today, doing my best and not comparing myself to others.

Who I am is important. I will not please others before I please myself.

I will not feel guilty for telling others no. My needs will come first.

I will not let worry or fear interfere with my social interactions.

I will realise that I am a human being and making mistakes is normal.

Today I will refuse to give others the power to control my emotions.

Self-will has not worked for me. I will now seek Gods will in my life.

I'm special. In all the world, there is nobody like me.

I refuse to dwell on my mistakes, instead, I will learn from them.

Today I will work harder to care about me as much as others care about me.

I love myself just the way I am.

I am a real person no matter what mistakes I have made.

Now choose five from the above statements and learn them by heart, repeating aloud in front of the mirror, seeing them with all your senses.

Recognising Negative Thoughts

"The soul becomes dyed with the colour of its thoughts."
—*Marcus Aurelius, Meditations*

Identifying your negative thinking is the first step towards letting it go. When you have a negative thought, your peace of mind vanishes and you begin to feel negative emotions, starting from discomfort and ending on depression. After having a negative thought, you often become discouraged and attract even more negativity. Procrastination becomes your second nature and your language starts to be negative. Eventually, you will develop another negative belief, as everything that you repeat enough times becomes permanent.

Negative thoughts are twisted in the same way as self-limiting beliefs. I have already presented you the ten twists in the chapter about beliefs, yet this classification is mainly used to define twisted thoughts. Let's see what kind of twisted thoughts you can have:

All-or-nothing thinking. Thinking in black and white categories, you do not accept any shades of grey.

Jumping to conclusions This distortion means concluding things are wrong without any definite evidence. This kind of twisted thinking includes fortune-telling (predicting that things will turn out badly) and mind-reading (if people are going to do wrong by you).

Overgeneralisation You think of a negative situation as a never-ending pattern of defeat.

Mental filter Ignoring the positives and dwelling on negatives.

Discounting the positives. Thinking this way, you insist that your accomplishments or positive qualities don't count.

Magnification or minimisation You blow issues way out of proportion, or you diminish their importance. For example, you can minimise the fact of being abused and magnify the good deeds the abusers have done for you.

Labelling You tell you, "I'm an idiot" or "I'm a loser" instead of saying, "I made a mistake."

Emotional reasoning. This kind of twisted thinking comes from how you feel: "I feel like a stupid person, so I must be one."

Blame You blame other people and overlook ways that you contributed to a problem yourself or for something that you were not totally responsible for.

'Should' statements Criticising yourself or other people with should, shouldn't, must, ought, and have-to.

Let's see what kinds of twists the following thoughts have:

Negative Thought - I can't do anything right today.
Twist - All-or-nothing, discounting the positive.

Negative Thought - Why do I always get all the red lights?
Twist - Overgeneralisation, discounting the positive, all or nothing.

Negative Thought - Can it get any worse?
Twist - Discounting the positive.

Negative Thought - Ugh! Do I have to get out of bed today?
Twist - All-or-nothing, mental filter, discounting the positive, labelling.

Negative Thought - I have the worst luck!
Twist - Discounting the positive.

Negative Thought - I hate it when it rains.
Twist - Fortune telling.

Negative Thought - I just know that I will make a mistake on this project.
Twist - All-or-nothing, fortune telling, discounting the positive.

Negative Thought - I will never be able to afford that.
Twist - Fortune telling, all or nothing.

Negative Thought - Now that I washed my car it is going to rain.
Twist - Labelling, blaming.

Negative Thought - My boss just called me into his office; this can't be good.
Twist - Fortune telling, mind reading, all or nothing.

Negative Thought - I am useless because I can't solve this problem.
Twist - Labelling, negative filter, discounting the positive.

Negative Thought - I am unlikable.
Twist - Labelling, negative filter, discounting the positive.

Negative Thought - I am an idiot.
Twist - Labelling, negative filter, discounting the positive.

Negative Thought - They think wrongly of me.
Twist - Mind reading, all or nothing.

Negative Thought - I am inferior.
Twist - Labelling, negative filter, discounting the positive.

Negative Thought - They don't like me.
Twist - Mind reading, all or nothing.

Negative Thought - I am weird.
Twist - Labelling, negative filter, discounting the positive.

Negative Thought- I look foolish.
Twist - Labelling, negative filter, discounting the positive.

Negative Thought - I can't change.
Twist - Fortune telling, all or nothing.

Negative Thought - I am stupid.
Twist - Blaming, labelling.

Negative Thought - I am boring.
Twist - Labelling, mental filter.

Negative Thought - I am no good.
Twist - Mind labelling, all or nothing.

Negative Thought - I will lose control and expose myself.
Twist - All or nothing, labelling, mental filter.

Negative Thought - I am odd.
Twist - Labelling, all or nothing.

Negative Thought- I am inadequate.
Twist - Labelling, mental filter, mind reading.

Negative Thought - Everyone is watching me because I'm feeling scary.
Twist - Labelling, negative filter, discounting the positive.

Negative Thought- I am trapped.
Twist - Labelling, negative filter.

Negative Thought - There is no hope for me.
Twist - Mental filter, mind reading.

Negative Thought - This is terrible.
Twist - Emotional reasoning, all or nothing.

Negative Thought - Everyone is judging me.
Twist - Labelling.

Negative Thought - People don't like me because I am quiet.
Twist - Labelling, mind reading.

Negative Thought - They can see how anxious I look.
Twist - Emotional reasoning, all or nothing, labelling.

Negative Thought - People don't like me because I am nervous.
Twist - Blaming, fortune telling.

Negative Thought - If the conversation doesn't go well, it is my fault.
Twist - Discounting the positive.

Negative Thought - I must appear interesting. Otherwise, people will not like me.
Twist - Overgeneralisation, blaming.

Negative Thoughts and Their More Positive Counterparts

Now I will give you a quick tip how to find the most uplifting thoughts. I have prepared some examples of negative thinking for you below. There are the most common negative thoughts which you may meet. Find your thought.

Negative Thought I can't do anything right today.
Alternative Thought I am sure I CAN do at least one thing that I have planned. I will handle it.

Negative Thought Can it get any worse?
Alternative Thought I feel... (name the negative emotion), but I am sure I can overcome it.

Negative Thought I don't feel good today. Ugh! Do I have to get out of bed today?
Alternative Thought There are plenty of blessings waiting for me today. I can't wait to experience them.

Negative Thought   I have the worst luck!
Alternative Thought The next time I will have a much better luck.

Negative Thought I hate it when it rains.
Alternative Thought Just before the rain the sunny day will come.

Negative Thought I just know that I will make a mistake on this project.
Alternative Thought Even if I make a mistake, I can learn something and the next time do it better.

Negative Thought I will never be able to afford that.

Alternative Thought When I start investing my money, I will be able to afford that.

Negative Thought Now that I washed my car, it is going to rain.

Alternative Thought The rain will wash my car for free.

Negative Thought My boss just called me into his office; this can't be good.

Alternative Thought My boss called me into his office to praise my work and maybe promote me.

Negative Thought I am useless.

Alternative Thought Even if I'm struggling now, I am excellent at some things _____ (name which ones).

Negative Thought I am unlikable.

Alternative Thought There are many people who like me.

Negative Thought I am an idiot.

Alternative Thought I am a smart person.

Negative Thought They think badly of me.

Alternative Thought I love myself no matter what other people think of me.

Negative Thought I am inferior.

Alternative Thought I am a worthy person, having equal rights as do other people.

Negative Thought They don't like me.

Alternative Thought Whether they like me or not, I am a decent person. I don't need other people's approval to feel loved.

Negative Thought I am weird.

Alternative Thought I am doing OK.

Negative Thought I look foolish.

Alternative Thought I look OK.

Negative Thought I can't change.

Alternative Thought I can change some things in my life.

Negative Thought I am stupid.

Alternative Thought I am smart at many things I do.

Negative Thought I am boring.

Alternative Thought I can be attractive to many people.

Negative Thought I am no good.

Alternative Thought There are people who see me as a great person.

Negative Thought I will lose control and expose myself.

Alternative Thought I will be able to keep control and not expose myself.

Negative Thought I am odd.

Alternative Thought I am OK.

Negative Thought I am inadequate.

Alternative Thought I am adequate, according to many people.

Negative Thought Everyone is watching me.

Alternative Thought Even if people are watching me, I am OK and liked by many of them.

Negative Thought I am trapped.

Alternative Thought I will find a solution soon.

Negative Thought There is no hope for me.

Alternative Thought I will take some action and will change my fate.

Negative Thought This is terrible.

Alternative Thought I don't like it, but there are many good things here.

Negative Thought I do not belong here.

Alternative Thought I am liked by some people here.

Negative Thought Everyone is judging me.

Alternative Thought Even if some people judge me, they think I am OK.

Negative Thought People don't like me because I am quiet.

Alternative Thought Talking is silver, but being quiet is gold, people appreciate that I am listening to them.

Negative Thought They can see how anxious I look.

Alternative Thought I can control my anxiety. People are too much bothered with themselves.

Negative Thought People don't like me because I am nervous.

Alternative Thought Everybody is nervous sometimes, and there are many individuals who like me.

Negative Thought If the conversation doesn't go well, it is my fault.

Alternative Thought I don't have to be perfect talking; everybody makes mistakes.

Negative Thought I must appear interesting. Otherwise people will not like me.

Alternative Thought There will always be people who like me and those who don't. I focus on those who find me attractive.

Negative Thought I am always doing the wrong thing.

Alternative Thought I do many things right and learn from some others.

Look at the list above and name five negative thoughts which you consider as true in your case. Learn by heart the positive alternatives and for thirty days write the positive statements down, filling out one page of your notebook.

Challenge A Negative Thought with Questions

Answer the questions below and see how many times you choose yes. The more times, the more negative is your thought. Test it on some of your thoughts.

My negative thought

…..

QUESTION

Am I confusing a thought with a fact? (Yes/No)

Am I assuming my view of things is the only one possible? (Yes/No)

Am I exaggerating the importance of events? (Yes/No)

Am I predicting the future instead of experimenting with it? (Yes/No)

Am I fretting about the way things ought to be, instead of accepting and dealing with them as they are?(Yes/No)

Am I taking something which has little or nothing to do with me personally? (Yes/No)

Am I assuming I can do nothing to change my situation? (Yes/No)

Am I overestimating the chances of disaster? (Yes/No)

Am I concentrating on my weakness and forgetting my strengths? (Yes/No)

Am I asking questions that have no answers? (Yes/No)

Am I thinking in all-or-nothing terms? (Yes/No)

Am I jumping to conclusions? (Yes/No)

Am I paying attention only to the black side of things?(Yes/No)

Am I blaming myself for something which is not really my fault? (Yes/No)

Am I expecting myself to be perfect? (Yes/No)

Am I condemning myself as a total person by a single event? (Yes/No)

Am I using a double standard? (Yes/No)

Am I confusing a thought with a fact? (Yes/No)

Am I assuming my view of things is the only one possible? (Yes/No)

Am I exaggerating the importance of events? (Yes/No)

Am I predicting the future instead of experimenting with it? (Yes/No)

Am I fretting about the way things ought to be, instead of accepting and dealing with them as they are? (Yes/No)

Am I taking something personally which has little or nothing to do with me? (Yes/No)

Am I assuming I can do nothing to change my situation? (Yes/No)

Am I overestimating the chances of disaster?(Yes/No)

Am I concentrating on my weakness and forgetting my strengths? (Yes/No)

Am I asking questions that have no answers? (Yes/No)

Am I thinking in all-or-nothing terms? (Yes/No)

Am I jumping to conclusions? (Yes/No)

Am I paying attention only to the black side of things?(Yes/No)

Am I blaming myself for something which is not my fault? (Yes/No)

Am I expecting myself to be perfect? (Yes/No)

Am I condemning myself as a total person by a single event? (Yes/No)

Am I using double standards?(Yes/No)

If you have discovered that your thoughts meet many of the criteria mentioned above (the questions to which you have answered 'yes'), then the time has come to change them.

10 Ways to Change Negative Thoughts

Here are the things which will help you to overcome your negative thoughts. You can use all the tips or just try one.

1. Smile. Stand in front of a mirror and force yourself to smile. It does help change your mood and relieve stress. Scientists proved that just changing your facial expression, you can turn into someone with a more positive attitude.

2. Modify the tone of your thoughts from negative to positive. For example, instead of thinking, "I am inferior," think, "I am a smart person in many fields of life." For the next week log all the negative automatic thoughts that come to your life. You will be surprised how many of them appear. Then look at the list with alternative views above and find a more positive statement.

3. Surround yourself with positive people. I have already mentioned that changing your circle of friends can change your life in a drastic way. Sometimes you will need to say goodbye to your cynical friends. Remember that even if you are changing, the negative people can infect you with negativity again. Avoid complainers, victims and critics. You will recognise them by focusing on problems or faults, without taking actions.

4. Meditate or do yoga. Check if there are yoga class in your town. It will take your focus away from your thoughts and will bring attention to your breath. Yoga is also very relaxing, which will help to ease your mind. You will stay present to your experience. Instead of jumping to what could happen, you will be brought back to the now, which is the only moment – the most important moment.

5. Stop playing the victim. Take responsibility. When you think in a negative way, you give control to the things which are bad, which you don't have. This frustrates you even more. Instead, think what action you could take to turn the situation to your advantage. Even if your living situation becomes unbearable, there is always a way out.

Read the chapters about making changes and taking responsibility once again and apply the tips described there in your life, right now.

6. Remember that no one is perfect and let yourself move forward. You can easily dwell on your mistakes. However, the only thing you can do now is to learn from them and move forward. Take your transformation diary and list all the things which you have learned within the last year. They can be your achievements, but also life lessons, like being more patient or understanding.

7. Help someone. Take the focus away from you and do something nice for another person. Think who you could assist right now. It may be your friend or family member, you might volunteer. You will become more proud of yourself for making other people happy.

8. Practice gratitude. Then you instantly focus on positive things in your life. List five things that you are grateful for right now. Being grateful helps appreciate what you already have.

9. Sing. When you sing, we show your feelings, and this provides an incredible stress relief. You focus on some uplifting music instead of negativity. Imagine how you feel going to a concert and singing with your favourite band.

10. Read positive quotes and books. Find some inspiring quote and place PostIt stickers with your positive thoughts on your computer, fridge door, mirror as reminders to stay positive. You can also read aloud the uplifting books of the self-help masters.

Change the Most Persistent Negative Thoughts

Sometimes you might need some more hardcore tips for your thoughts to be changed. Be aware that the tips I will give you below need some time to bring fruit. To make the most of these tips, make notes in your transformation diary for at least 30 days.

1. Stop. When a negative thought attacks you, the first thing which you can do is say: **"Stop!"** **"Enough already!"** These are the most efficient snippets used in an emergency. Depending on the type of your negative thoughts, you can use the following phrases:

TYPE OF THOUGHT	STOPPING SNIPPET
Overgeneralisation	No absolutes!
	What evidence do I have to draw this conclusion?
	Do I have enough data to make the rule?
	I can't predict the future.
Labelling	Stop! That is just a label.
	No more labels – be accurate.
	Enough already!
	Exactly, what do I mean by (idiot, stupid, etc.)?
	I have far more good points than bad.
All-or-nothing thinking	Nothing is totally everything.
	Remember the grey zone.
	No more absolutes!

Slow down now.

What are the percentages?

Blame

No more blaming!

No more brooding! The past is over, and I can do no more about it.

Stop bad-mouthing yourself.

I don't have to blame myself for others' behaviour.

Mental filter

Hold it! No comparisons!

Assume nothing.

Stop being paranoid!

Everybody else is too concerned with their own behaviour. They're not watching me.

Stop comparing!

Everybody is an individual, with unique strengths and weaknesses.

Mind-reading

Stop nonsense.

Assume nothing.

What are the facts? Spell them out.

I have no way of knowing what they're thinking.

Emotional reasoning	Lies! My emotions are lying to me.
	Look at the underlying thoughts.
	Stop! Just stop it right now.
	Correct the thoughts and the pain will go.
	Distrust all sudden feelings.

Choose three of your thoughts. Find which category of twists they represent (i.e. some of the ten ways of twisted thinking). Then select one snippet from the list above for each thought and learn them by heart, so that you will be able to use them whenever the negative thought suddenly attacks you.

2. Do a cost-benefit analysis. Is it worth it to think the negative way? If you are flooded by negative thoughts, write them down. Always have a small notebook and a pen where you can do the logging, this time of your negative thoughts. When you already have some of the thoughts, do the cost-benefits analysis: List all the costs and all the benefits of thinking that way and mark the importance of them. Add up the score and you will see in most cases that thinking the negative thought costs you more than the profit it gives you.

My negative thought is ....
....
....

COSTS   **BENEFITS**

3. Think in the shades of grey. It is especially useful in case of all-or-nothing thoughts. Write some of them in your transformation diary now. Answer the questions:

• What are the alternative options?

• How would it look in the shade of grey?

List at least three options of the shade of grey for your negative thoughts. Think of the cases when an absolute thought has become grey or hazy. A grey thought is an unclear one or one that you are unsure about. The shade of grey is determined by the strength of the thought.

4. Test your thought. Act like a scientist. For example, notice if people are watching you or would rather talk to each other, totally ignoring you. While doing this, try each approach on different occasions and remember to monitor each social exposure. This would give you objective feedback about whether they are watching you. Take your negative thought and plan three small experiments which you will make to question if this thought is true. List the tests now.

1. ....
2. ....
3. ....

For example, in the case of being afraid if people are watching you, go out for a walk in the city centre, have a coffee in a busy café and then go to a luxury boutique. When you do the three tests, analyse your observations.

Who has watched me?

Test 1 ....

Test 2 ....

Test 3 ....

Even if somebody watched me, was this person interested in me? How long were they watching me?

Test 1 ....

....

Test 2 ....

....

Test 3 ....

....

5. Pretend that you are a journalist. Interview people. Ask your friends – in the real world and online, what they think about your thought. You can also ask strange people, who you started a conversation with. For example: What do you think about people watching you? Were you embarrassed? Do you think that people were interested in your life?

Try it in writing now, but then combine asking questions with doing behavioural experiments (a tool described above). Prepare three questions for the survey.

Your questions for the survey:

1. …………………………………………………………………………
2. …………………………………………………………………………
3. …………………………………………………………………………

6. Use two standards for your thought. We are usually overly critical of ourselves, while we are more compassionate to our friends. Write down three negative thoughts below and what you would say to your friend instead.

MY NEGATIVE THOUGHT

WHAT WOULD I SAY TO MY FRIEND

For example, instead of saying 'You should have...' you would say 'You've done..., but you can learn from that. What would you improve right now?'

7. Define the terms of your thought. It is especially useful in case of labelling and overgeneralisation. Now choose three of your negative thoughts. Write them down below and define what each of them means.

Thought …………………………………………………………………
What does it mean?

…………………………………………………………………………

Thought …………………………………………………………………
What does it mean?

…………………………………………………………………………

Thought ....

What does it mean?

....

For example: Thought: *"I am stupid."* What does it mean? *"I cannot write a good report and make typos."*

8. Question your thoughts. You can do it in two ways: use a goal-directed thinking and putting your thoughts in perspective. Answer the following questions in writing.

My negative thought is

....

Is there something I can learn from this situation, to help me do it better next time?

....

What can I do that will help me solve the problem?

....

Is thinking this way helping me to feel good or to achieve my goals?

....

Then put this thought into perspective.

What is the worst thing that could happen? How likely is it?

....

What is the best thing that could happen?

....

Is this situation as bad as I am making out to be?

....

What is most likely to happen?

....

Will this matter in five years' time?

....

Is there anything good about this situation?

....

Changing your thoughts is a process and takes some time. You need to create some new habits, like using the snippets every time your negative thought appears or asking questions undermining this thought. I will help you how to establish these habits in Chapter Eight. If you need to know these tools now, go to that chapter and apply them as soon as possible.

Chapter 6
Master the Happiness Language

"But if thought corrupts language, language can also corrupt thought."
— George Orwell, 1984

Tina used the victim language and put herself under tremendous pressure. Every time there was something to do, she said 'have to' automatically. It took her few months to create a new habit of using the more positive, in other words, 'happiness' language. You can do the same.

This chapter will show you:

- An example of the happiness and unhappiness language.
- The features of the happiness and unhappiness language.
- Why communication is so important in creating happiness.
- Some common expressions of the unhappiness language.
- Examples of the unhappiness language.
- Metaphors of the unhappiness language.

- The vocabulary of happiness.
- The metaphors of happiness.
- The uplifting questions.
- To neutralise the unhappiness language.
- To accelerate the happiness language.
- To use affirmations to be a permanently happy person.
- Examples of powerful affirmations.

Language is an exceedingly powerful tool. Communicating orally, or in written form, you need to be aware that your message and its language will affect whether it is received positively or negatively. Even when you are conveying unpleasant news, the impact can be softened using what we call positive language. I will also call it happiness language.

Let's look at these two examples of official letters to someone starting a new business and applying for a loan:

"We <u>regret</u> to inform you that we cannot process your application to grant you a loan because you have <u>neglected</u> to provide sufficient information. Please complete ALL sections of the attached form and return it to us."

*"**Congratulations** on your new business. To start processing your application for a loan, we need some additional information. If you return the attached form, with the highlighted areas filled in, we **will be able to** further discuss details of granting you a loan within three weeks. We **wish you** success in your new endeavour."*

The words which are underlined out in the first message are the examples of negative language, in other words – unhappiness language. I deliberately underlined these words out so you can instantly learn to eliminate them from your daily speech or writing. You will find more examples of unhappiness words, metaphors and questions later in this chapter.

The second message is positive because it contains the elements of happiness language. You can see the words in **bold font** which show praise and one indicates that taking action is possible. Start using them as often as possible.

It is very easy to fall into the unhappiness language pattern. You do so without being aware of it, particularly in written communication. But unhappiness language is also harmful when you talk to other people or yourself. In the first case, you undermine your relationships with others while in the second you destructively criticise yourself.

The Unhappiness and The Happiness Language

You will soon learn particular words, metaphors and questions which can uplift you or impair your happiness. Let's look at the main features of each of them, before you start learning the new, positive language and avoiding the negative one.

Unhappiness Language

- Unhappiness language tells the recipient what cannot be done. And this sabotages your happiness as the feeling of incompetence can be very overwhelming.
- Unhappiness language has a subtle tone of the blame. I have written in many cases that blaming destroys happiness.
- Unhappiness language criticises without giving you suggestion what to improve. The negative message can be both spoken and written, directed to others or yourself.

On the contrary, happiness language has the following qualities:

Happiness Language

- The message is easy to understand by your receiver. Nothing frustrates us more than the need to figure out what the sender's message meant.

- Happiness language suggests the recipient what to do. Then even if you have done something wrong, you have an opportunity to learn from your mistake and to make progress.

- Happiness language suggests alternatives and choices are available to the recipient, which gives them the sense of having control over the situation, even in the case of making mistakes.

- Happiness language sounds helpful and encouraging. As you could read in the second message, congratulating success is the example of encouragement.

- Happiness language stresses positive actions and positive consequences that the recipient can anticipate. If you read the second message again, you will notice that the bank precisely indicated what happens when the application is filled in correctly.

Why Is the Language So Important to Creating Happiness?

Do you remember this quote: "Watch your thoughts as they become your words, watch your words as they become your beliefs, watch your beliefs as they become your actions...?" Yes, before you create a belief, you have probably heard the statement spoken many times by you or your parents and friends.

Therefore, it is so important to pay attention to how you are talking to yourself and to others, avoid contact with negativity – especially the unhappiness language, stay around positive people. You already know the general features of the happiness and unhappiness language. Now time has come to tell you more about this topic.

Language is created by words and phrases (often metaphors) which form statements or questions. Changing each of the above-mentioned elements of language, you can dramatically increase the level of your happiness. And if you consistently use the happiness language, you can transform your beliefs and your life.

Suppose that you are using "I can't do it" very frequently. What happened to your actions and belief in success? They vanish because 'can't' is an example of helplessness language. If you say **"If I try I will learn. I will overcome this challenge, either by myself or with the help of others. I will handle it."**, you focus your mind on taking action and regaining control over your life.

Metaphors are also very powerful. How do you feel when 'life is an adventure' instead of 'life sucks, and then you die'?

Questions are even more compelling as they set your mindset and generate your thoughts. Suppose that you are diagnosed with cancer and say "Why has it happened to me?" you will activate the avalanche of negative thoughts, start blaming yourself or others and eventually feel even more helpless.

Now let's say that you change your question and say **"What can I do right now to enjoy my life despite my illness?"** in the same situation. You would take as much action as possible.

Common Unhappiness Phrases

Unhappiness language is very subtle and often difficult to discover because no one teaches you how to recognise it. The literal meaning of the word, phrase or question is not the only factor determining positivity or negativity. However, we can distinguish some categories of unhappiness language. Some are so negative that I deliberately crossed them out.

The language of inability, failure, and helplessness. Stop using them:

~~I can't~~	~~failure~~
~~problem~~	~~I fail to~~

~~You fail to understand~~	~~I'm stressed~~
~~I've lost~~	~~loss~~
~~unfortunately~~	~~it's impossible~~
~~unable to~~	~~I'm paralysed~~
~~I'm defeated~~	

The language of pressure. Substitute them with other phrases.

~~Must~~	~~sick~~
~~have to~~	~~should~~
~~ought to~~	~~are supposed to~~

The language of incompetence. Eliminate them, using more neutral counterparts.

~~stupid~~	*mistake*
~~an idiot~~	*error*
~~a jerk~~	*damage*
~~you are wrong~~	
~~unworthy~~	

Overwhelming negative emotions. Neutralise them with alternative phrases.

overwhelmed	*destroyed*
helpless	*anxious*
furious	*dreadful*
mad	*hurt*
crazy	*hate*
depressed	*rejected*

Pejorative labels and blaming.

lonely

terrible

it's your fault

selfish

miser

Unhappiness Questions

In general, all the questions starting with "why" when you are frustrated and unhappy are undesirable. Let me give you some examples:

- Why does it have to be the red light when I'm in a hurry?
- Why is he so selfish?
- Why can't she make love more often?
- Why is the boss so demanding?
- Why did it happen to me? (having a long-term illness, someone close died).

All these questions focus on analysing the past and blaming while happiness is the result of taking action, even in a challenging situation.

Metaphors of Unhappiness

You hold language and pictures in your mind. Creating a vision and holding it in your head will steer you towards the emotions and feelings that you associate with this picture. When you add emotions to that picture, you will start creating a new reality.

When you start believing in the picture created by your mind and project it many times, it will become reality, and you will start attracting happiness or unhappiness – the people, circumstances by your state of mind.

Metaphors shape your overall experience because they filter what you perceive and influence how you make meaning. The truth is that you are the most important sense because even a neutral metaphor can become negative in context. Why are metaphors so important?

They shape your experience and are part of our language and like single words and phrases, have an impact on your thoughts and emotions.

The metaphors of happiness empower you to change how you think and feel, on condition that you are using the positive metaphors. In the case of the negative ones which you will learn of in a minute, metaphors can disempower and destroy you.

Unhappiness metaphors have some features in common: they disempower you and make you feel bad. Here are some examples of the metaphors to avoid in your everyday language if you want to be a happy person. I have given you some general examples and those attributed to some everyday issues of life. Here are some unhappiness metaphors in sentences:

- A stitch in time saves nine.
- Life sucks, then you die.
- That ship has sailed.
- It's raining cats and dogs.

You can meet many expressions which are abstract, but frequently used. Here are some of them:

- hitting a wall
- up the stream without a paddle
- wicked problems
- 1800-pound gorilla
- flogging a dead horse
- a late bloomer
- the point of no return
- uphill battle

- chicken on the egg
- the elephant in the room
- swimming upstream
- broken hearted
- time is a thief
- the stench of failure
- Life is like: .... a poker game, a horror, a maze, a jigsaw puzzle.
- Life is: ... a roller coaster, a struggle, hard, unfair, a tragedy, a mountain to climb.
- Love is: ... a cloud, a clash of lightning, a dirt road, a fire, an exploding cigar, a beggar, a truck and a wall, a mental disease, a homeless guy, a madness, a (fierce) flame, a fever, an addiction, a debt, a battlefield, a weapon, a volcano, a loaded gun.
- Money is the root of all evil.
- More money equals more problems.
- Poverty is no sin.
- She is fishing in troubled waters.
- He drowned in a sea of grief.
- Success is a bastard as it has many fathers; failure is an orphan, with no takers.

Happiness Vocabulary

All the words which uplift you can be listed here. However, I have chosen only the most uplifting ones, so you can learn them quickly and use them on an everyday basis. Later you will learn how to turbo transform your language.

amused	gratified	sunny
awesome	ballistic	fabulous
beaming	on cloud nine	merry

tickled pink	upbeat	booming
gorgeous	outrageous	brilliant
invincible	ecstatic	centred
raring to go	energised	charged up
empowered	impassioned	cheerful
ebullient	overjoyed	confident
smashing	unbelievably	cosmically charged
sumptuous	just tremendous	emboldened
superb	excited	fascinated
gifted	great	glad
thrilled	exhilarated	carefree
walking on air	enraptured	contented
exultant	grinning	in a good mood
blissful	content	invigorated
chirpy	light-hearted	jocular
gleeful	cheery	jolly
delighted	in good spirits	jovial
blithe	euphoric	optimistic
jubilant	chipper	outrageous
satiated	unstoppable	over the moon
buoyant	in seventh heaven	satisfied
on top of the world	untroubled	smiling
elated	mirthful	turbo-charged
serene	explosive	joyous

Uplifting Metaphors

You can find many uplifting metaphors in the dictionary. I have chosen only some of them because you will be able to learn how to use the new metaphors gradually. You can choose some of them and use them on a regular basis. The first group is with comments to help you better understand the meaning of some common terms. They are important for every person.

Life is...

...10% of what happens to you and 90% of how you respond to it.

... crazy only for those who have no plans for it.

... a comedy for those who think and a tragedy for those who feel.

... like a room full of open doors that close as you get older.

... unfair if you don't have the wisdom to understand it.

Life is like...

...a game of tennis, photography, a building, a mine, money, a grammar lesson, an onion, a pencil, a seed, a novel, eating grapefruit, magic, adventure, cooking, mission, a banana.

Money is...

...energy, the life blood of society but charity is the soul.

Money...

... follow the money, makes money.

Love is...

...a flame and burning coals, a tree, a fruit, a concerto, a plant, a wild plant, a poetry of the senses, a rose, a spice, a garden, the only disease that makes you feel better, a work of art.

Now let's meet some fixed phrases. Some are used in sentences.

- Your ship is sailing, and you're on it.

- Your ship has come in.
- Chipping away at the stone.
- Grab the bull by the horns.
- Bubbly personality.
- The apple of my eye.
- Expedition.
- Eye of the tiger.
- The light of my life.
- Destroy the blocks.
- Break down the wall.
- Let go of the rope.
- Dance your way to success.

Uplifting Questions

You can find many uplifting questions which will help you to transform your life. I have already mentioned what kind of questions happy people don't use. Now read carefully and start using the uplifting questions. I have gathered them in categories.

1. Questions for solving problems

What is good in this situation?

How can I make the most of the situation?

If there are no good options, what's the best play I can make for this scenario?

What's right with this picture?

What can I do to ensure that the situation will be in line with my plans?

What can I do to turn that situation around?

What can I stop doing to turn the situation around?

What can I do differently to turn that situation around?

What action could be taken to give the simplest and the fastest result?

Now, what are you going to do about it?

Who can help me?

Who else shares this problem?

 Who would solve this issue well?

What would (famous or interesting person XYZ) do?

What can you be the best at in the world?

How would I respond if I was (famous or interesting person XYZ)?

What kind of life lesson can I learn from this situation?

What will I gain solving this problem?

When was the last time I successfully dealt with a situation like this?

What could I change here to succeed?

How can I change it?

What's the way forward?

Will it matter in 100 years?

So, what? Now, what?

2. Questions to ask when setting and achieving goals

Am I choosing for my story or someone else's?

What am I pointing my camera at?

Who do I want to be and what experiences do I want to create?

How does that serve me, regarding who I am and who I want to be?

What precisely do I want?

What do I want to accomplish?

What do I want to do more of each day?

What am I committed to in my life right now?

What am I willing to receive?

How much time do I have?

What am I making time for?

How fast can I do it?

Where am I on the map?

If I had all the time in the world, how would I spend my time?

What do I need to be successful in this situation?

What energy am I willing to receive that would create success in my life?

Do I find myself influencing my world, does it have an impact on me or does it control me?

What are my talents? How can I use them?

How does it get better than this?

What magic could show up for me and my business today?

What else is possible?

What will I lose if I achieve my goal?

What does my current behaviour give me?

What permission do I need/want to move forward?

What else do I need to know here?

Who do I need to talk to?

3. Questions measuring progress

How has today added to the quality of my life?

How can I use today as an investment in my future?

Am I doing what you believe in or settling for what you're doing?

What did I learn today?

Does your schedule reflect my priorities?

Are you creating the results you want?

Do any of the things that used to upset me a few years ago matter at all today?

What's changed?

What's best for me?

What's the best thing for now?

What's the next best thing to do?

What's wearing me down?

What's lifting me up?

Am I giving my best where I have my best to give?

What's the most practical thing for me to focus on?

Can I teach it to someone else?

4. Questions for generating wealth

What do I love about money?

(paying bills) Was this expense for now or the future?

If joy became the national currency, what kind of work would make you wealthy?

If the money weren't the issue, what would I choose?

Would I rather have less work to do or more work I enjoy doing?

What else can I add to my business?

What would people pay me for?

What would it take for me to increase my income?

What can I add to the services I offer?

If I had all the money in the world, how would I spend it?

5. Questions for overcoming worry

Which worries me more – doing things right or doing the right things?

What is the worst thing that can happen?

How can I turn things around?

How likely is the thing I worry about?

6. Questions which are helpful in case of fear and anxiety

What risk would I take if I knew I could not fail?

What if I succeed?

If this situation were never to change, what's the one quality I need to enjoy it?

Which is worse—failing or never trying?

What am I avoiding?

If not now, when?

If not me, who?

If I knew I couldn't fail and would succeed - what would I do?

What is my greatest strength? Have any of my recent actions demonstrated this power?

7.Questions generating love and gratitude

What would make life more wonderful for me?

What are the top five things I cherish in my life?

What am I most happy about in my life at the moment?

Who do I love? Who loves me?

What excites me the most about life at the moment?

What can I contribute to others?

What can others contribute to me?

What am I most proud about in my life at the moment?

At what time in the recent past have I felt most passionate and alive?

Have I been the kind of friend I'd want as one?

What am I most grateful about in my life now?

What have I given to others today?

What do I most connect with? Why?

What am I enjoying most in my life at the moment?

8.Question which help to overcome negative thoughts

Is it a fact or opinion?

Who said that and is he/she an expert in that field?

What would my friend say for that?

9.Other useful questions

How old would I be if you didn't know how old I am?

What one piece of advice would I offer a new-born child?

What is the one job/cause/activity that could get me out of bed happily for the rest of my life? Am I doing it now?

What would I say is one thing I'd like to change the world?

Neutralising the Unhappiness Language

You have learned how the language of happiness and unhappiness looks. Now the time has come to use all the knowledge for your good. Firstly, you will learn how to eliminate the unhappiness language and then how to accelerate happiness vocabulary and questions. Let's start then.

Do all the steps in writing so you will be able to refer to your notes, recall what words to change and notice your progress. We will start with the three most disempowering phrases, and then you can apply the same steps to another word, questions, and metaphors.

Step 1. Analyse your current language.

For the next three days, notice when and how often you use the unhappiness language. Let's choose the following examples:

~~I can't~~

~~I should~~

~~I have to~~

~~idiot/jerk/stupid etc.~~

I deliberately crossed them out because you will do the same in your transformation diary. Don't go to the next steps until you find your pattern of using these devastating phrases. Your log may look like this:

Negative Word /Phrase	Times of use (Mark with dots)	Comments (What are you thinking /Feeling/How you behave)
~~I can't~~		
~~I should/ have to~~		
~~Stupid/idiot~~		

You can also log other examples of unhappiness language. Often refer to the list at the beginning of this chapter.

Step 2. Transform the negative language with positive counterparts.

I have chosen only three examples, but you will be able to transform more of them later. Because you need to learn using new expressions, like driving or writing, the process will take some time. You need to create a new habit. Now let me show you how you can neutralise the disempowering phrases you were observing. Choose one alternative of the examples:

I~~ can't do~~	**I'll handle it/I can do it/I'm capable of doing it**
I~~ should do~~	**I could**
I~~ have to do~~	**I need to/I will do/I choose to do/I get to**
~~stupid/idiot~~	**smart/learning/doing a homework**

Since I have given you more options of transformation the disempowering examples of language, choose only one alternative at first. For example, you might feel resistance for saying "I choose" when 'have to' rules your language. Then "I need to do" is more acceptable in your subconscious. Now I will show you how to learn the new language:

(i)   Written transformation.

Note down some automatic sentences in which you use examples of the unhappiness language listed above. Do it for one day, write them down with each of the examples crossed out in your transformation diary.

Do each exercise for a minimum of 30 days, but it is advisable to continue it for the next 60 days in order to crystallise the new habit. You can choose a particular time of the day for learning the new language or write the happiness sentences every time you start thinking negatively.

Here are some ways in which you can transform your language in writing.

Writing alternatives together with the disempowering sentences. When you have the sentences ready, write the options with the new phrases. Remember to cross out the old negative vocabulary, even more than once and underline the alternatives. Write the new negative sentence once and cross it out, then the alternatives 9 or 27 times underlining each line to program them to your sub-consciousness.

<u>Finishing sentences technique.</u> Write five endings to each of the beginnings below:

I could do……..

I need to do …………

I am smart because …….

Again, use this exercise every day for 90 days to create a new habit.

(ii)   Listening to the happiness language.

If you have done the exercises described above for a few days, you can empower the learning process by recording audio of the written script. Choose relaxing music as a background and record you. You can use Audacity or another program for recording audio on your computer. Speak slowly. At first, you might not like your own voice, but I can assure you, after some time you will also handle this challenge.

You can listen to the new language when travelling on public transport to work, walking or doing housework. Do it as often as possible. You have heard the disempowering phrases million times, so now it is necessary to listen to the new, happiness counterparts even more times.

Step 3. Use the new happiness language as often as possible.

It is the same as learning any foreign language. You need to repeat the new words and use them as often as possible, whenever the old sentences appear. Not only learning the new phrases by heart but regularly reading sentences using them.

Remember that you have committed 100% to the life transformation by reading this book. Hence, do your best to continue the process of changes and you will enjoy the fruits of your efforts later, despite obstacles.

Step 4. Eliminate the obstacles.

There will be challenges on your road to speaking the happiness language. I will describe the biggest obstacle below and I will give you some tools helping you to overcome it. The obstacle I am writing about is... your own motivation. Yes, there will be the times when you become discouraged and unwilling to do the exercises. Here are some tips I am giving you to overcome this:

The cost-benefit analysis I have mentioned some times where this tool is useful for dealing with obstacles and it also works here. List, in writing, all the benefits of speaking the happiness language and all the costs of using the disempowering one. Do it now and don't continue reading until you finish this exercise:

Costs of using the disempowering language	Benefits of using the happiness language

Before writing down the new, uplifting sentences, read aloud the cost-benefits analysis so you will stay motivated. Do this exercise every day.

You can accelerate the process of conditioning your mind by using these techniques.

List all your reasons why you want to use the happiness language.

These are your benefits but formed in a slightly different way. Write down five answers to the question: Why do I want to speak the happiness language?

1. ....
2. ....
3. ....
4. ....
5. ....

Visualise the 'why' reasons Now imagine all the benefits of using the happiness language. Do it after waking up and before falling asleep. You can use sticky notes to remind yourself of the new language and read them aloud, e.g. in the bathroom.

Regular monitoring of your progress is essential.

Limit contact with the people who put pressure on you Even if you master the happiness language, there still will be people who use the unhappiness one, often unconsciously. Then every time you hear 'have to', 'it's/you are stupid' or 'you can't do it' learn to automatically use the happiness counterparts – 'I need/ choose...', 'I'm smart because...' and 'I'll handle it.' However, some people are masters in using disempowering language so you'd better avoid or at least limit contact with them for everyone's sake.

Treat changing your language as a mission When you destroy the negative words or metaphors, you start noticing more opportunities around you. It is like fighting with evil. The unhappiness language is a challenge to take and win. Treat each step of transforming your language as a personal victory, a completed successful mission.

Negative thinking and negative beliefs are other reasons impairing the process of learning and using the happiness language. You can cope with them doing the exercises described in Chapter Four and Five, setting some compelling goals and surrounding yourself with positive people.

Step 5. Make changing your language the long-term journey.

Changing three of the most negative examples of language is a good start. However, it is just the beginning of transforming your language in the long run. Many of my clients asked me what to do with negative emotions. Follow the same steps and choose three most negative emotions you will neutralise. Here are some examples:

Negative emotion	Neutralising word or phrase
disgusted	uncomfortable
irritated	stimulated
dread	little disgusted
rejected	misunderstood, overlooked
uncomfortable	anticipating
lonely	temporarily on my own
angry, furious	frustrated, disappointed, irritated
afraid, anxious, fearful,	uncomfortable, anticipating
hurt	confused, uncomfortable
hate	irritation
insulted	uncomfortable

irritated	uncomfortable, disappointed,
jealous	a little concerned
overwhelmed	expectant
humiliated	exhausted, tired
terrible	surprised, bothered
painful	uncomfortable
stressed	challenged, busy, I have lots of energy
sadness	sorting my thoughts
I'm paralysed	I've temporarily stopped searching for a solution
sick	a little disgusted
challenged	questioning

If you start working only on three phrases per month, within a year there will be thirty-six new words you will start using differently. Just choose a set of new words every month, still working on the ones you are already changing.

Apart from negative emotions, you can also transform some statements meaning failure and defeat:

Negative statement	Neutralising statement
It's impossible, unable to	I'm looking for a solution
I'm defeated	I have a lesson to learn
I fail to	I'm doing homework, I'm learning
you fail to understand	you learn to understand
I've lost	seeking a solution
failure	lesson

problem	challenge, lesson
unfortunately	because of unpredicted circumstances

It is not a complete list. If you find any interesting example of a negative emotion which is not mentioned here, let me know. Now time has come to transform some of the metaphors listed in this chapter. I have deliberately chosen only some of them because even this number of metaphors may be overwhelming if you start using them all straight away. I have opted for some general metaphors, and those about life and love as these two things are crucial to being a happy person.

Negative metaphor	Uplifting metaphor
hitting a wall	looking for a solution
up the stream without a paddle	seeking a new paddle to go down stream
wicked problems	intriguing challenges
1,800-pound gorilla	a big challenge
a late bloomer	a sage
point of no return	sailing on a new ship
uphill battle	working on a challenge
elephant in the room	challenge
swimming upstream	taking challenges
broken heart	life lesson
flogging a dead horse	learning the lesson, working
life sucks then you die	life is an adventure
Time is a thief	Time is a teacher
It's raining cats and dogs	There are many challenges here

Victoria Herocten

Life is like a poker game
Life is like a maze
Life is a roller coaster
Life is a struggle
Life is like a jigsaw puzzle
Life is hard, no one makes it out alive
Life is like a movie

Life is unfair

Life is a mountain climb

Love is a cloud
Love is a clash of lightning

Love is a dirt road
Love is a fire
Love is an exploding cigar
Love is a beggar
Love is a truck and a wall

Love is a mental disease
Love is a madness
Love is a (fierce) flame
Love is a fever
Love is an addiction
Love is a debt
Love is battlefield

Life is an opportunity
Life is like a pathway
Life is like sailing the ocean
Life is full of lessons to learn
Life is an opportunity
Life can be challenging, but can be happy
So act your role as well as you can

Life is different depending on your destiny

Life is a pathway with challenges and victories

Love is a mission
Love means overcoming the downs and enjoying the ups

Love is a mission
Love is a teacher
Love is a task to solve
Love is an ally
Love may be a challenge solved by two people

Love is mind transformation
Love is mind transformation
Love is a challenge to handle
Love is a challenge to handle
Love is mind transformation
Love is a mutual give-take
Love is a school of life

Love is a weapon

Love is a volcano

Love is a loaded gun learn to handle

Love is a way to happiness

Love is a challenge to handle

Love is a thing which you

Accelerate Happiness by Using Mega Uplifting Language

Apart from learning how to eliminate unhappiness language, you can also learn how to speak and think with more enthusiasm, to be even happier. Many words can be amplified, so their positive meaning is empowered. How to do it?

Step 1. Discover your language

Now, for three days, record all the positive words which you use (hopefully there will be many of them). Just doing this exercise will transform your life as you switch your focus to the most positive side of life.

Step 2. Change the language you use

Look at the list below. Which of the words used by you on an everyday basis can you amplify to feel even happier?

Positive word	The word of mega happiness
Good	
all right, not too bad	grand, superb
good	dynamite, better than excellent,
good	just doesn't get any better
nice	spectacular, fantastic,
okay	perfect, energised, fantastic

pretty good	great
fine	awesome
tasty	sumptuous
not bad	couldn't be better
cool	outrageous
pleasant	monumental
interesting	captivating
feeling good	cosmically charged, tremendous
great	exhilarated, phenomenal, vibrant, incredible
fantastic	fabulous
super	blooming
attractive	gorgeous
perfect	extraordinary, superb, brilliant

Efficient

alert	energised
fast, quick	ballistic, explosive
awake	ready to go
curious	fascinated
paying attention	focused
focused	energised

Confident

confident, determined	unstoppable
strong, powerful	invincible
smart	gifted
motivated	compelled, driven to

moving forward	moving at warp speed
resourceful	brilliant

Happy

comfortable	smashing
glad	over the moon
peaceful	serene
happy	jazzed, ecstatic, totally blissed
excited	outrageous, impassioned, ecstatic
loving	passionate, exuding love
interested	enthralled
intense	laser-like
terrific	ecstatic
stimulated	charged up

Safe

secure, safe	emboldened, confident, empowered, centred,
fortunate	unbelievably blessed

Step 3. Choose three mega powerful words used everyday

Learn them by heart. Let's say that you often use the phrase "I'm OK" or "good." What are the examples of 'happier' language?

"I'm dynamite!"

"I'm better than excellent!"

"It just doesn't get any better!"

"It's perfect!"

"It's energised!"

"It's fantastic!"

Choose one of them and use as often as possible, even if it might sound funny at the beginning. Write them down.

My frequently used positive word is:

....

It's more uplifting counterpart is…

....

Step 4. Practice

Practice, practice, practice. As in the case of eliminating unhappiness language, also here you need to use the new words on a regular basis. How do you do it? Use the same methods which you learned earlier in this chapter.

Write down a powerful manifestation: some sentences with the new, more empowering words. Place them in your wallet, on your mobile, hang them in the bathroom or the kitchen.

Read aloud the sentences with the new words: It will accelerate the process of learning the more powerful and happier language. You start noticing things and yourself as excellent. Record a powerful manifestation and listen to it every day for 90 days.

Step 5. Monitor your progress.

As with each goal, this goal to change your language for the mega happiness one requires monitoring your progress, use Habit Bull or the sheet provided in the book to mark how well you are doing while changing your language.

Use Affirmations to Become a Permanently Happy Person

Affirmations work to help us change. They are positive assertions. You can use them as one of the tools to transform your life for a happier one: changing your beliefs, negative thoughts, and neutralising negative emotions. How to use them?

1. Choose the three most often used phrases or one most negative thought or belief.

It depends on which of them are the most destructive in your life. Usually, it is advised to work on your beliefs and thoughts first, as changing them will bring you more significant happiness. However, as I have already written in this chapter, even turning three negative phrases (like "I can't", "an idiot" or "I should/have to") will help you to be a happier person.

I remind you once again to choose only one category for changing (i.e. either your beliefs or your thoughts, or your language). If you want to work on each of them, create three separate affirmations and treat them as three different goals.

As a short exercise, write your belief, thought or a word now:

…..

2. Identify your negative self-talk, beliefs or language.

You have already done this step when reading the previous chapters and part of the present one. Choose one category for making changes at first: your thoughts, beliefs or language. Write three of your thoughts, words of beliefs now. After writing them down, cross the phrases out like in the example given:

a. …...

b. …...

c. …...

For example: "~~I'm an idiot~~", "~~I can't do it~~", "~~I'm not worthy~~"

Do this in handwriting, rather than using a computer because it is important to connect your physical self with your neurons and psyche and intuition. Our subconscious learns from what our bodies do. So, for the next three days log all the examples of negative beliefs, thoughts and language. After you think you have written them all, wait. There will be more thoughts, beliefs or words that will come. While you are emptying out the top layer in your mind, the next layer will be revealed and released.

3. Create an alternative to your beliefs, thoughts or language.

I will give you some examples of powerful affirmations later. You can also find many of them on the Internet. However, if you would like to create your affirmation, follow these rules:

The affirmation should be positive.

Transform all the negative words to positive ones. For example: "I'm an idiot" can be transformed into **"every day I'm becoming smarter and smarter."**

One note of caution: Not only avoid the words that have a negative meaning but also the negation of the whole sentence (i.e. not, no, neither, nor). Stay away from words that imply loss, such as get rid of, give up, lose, quit, stop, refrain, avoid, etc. Keep away from words like I wish, I want, I wish and I would like because they imply a lack of something. Affirm the positive states of doing, being, or having instead. Words which suggest the negative issue you are trying to change also should not be used in affirmations. For example: "I'm less and less anxious every day" is not a good example. Substitute it with "anxiety-free" or even better "more and more confident."

The affirmation must be personal.

Start them with "I" because it is your personal statement. If you fear high resistance writing and saying an affirmation starting with "I," use the third person. For example: "People say that I am wiser and smarter every day."

Affirming what others will do, be or have is a waste of time as you can only change yourself. Even if you have the best of intentions, your idea of what is right for another person may not be what they want or need. The only beliefs, thoughts and language that you can change are your own.

Affirmations which others write are a good starting point. However, always change any words or phrases which you feel uncomfortable with.

Affirm in the present.

Doing so you already experience the benefits of what the affirmation means.

Saying "I will be rich" or "I am going to be rich" is placing your desire somewhere out there, just beyond reach. Remember, the future doesn't exist. Change only happens when you focus on the present.

By affirming in the present tense, it is also easier for you to generate the necessary emotions and visualisations that support your affirmations. There is a significant difference between saying "I will be so rich when ..." and saying "I am so rich now that ..."

Affirmations must be precise, in theory.

In the beginning, when you start changing and in the case of core beliefs, general affirmations work better. However, as you grow, start to create more powerful affirmations – more precise and relevant to you.

Describe your desire in detail and the more accurately you can describe it, the better. Add as much detail as possible. You can add all the benefits that attaining your goal would bring. Your subconscious mind needs a clear picture to work on.

Use comparatives wisely. Words such as 'more', 'better', 'greater' or 'best' should only be used if they precede more detail. When you use comparative words, the subconscious mind is forced to compare what you want with what you don't want. Therefore, you end up putting as much energy behind the negative as the positive.

Remember to avoid ambiguous words. It will create ambiguous results and if you are affirming for a larger salary, would you be happy with an increase of 1%? Be precise and declare for the best outcome that you feel comfortable with, but make your affirmations realistic. Choosing "I have a 100% larger salary" will not work when there is little hope for promotion or your business is not growing fast at the moment.

Use your words if possible. There are many words you can use in affirmations that are acceptable. However, these affirmations should be clarified in our statements. Words like: health, happiness, wealth, prosperity and success are all good words to use. But try to go a bit further. For example, you can say 'able to travel around the world' for 'wealthy'. Define these words in your terms.

Amplify your affirmations. Use humour, some energising words. Choose some from the list: energised, ballistic, explosive, ready to go, energised, unstoppable, invincible, fascinated, gifted, driven to, over the moon, on cloud one, smashing, brilliant.

Begin using the new affirmation statements.

Practice, practice, practice. And you can use the same ways of conditioning your subconscious mind like while transforming your language. Let me list them once again:

Write down a powerful manifestation. You can do it every day and then repeat every day. Place them in your wallet, on your mobile, hang in the bathroom or the kitchen.

Read aloud sentences with your affirmations. This will accelerate the process of learning the more powerful and happier language. You start noticing things and yourself as excellent.

Record a powerful manifestation and listen to it every day for 90 days. If you catch yourself thinking or saying any of your old (negative) beliefs, thoughts or words, stop yourself. Use the tools described in the chapter about beliefs, thoughts and outlined in this chapter. But you can also write the negative beliefs, words and thoughts down, then cross the negative belief out and burn or shred the page.

Powerful Affirmations

You can find hundred positive affirmations on the Internet or in the self-help books. That may be overwhelming. As I wrote earlier, remember to choose the one which will suit you, your circumstances. To inspire you, I have listed some the most powerful and the most common, with mentioning when these affirmations can be used.

Health

People admire my healthy lifestyle choices.

I take care of my body with respect and love.

I respond to my body's messages with patience and understanding.

I manifest perfect health by making smart choices.

I love taking care of myself.

I like every cell of my body.

I look forward to healthy old age because I take care of my body now.

I give myself permission to have perfect health.

I enjoy being healthy, happy and whole.

I deserve to live a healthy life.

I create the exact style of life with enthusiasm.

I attract pure health and wholeness every day.

I am ready to enjoy perfect health.

I am grateful for the healing that is happening to my body.

I am capable and prepared to heal my body.

I am surrounded by people who encourage me to be healthy.

Every day, in every way, I'm getting better and better.

Perfect health is my divine right and I acclaim it now.

Happiness

The whole process of living makes me happy.

Moving towards my goal makes me happy.

Miracles and magic surround me wherever I go.

I spread happiness to others and absorb happiness from others.

I enjoy every moment of the day. Be happy is my motto.

I choose happiness and health in my life.

The future is good. I look towards it with hope and happiness.

I celebrate life every day.

I am kind, I am loving, I am happy.

Happiness is my birth right.

Being happy comes easy to me. Happiness is my second nature.

Wealth

Wealth continuously flows into my life.

My finances improve beyond my dreams.

My actions create constant prosperity.

The money will have a positive influence on my life.

Money is the root of joy and comfort.

Money is my servant.

Money expands my life's opportunities and experiences.

Money creates a positive impact in my life.

I welcome an unlimited source of income and wealth in my life.

Money comes to me in expected and unexpected ways.

Money comes to me easily and effortlessly.

Money and spirituality can co-exist in harmony.

I use the money to improve my life and the lives of others.

I constantly attract opportunities that create more money.

I take advantage of any opportunity to make money.

I release all negative energy over money.

I move from poverty thinking to abundance thinking.

I have a natural money consciousness.

I embrace new avenues of income.

Self-confidence

My self-esteem grows every day.

My positive mental attitude is consistent at all times.

I see the bright side of any situation.

I remain confident in all situations.

I keep a positive attitude at all times.

I have a high level of self-esteem.

I am positive.

I have a strong, positive self-image.

I have a strong level of self-belief.

I have a natural level of self-confidence.

I have a natural and healthy level of self-esteem.

I have a bright, positive future ahead of me.

I focus on the good things in my life.

I believe in myself.

I am self-assured and happy within myself.

I am grateful for all the right things in my life.

I am comfortable just being myself.

I am comfortable in my skin.

I am always optimistic.

I always think positively.

Good Relationships with People

I have a successful relationship.

I am happy with my partner.

I am greeted by love whenever I go.

I deserve to have a healthy relationship.

I always count the good things in my relationship.

My relationship will last because I am in a loving relationship.

I am very grateful for all the love I receive in my life.

I am totally committed to my partner and our relationship.

I fully trust and love my partner.

I can respectfully communicate my feelings.

I do anything possible to nurture the love I have for my partner.

My partner respects and cherishes me.

Having a healthy and loving relationship is just a regular part of my life.

I am focused on making my relationship work.

Drawing boundaries and fostering respect is important.

It is worth any effort to build a happy relationship.

Listening to my partner's feelings is crucial to me.

Having a healthy relationship is very important to me.

I choose to see clearly with eyes of love. I love what I see.

Love is around every corner and joy fills my entire world.

I want to stay with my partner and make my relationship work.

I have come to this planet to love myself more and to share love with all those around me.

Honest communication is one of my natural strong points.

My partner and I love each other.

I give out love and it comes back to me. I choose to give love.

I always see mainly the positive aspects of my relationship.

I rejoice with the love I encounter every day.

I am worthy and wanted.

I have a fantastic lover, and we are both in love and at peace.

I am in a loving and happy relationship.

I am in a happy intimate relationship with a person who loves me.

I am beautiful, and everybody loves me.

I am surrounded by love.

My heart is open. I speak with loving words.

I am safe in my relationships, and I give and receive lots of love.

I attract only healthy relationships, and I people always treat me well.

Other Useful Affirmations

I will handle every challenge in my life.

I will handle every challenge myself or with the help of other people.

I attract helpful people to my life.

I am a success magnet, attracting success in whatever I do.

I am a happiness magnet, and I attract happiness in whatever I do.

I am solution oriented. All problems are solvable.

The power is within me.

I live in the now, learn from the past, and plan for the future.

I am in charge of my life.

I always make the correct decision, which always leads to happiness and success.

All my actions are focused on reaching my goal.

I achieve my goals one after the other.

I always prepare for taking action. Hence, luck always favours me.

I always spot opportunities and utilise them. New doors are always opening for me.

I am free of negative thinking. I embrace only positive thoughts.

I see success and happiness in everything I do. Small successes build up into large success and happiness for me.

I am in charge of my desires, emotions, and abilities. I focus only on love, happiness, health.

I am a person of action and vision.

Success is the only outcome of whatever I do.

Success is my birth right, and I believe in achieving it.

I deserve to be successful. My good fortune and my good life is the result of my success.

Affirmations for particular challenges

Anxiety and Fear

All is well in my world.

I am safe.

When I breathe in, I calm myself; when I breathe out, I release all the tension.

I am prepared for change.

I am confident about solving the problems of my life successfully.

I am cool, calm and collected.

I am free of anxiety.

I am social.

I like meeting people.

I overcome my fear of anything and everything.

I live my life courageously.

I transcend stress of any kind. I live in peace.

Life is wonderful.

I trust in God/the Universe to live a well-fulfilled life.

With every breath, I release the anxiety within me and I become more and calmer.

Every cell in my body is relaxed and oozes calmness.

Self-acceptance

I love myself deeply and unconditionally.

I love and approve of myself.

I love you no matter what.

Anger, Frustration, Disappointment

I remain calm even under intense stress.

I control my anger by expressing myself in a firm yet positive manner.

I am in control.

I am calm, focused, and relaxed.

I have the power to regulate my emotions.

I can diffuse my anger and channel it in a more productive way.

I can calm myself down and detach from anger.

I always stay calm in difficult or frustrating situations.

I always speak my mind rather than let frustrations build up.

I allow myself to acknowledge angry feelings without losing control.

Guilt

I take full responsibility for my shameful acts.

I release all guilt and pain.

I release all my unexpressed and unresolved guilt.

I release all the ways I am holding onto guilt.

I release all my conscious or unconscious thoughts and feelings of guilt.

I remove all the ways I dwell in guilt.

I am leaving the past behind.

I am letting go of my shame.

I release all the emotional shocks and traumas.

I am at peace with my guilt.

I am a better person because I have learned from my past.

I accept and acknowledge what I have done.

I accept my guilt, and this helps it melt away.

Bereavement

With every breath I take, I am sending, love, gratitude, and healing to every single cell in my body.

I will handle my bereavement and start a new life again.

I release trauma.

I release the belief that I will never recover from this.

I release grief.

I release all the ways I feel responsible.

I release all painful, unrelenting thoughts and emotions.

I release all my feelings of isolation.

I release all my feelings of injustice.

I learn from the loss to be happier.

I remove all the ways this should not have happened to me.

I attract people who love me into my life

I attract helpful and loving people into my life.

I am surrounded by the people who love me.

Worry

Whatever happens, I will handle it.

My mind is relaxed and thinking clearly.

My mind is peaceful and focused.

I let go of worries because I know that I can always come back to them later.

I am working calmly towards resolving my problems and concern.

I am relaxed even when life becomes difficult or stressful.

I am letting go of my worries.

I am free from worry.

I am calm even when I have a problem to solve.

I am at peace with myself.

I can resolve problems and worries logically.

Stopping Addiction

I successfully quit smoking. I am now healthier, happier and relaxed.

I successfully quit drinking. I am now healthier, happier and relaxed.

I successfully quit computer games. I am now better organised, happier and richer.

I prefer love over loneliness. I refuse to give over to watching porn.

I prefer life over death. I refuse to give over to taking drugs.

I prefer life over death. I refuse to give over to smoking.

I prefer life over death. I refuse to give over to drinking.

I prefer happiness and riches over poverty. I refuse to give over to playing computer games.

I choose wealth over playing computer games, freedom over addiction and happiness over depression.

I choose health over taking drugs, freedom over addiction and happiness over depression.

I choose health over smoking, freedom over addiction and happiness over depression.

I choose health over drinking, freedom over addiction and happiness over depression.

I cancel smoking out of my life.

I am smoke-free and craving free from nicotine.

I am robust and healthy. I repel computer games/Facebook etc. and playing/ using them does not attract me.

I am robust and healthy. I repel cigarettes and smoking does not attract me.

I am robust and healthy. I dump bottles of whiskey/vodka/beer, and drinking does not attract me.

I am porn free and enjoy a happy relationship with my partner.

I am drugs free and enjoy healthy life.

I am drinking-free and enjoy good social life.

I am computer games free and enjoy success at my job/business.

I am a quitter on porn. As a result, all my relationships are in their perfect condition.

I am a quitter on smoking, therefore, all my senses are in their perfect condition.

I am a quitter on playing computer games. As a result, my business/ job is in their excellent condition.

I am a quitter on drinking. As a result, all my senses are in their perfect condition.

Every new day takes me away from smoking and towards a new, healthier me.

Every new day brings me away from playing computer games and towards a new, wealthier me.

Every day the amount of nicotine in my body is becoming lesser and lesser, and my lungs are becoming cleaner and cleaner.

Every new day takes me away from drug taking and towards a new, healthier me.

Every new day brings me away from drinking and towards a new, healthier me.

Chapter 7
Use the Power of Your Emotions

"Reason is the gatekeeper, but it cannot resist the rushing torrents of emotion"
— *Bangambiki Habyarimana, The Great Pearl of Wisdom*

Tina had a big problem with negative emotions. She just could not manage them. Instead of letting them go, Tina suppressed these feelings and suddenly lost control. Anger was the top emotion which she could not manage.

Tina was also not sure what she was feeling. Sometimes she assumed that guilt was a disappointment. I have worked with her on that issue for some months, and now Tina has made enormous progress.

You can do the same, doing some exercises described in this chapter. By the way, I am just writing another book, which also will be about handling specific negative emotions. This chapter will help you to make you the start step. You will learn:

- The eleven most common negative emotions.
- The words describing emotions.
- The destructive ways of dealing with emotions.
- To release negative emotions.
- To use mindfulness to improve emotional health.

Common Negative Emotions

I am sure the list is much longer. However, you have probably faced at least once with one of the following negative emotions. Wikipedia and most dictionaries define these emotions as follows:

1. Anger is an intense emotional response. It is a normal emotion that involves a strong uncomfortable and emotional response to a perceived provocation. Often it indicates when one's personal boundaries are violated. Some have a learned tendency to react to anger through retaliation. Some self-development gurus treat anger as something wrong, the destroyer of your peace of mind. Yes, anger can make you blind.

However, anger is a completely normal, and often healthy, human emotion. The problem starts when it gets out of control and turns destructive. Then it can lead to problems in your personal relationships, at work, in the overall quality of your life.

2. Worry refers to the thoughts, images and emotions of a negative nature in which mental attempts are made to avoid anticipated potential threats. You can handle worry by postponing or questioning it. More about how to manage worry will be in my next book.

3. Guilt is "a cognitive or an emotional experience that occurs when a person believes or realises—accurately or not—that he or she has compromised his or her standards of conduct or has violated a moral standard and bears significant responsibility for that violation. It is closely related to the concept of remorse."

4. Pain The International Association for the Study of Pain's widely used definition states: "Pain is an unpleasant sensory and emotional experience associated with actual or potential tissue damage, or described regarding such harm." In medical diagnosis, pain is a symptom.

Emotional or mental pain is an unpleasant feeling of a psychological origin. It is the result of losing something: e.g. a job, after a breakup, when somebody close dies.

5. Discomfort is "a feeling of being uncomfortable physically or mentally, or something that causes this." In other words, it is everything which is not pleasant. In particular, it can be boredom, impatience or annoyance, anything that communicates you that something is wrong."

6. Frustration "is a common emotional response to opposition. Related to anger and disappointment, it arises from the perceived resistance to the fulfilment of individual will. The greater the obstruction, and the greater the will, the more the frustration is likely to be."

However, according to some self-development leaders, frustration is a positive sign as it mobilises you for taking action. However, when neglected, frustration turns into disappointment which is a very negative emotion.

7. Disappointment "is the feeling of dissatisfaction that follows the failure of expectations or hopes to manifest. Similar to regret, it differs in that a person feeling regret focuses primarily on the personal choices that contributed to a poor outcome, while an individual who is disappointed concentrates on the issue itself."

Disappointment must be handled quickly as possible. Otherwise, it will cause destruction in your mind. Disappointment means that you feel sad because you have expected more than you had achieved.

8. Being overwhelmed Something which is overwhelming is very intense and hard to deal with. It is manifested by sadness, helplessness or depression. You can be overwhelmed by your job, your boss, your spouse or children. But you can also be overwhelmed by your thoughts, putting pressure on yourself. It's challenging to overcome overwhelming things. However, it is possible, and you can easily apply efficient tools to achieve peace of mind again.

9. Shame "is a painful feeling of humiliation or distress caused by the consciousness of wrong or foolish behaviour. The person feeling shame manifests comparison of the self's action with the self's standards. However, shame may equally stem from a comparison of the person's state of being with the ideal social context's standard. Therefore, shame may arise from volitional action or simply self-regard. Although usually considered as an emotion, shame may also variously be seen as cognition, state, affect, or condition."

10. Fear and Anxiety Most of us make some distinction between fear and anxiety. Sometimes it's merely a matter of linguistics. We say we have a fear of something (flying, ageing) and anxiety about something (flying, ageing).

However, there is a big difference between these two terms. While fear is the natural response to survive, anxiety is the illusionary apprehension, which means that you are afraid of things that don't happen.

Sometimes you can distinguish these two emotions by your bodily experience. For example, the sudden re-arrangement of your guts when an intruder holds a knife to your back manifests fear, while dizziness, when you are about to make a difficult phone call, indicates anxiety.

11. Sadness and Depression Feeling sad can be a normal reaction to life's struggles, loss or an injured self-esteem. However, when feelings of intense sadness include feeling helpless, hopeless and worthless last for many days, even weeks, and keep you from functioning normally, then you are struggling with depression.

Some psychologists say that negative emotions can be healthy, i.e. justified and unhealthy, unjustified. Even if the negative emotions can exist for positive reasons, they always cause discomfort. How you will handle them is another question.

Apart from the ten most common negative emotions described in this chapter, you can find many other words describing negative emotions. Here are examples, the list was created by Steve Hein.

Dignity/Respect/Self-Worth

ashamed	beaten down	cut down
criticised	dehumanised	d i s r e s p e c t e d
embarrassed	humiliated	inferior
insulted	invalidated	labelled
lectured to	mocked	offended
put down	resentful	ridiculed
stereotyped	teased	underestimated
worthless		

Freedom/Control

bossed around	controlled	imposed upon

imprisoned

inhibited

invaded

forced

manipulated

obligated

over-controlled

over-ruled

powerless

pressured

restricted

suffocated

trapped

Love/Connection/Importance

abandoned

alone

brushed off

confused

disapproved of

discouraged

ignored

insignificant

invisible

left out

lonely

m i s u n d e r s t o o d

neglected

rejected

uncared about

unheard

unknown

unimportant

uninformed

unloved

unsupported

unwanted

Justice/truth

accused

blamed

cheated

disbelieved

falsely accused

guilt-tripped

interrogated

judged

lied about

lied to

misled

punished

robbed

Safety

abused

afraid

attacked

defensive

frightened

insecure

intimidated

over-protected

scared

terrified

threatened

under-protected

unsafe

violated

Trust

cynical	guarded	sceptical
suspicious	untrusted	

As you can see, you can name the same negative emotions in some different ways. For example, anger can be exasperation, fury or intense annoyance.

Exercise:

Now an exercise for you. Become more aware of your negative emotions. Name ten negative emotions below. The table above can help you.

List ten negative emotions

....

....

....

....

....

Destructive Ways of Handling Negative Emotions

You can handle negative emotions in two ways: constructively and destructively. I will tell you about effective methods later, but first meet the fourteen inefficient ways.

1. You ignore your feelings. So, you just pretend that your negative emotions do not exist. However, by doing so you deceive yourself, and you are not authentic. Remember that other people will notice it at once, and your relationships will be affected.

2. You bury angry emotions under the mask of peace and love. It is a very tricky way of avoiding negative emotions. Hiding emotions will not work for long as these emotions will break out earlier or later, which means that instead of love you will cause a fierce argument.

3. You always intellectualise and analyse. Do you know the kind of people who are ruminating about one and the same subject? Guilt is the most common here. If you feel it because of having done something wrong to someone, just apologise and ask how you can redeem this wrong.

4. You always keep busy and work excessively so you can't feel. This common way of handling negative emotions is destructive because your emotions can burst out suddenly, and you also risk health problems, like a heart attack.

5. You pretend something has not happened. You just pretend that nothing has happened when your partner asks you what is wrong. However, if you lie, it will lead to creating another lie, and eventually, you will have to lie all the time.

6. You drink alcohol excessively. It is a very common way to forget about pain, remorse, guilt and any other emotion that causes discomfort. However, it is a quick fix, and the hangover (not only the physical one) is more painful that the feelings before drinking. Also, you are at risk of alcoholism.

7. You overeat. Food, the same as alcohol or coffee, can also comfort your negative emotions and soothe you for a while. It is also a kind of quick fix. You don't enjoy the food as you are full, but are still eating. You risk obesity and many diseases related to it.

8. You use recreational drugs excessively. Who would not like to feel good and stress-free? And you are just struggling with some negative emotions. So, another Coke or other drink will help you for a while to keep a positive spirit. However, what will you do when they stop working?

9. You eat foods loaded with sugar and fat. Carbohydrates are very addictive. Scientists have proved that cutting on sugar can cause discomfort because of withdrawal symptoms. And who wouldn't like to reach for another bar of chocolate or a packet of crisps? The only problem with eating sugary and fatty foods is obesity which will cause another flood of negative emotions. And you will end up in a vicious circle.

10. You have excessive sex with or without a partner. This method is so popular because sex gives you lots of pleasure and orgasms indeed help to relax you. However, everything in excess harms and the same rule applies to sex. In more serious cases, excessive sex means cheating, which means that you also hurt other people and provide yourself with another portion of negative emotions.

11. You behave compulsively. Checking if the door is locked many times, washing your hands fifty times per day, biting nails, picking your nose are only a few examples of compulsive behaviour which itself causes stress. Creating new habits will help you to stop behaving in this way. Go to Chapter Eight to start your transformation.

12. You exercise compulsively. Practising a sport is always beneficial. But if you go running to forget about the last argument, then chances are that you risk an injury, because your muscles will be stiff when you try to hide the emotions and because you will overtire your muscles.

13. You use prescription drugs such as tranquillizers or Prozac. It is a more severe case of dealing with negative emotions. You are probably very overwhelmed with sadness, helplessness and put too much pressure on yourself. Remember, that drugs are also a quick fix and will not solve the underlying problem.

14. You keep conversations superficial. To avoid the pain of negative emotions, you only choose some neutral topics. Instead of discussing the problem and find a solution, you change the topic and therefore, avoid pain.

How to Release Negative Emotions

1. Name the emotion. Recognising that a negative emotion has arisen is the first step. Doing so, you can give a label to this feeling in your mind. So, it can be fear, anxiety, guilt, shame, anger. Some scientists proved that just naming the negative emotion or any other challenge decreases its intensity by 50 percent. The remaining fifty can be managed by using the self-development tools. Some of them are presented in this chapter.

However, it is important to label the emotions in the right way. Never say "I'm angry" or "I feel anger." Instead use the phrases "anger has arisen" or "anger is here." Do you see how just changing the words already creates a different perspective and more space? This is just one of the examples of how changing the language can change your life. Now choose one negative emotion that you frequently feel and name it: …..

2. Pray for the people who have done you wrong. It is especially useful in case of resentment. Wish them blessing and luck in all things. In this way, you will attract them to your life, according to the Universal Law of Boomerang. If you are a religious person, go to church and offer a mass for them.

You can also write about the people who hurt you: all their negative qualities you see. Then write about the positive qualities you notice in them. By writing about their positive qualities, you will regain peace of mind.

Also, write about the situation: what these people have done to you, how it affected you and how it made you feel. Write about your reaction to this situation, what you said and what you did. However, be careful not to sink into rumination, just acknowledge the facts.

3. Release. Let the emotion go. There are some ways which will help you to release your feelings: using your hands, physical activity, screaming, talking to a friend.

Screaming. Go into an empty room or for a drive alone. Scream as loudly as you can. Scream the words which name the emotion: "I hate", "I'm screwed" etc. Unfortunately, many people have never screamed out their hurt or rage. Continue screaming until you feel the peace inside of your mind again. Also, allow yourself to cry your feelings if you need to.

If you cannot scream aloud, *imagine that you are screaming* your hurt, rage, and pain. Imagine it, using all the senses. See your mouth open and feel how the vibrations of your voice are destroying the anger, hurt or pain. Feel the razor of your sounds chopping the emotion into small pieces.

Physical activity is another way of releasing negative emotions. Take a pillow and keep hitting your bed or a chair, feeling your hurt or fury every time you hit the object with that pillow. While doing so, say the words "I hate" or "I am frustrated" or whatever it is that you are feeling. You can combine using the objects like a pillow with screaming.

Take your fists and keep pounding a table saying, "I hate." Continue doing it until you feel better.

Getting yourself a punching bag and hanging it in your attic or cellar is another way of using the physical method. When you feel pain, anger or fury, take the time to keep hitting that punching bag to release your negative emotion. You can also join a kick-boxing classes. It is a perfect discipline for people with a short temper.

Use your hands and write about how afraid you are, write about your hate, write about your anger, write about how hurt you are. Describe what you have lost, what happened and how it is affecting you today. Write about what you have never had that has hurt you so deeply. You may also cry or scream when discovering your emotions.

Remember that one negative emotion can mask another. Anger and hurt often manifest an underlying fear. It happens because we don't want to show fear, being vulnerable then. It is easier to show the most potent emotion like anger, or even use this emotion to manipulate other people.

Focus on the emotion rather than what caused it. While releasing your negative emotions, forget who did what that caused the emotion, about the individual who did something to you. Instead, concentrate on the "I hate," "I am so hurt," "I am angry." It's the emotion you need to release.

Talk to your friend. To release emotions, tell someone about the situation that caused the feeling buried within you. Explain in detail what happened, your feelings around this experience, and how this experience is affecting your life today. However, never play the victim, ruminating on the problem.

You may often hide your feelings and life's happenings because you are ashamed. You can also make yourself guilty and somehow feel things happen to you because you are 'a bad person'. Telling your story to a friend will help you to gain a healthier perspective on the situation.

Bear in mind that if you keep repeating the story to different people, talking about it many times, thinking about it repeatedly, then you will create a recurring negative thought and even a belief. Then this new belief or negative thoughts pattern becomes another problem rather than part of the solution.

4. Shift your perspective. Life brings bad luck, injustice, abuse and emotions of anger, self-pity, hurt and depression. It's quite easy to look at what others have done to you and to consider it as wrong. However, it is not hard to look at your response to the real wrong or injustice that was done to you.

Someone might have demeaned you. What did you do – punish them in some manner for their behaviour or take responsibility for your reactions? Did you respond to the situation in a healthy and loving way or were you critical and retaliated?

Emotions around injustice of any kind are complex. Once you accept personal responsibility for your reactions, the emotions around a given situation will lose their hold over you. Admit that an injustice has occurred, but be ready to release that from your life. This involves looking at your behaviour, and accepting responsibility for your actions.

5. Detach yourself. This technique is good when your emotions are running high, and you are having difficulty reducing the intensity. Then detach yourself from the situation and the emotion.

Imagine that somebody else is feeling the emotion, has been hurt, demeaned, etc. See if your behaviour would be the same if someone else put on your shoes. If the answer is yes, then begin to see that experience as not necessarily concerning you. The other person is probably acting unconsciously, while you happen to be the individual in their way.

Detaching yourself in this manner can help you move through tough situations without taking the abuse personally. You will make the case void as your detachment allows you to look at things more rationally and quietly.

6. Accept responsibility for your emotions. You have learned this happiness skill in reading Chapter Three and doing all the exercises described there. As you are responsible for expressing your emotions and handling them, do your best to take care of your mental health by instantly releasing your negative emotions or detachment from them. Emotions are not right or wrong, they just are. So be careful and stop punishing yourself or being too hard on yourself. Balance is the key word.

Use Mindfulness to Release Negative Emotions

Here are some definitions of this term, so popular today: "Mindfulness means paying attention in a particular way; On purpose, in the present moment, and non-judgemental." According to Jon Kabat-

Zinn, "It doesn't mean blanking out your mind. People think it's about going into a trance, but it's not. It is also an emotionally non-reactive state. It's a way of training the mind to reduce stress and develop greater clarity. It also helps us deal with our emotions better. It's about focusing on the present moment, feeling less controlled by our thoughts and having more mental freedom."

Mindfulness is becoming a vital and influential part of many psychological treatments: anxiety, post-traumatic stress disorder, depression, bipolar disorder and relapse prevention for addiction.

Mindfulness also raises your subjective well-being. It is commonly known as happiness! Even a few weeks of mindfulness practice can create positive changes in the brain. Long-term mediators display levels of prosperity far higher than average.

Consider for a while how you relate to your emotions. Stop thinking of them as an experience to be embraced or do you shy away from them. You may try to fight or push away your negative emotions, yet as you already know, it does not work.

So how can mindfulness help you? It encourages you to be simply aware of your feelings with mindful attitudes, such as compassion, curiosity, acceptance and openness.

Go with the flow. In a mindfulness meditation, once you establish concentration, you observe the movement of emotions, bodily sensations and inner thoughts without judging them as good or bad.

Pay attention. You also notice external sensations such as sounds, sights and touch that make up your moment-to-moment experience.

Imagine that you are feeling anxious at the moment. By thinking about something you are a bit concerned about, you can even try evoking some anxiety right now. Now let's see how awareness, self-compassion, curiosity openness and acceptance can help you:

Awareness helps you feel the emotion in your body. Without being aware of them, your emotional response is automatic and can't change. You are already aware of your goals, values, life mission and life path. Now let's focus on the present. Notice where in your body you feel the feeling itself.

Curiosity helps you to shift your attitude from unhealthy avoidance to a healthier approach state. Become interested in what the emotion is like: become aware of its size, possibly associated colour, scent, shape, and texture. Notice whether the human emotion is getting bigger or smaller with each breath you take.

Acceptance helps you process the emotion. Make an attempt to say to yourself, "The feeling is already here . . . It's okay . . . Let it be." In this way, you acknowledge the emotion. Check Chapter Two of this book for more tips on how to practice acceptance.

Self-compassion helps you to be understanding of the fact that you are feeling anxious, angry or sad. Treat yourself as your best friend. If they were feeling anxious, angry or sad, what soothing words would you say? Now say those words to yourself. Then gently place your hand on the area of the emotion in your body in a caring, loving way. You have already learned how to be compassionate while reading Chapter Two.

Openness will help you to shift your perspective. Step back from your emotion and make space for it just to be there. Become a curious but dispassionate observer and say, "I'm watching this anxiety, anger, sadness . . . I'm the observer . . . The witness."

Chapter 8
Transform Your Habits

Your net worth to the world is usually determined by what remains after your bad habits are subtracted from your good ones.
Benjamin Franklin

Tina was a chain smoker. It was her way to cope with stress. She also picked her nose and went to bed late, being short of sleep the next day. I have helped her to get rid of smoking and change her undesirable habits. This chapter will teach you:

- The difference between a habit and addiction.
- To recognise that you are addicted.
- The principles of successful treatment of addictions.
- How to treat an addiction.
- The groups helping to cope with cravings (Uk, Ireland, USA).
- What are habits.
- How to create a new habit.
- The phases of creating a new habit.
- To accelerate creating a new habit.
- Which patterns are desirable to develop.

The Difference Between a Habit and An Addiction

According to Wikipedia: "**habit** is a routine of behaviour that is repeated regularly and tends to occur subconsciously."

The American Journal of Psychology (1903) defines it this way: "**A habit**, from the standpoint of psychology, is a more or less fixed way of thinking, willing, or feeling acquired through previous repetition of a mental experience."

Scientists proved that old habits are easy to form, yet hard to break, and new habits are hard to form and easy to break because the behavioural patterns we repeat are imprinted in our neural pathways.

Habits are not necessarily an addiction, yet they can also have a severe impact on your life, like negative thinking. However, habits associated with addiction are typically characterised by short-term reward, coupled with delayed lethal effects.

"**Addiction** is a brain disease that is characterised by compulsive engagement in rewarding stimuli, despite adverse consequences. The two properties that characterise all addictive stimuli are that they are reinforcing (i.e. they increase the likelihood that a person will seek repeated exposure to them) and intrinsically rewarding (i.e. perceived as being positive or desirable)" Wikipedia

Addiction has a negative impact on individuals and society because of their direct adverse effects, which also include associated healthcare costs, long-term complications (e.g. liver cirrhosis with drinking alcohol) and loss of productivity. Here are some examples of drug and behavioural addictions:

- alcoholism
- food addiction
- nicotine addiction
- cocaine addiction
- amphetamine addiction

- opiate addiction
- benzodiazepine addiction
- sexual addiction
- gambling addiction

How to Recognise That I Am Addicted

Here is a short test which will help you to define if you have an addiction. Read the statements listed below and mark if they are true (you agree), somewhat true, or false (you disagree).

Statement	True	Some-What True	False
I cannot function without alcohol, drugs, benzodiazepines, etc.			
I cannot stop taking the substance.			
I have withdrawal symptoms (e.g. insomnia, dizziness, seizures and delirium tremens).			
I give up some activities because of addiction.			
I buy the addictive substances in bulk to have enough supply of them even if I am short of money.			
I take the elements alone.			
I deny that I am addicted.			

Statement	True	Some-What True	False
I drop hobbies and activities for taking the addictive substances, compulsory behaviour.			
I lost control over the frequency and amount of taking a drug, drinking, doing something, spending money.			
I have problems with the law (theft, aggression, etc.)			
I have problems with my relationships.			
I take too many risks after using some substances.			
I have to do some things many times, even if it is not necessary. (checking if the doors are locked, wash my hands, etc.)			

Calculate your score: true – 3 points, somewhat true – 1 point, false – 0 points.

Your score:

0-7 points You are at low risk of being addicted. However, pay attention to the statements with which you agreed, even partially and talk to someone to prevent the development of addiction.

8-15 points You are at high risk of addiction. If you answered most of the questions 'somewhat true' and at least one as 'true', the chances are that you are unaware of your addiction. It is still not too late to start treatment and prevent more serious adverse effects of your life.

16-26 points You are seriously addicted and have totally lost control over your life. You need the immediate help of professionals, like medical staff or a psychologist. The earlier you take action, the better for you.

Principles of Effective Treatment

Scientists have proved that by doing research since the mid-1970s that the following fundamental principles should become the basis of any effective treatment program.

It is commonly known that addiction is a complex but treatable disease that affects brain function and behaviour. Hence long-term treatment is necessary to change the neuro associations which are responsible for addictive behaviour

No single treatment is right for everyone. As in the case of taking regular medication, also in the case of addiction, the brain's reaction will be different for each person. Therefore, while treating the withdrawal symptoms, the patient's reactions may vary. Also, an individual will react differently in the case of an advanced phase of addiction to when the disease is at the early stage.

People need to have quick access to treatment. It is especially important when the addiction is severe, and there is the risk of death or serious social problems. However, in the case of the early stage of addiction, it is also better to treat it as soon as possible, to avoid bigger damage to the body.

Effective treatment should address all the patient's needs, not just his or her drug use. Addiction is a complex illness and usually starts because of other reasons, like environmental (parents also taking drugs), loneliness or a current situation (problems at work, in the relationship, trauma). In these cases, the individual also needs help to cope with the background issues of the addiction.

Staying in treatment long enough is critical. Addicts develop habits and to treat them, the change of neuro associations in the brain are needed. It is a long-term process. Also, eliminating the addictive substance from the body takes time, as well as learning the brain to stop cravings. Shortening the treatment period brings the risk of relapse of the addiction.

Counselling and other behavioural therapies are the most commonly used forms of treatment. This is because taking drugs or drinking is a complex process, with the underlying background. Therefore, the addicted person also must learn how to cope with stress, discomfort and how to solve his or her problems.

Medications are often an important part of treatment. It is especially important when they are combined with behavioural therapies. Medication administration is especially important at the beginning of treatment, to ease withdrawal symptoms and decrease discomfort (stabilising the mood – depression and anxiety). However, to change addictive habits, the individual also must undergo psychotherapy to change his or her behavioural patterns. When the individual improves, the doctor may consider withdrawing medication.

Treatment plans must be reviewed often and modified to fit the patient's changing needs. Overcoming an addiction is a dynamic process, which needs flexibility. There will be ups and downs, the dose of medication administrated can vary, depending on the mood and the risk of relapse. During psychotherapy, the patient may discover new areas of problems to work on, which will be of higher priority than the ones he or she has started working at the beginning of the treatment.

Treatment should address other possible mental disorders. Taking drugs or drinking can be the result of other mental illnesses, like depression or anxiety, or when the patient searches for quick fix means, to alleviate his or her discomfort. In this case, the treating of other mental illnesses is a must to conduct a successful recovery from addiction.

Medically assisted detoxification is only the first stage of treatment. As you will read later, there are some steps to changing addictive behaviour and reactions. To achieve successful recovery, the patient must go through all the stages of treatment.

Treatment doesn't need to be voluntary to be effective. In the case of extremely high danger of death or self-harm, involuntary treatment can be conducted, and it is effective in the same way as the voluntary one.

How to Treat an Addiction

Now when you know if you are at risk of addiction or even addicted, time has come to either prevent becoming addicted or to treat the current addiction, which is not simple, but possible. Addiction is a chronic disease, so people cannot only stop using drugs for a few days and be cured. In most cases, long-term or repeated care is required to stop using completely and recover their lives.

1. Detoxification

This is the process by which the body rids itself of a drug. Medications can be used to prevent relapse, manage withdrawal symptoms, and treat co-occurring conditions.

Patients can take medications to help re-establish normal brain function and decrease cravings. In this way, the drug prevents relapse of the addiction.

Medications are available for treatment of alcohol addiction and opioid (heroin, prescription pain relievers). Scientists are developing other medications to treat cannabis (marijuana) and stimulant (cocaine, methamphetamine) addiction. People who use more than one drug need treatment for all the substances they use.

Medications help suppress withdrawal symptoms during detoxification. However, remember that detoxification is only the first step in the recovery process. People usually resume their drug use in case of not receiving any further treatment after detoxification. It may happen in almost 80 percent of detoxifications.

2. Residential Treatment

Individuals may attend long-term treatment where they are involved in intensive and structured treatment. The treatment lasts about six months to a year. In the case of short-term programs, participants stay at the treatment centre for three to six weeks followed by psychotherapy and participation in a self-help group.

3. Outpatient treatment

This includes a variety of programs for patients who visit a psychologist regularly. Most of the programs include individual or group drug counselling, sometimes both. Treatment is sometimes intensive at first. Patients attend multiple outpatient sessions each week. After completing intensive treatment, patients meet the psychologist less often and for fewer hours per week to help sustain their recovery.

Sometimes inpatient or residential treatment may be necessary, especially for those with more severe problems. Therapeutic communities are highly structured programs in which patients remain at a residence, which typically lasts for 6 to 12 months. The entire community act as key agents of change, influencing the patient's attitudes, understanding, and behaviours associated with drug use.

4. Self-help groups

They may help the people recovering from addiction meet other people having the same problem, which often boosts motivation. Self-help groups are useful source of education and information. Some of the self-help groups are listed below.

Alcoholics Anonymous, Narcotics Anonymous, and Cocaine Anonymous implement the 12-Step Programs, which can help individuals with addiction. The goal of the 12-Step Program is for people to achieve and maintain abstinence. People accept that they have a disease, surrender it to a higher power and actively participate in all twelve steps.

Family Therapy. Sometimes it is appropriate that also the patient's family take part in therapy. There are several types of treatments that are useful for younger sufferers. Family therapies focus on interactions between the members of a given family and on the cases which might worsen abuse or behavioural problems.

5. Doing exercises

Scientists have proved that exercise, in addition to traditional treatment, helps with smoking cessation, because it boosts mood and decreases stress. Many experts believe it may help with other addictions, too.

6. Evaluation and treatment for co-occurring mental health issues

They include depression and anxiety. The assessment is done by a psychiatrist and the person recovering from addiction.

7. Long-term follow-up to prevent relapse

People recovering from addictions undergo regular check-ups by the psychiatrist and attend counselling sessions.

Groups Helping with Addiction, Anxiety and Depression

GROW

http://grow.ie/ Members attend a weekly meeting which lasts for about two hours. During this time, a specific Group Method is followed which enables the members to learn a practical psychology of mental health, and is called the GROW Program. Members provide mutual support in undertaking certain tasks that encourage a healthy change in thinking, behaviour and relationships.

GROW Group meetings are chaired by ordinary members. However, each Group has an Organiser and a Recorder, or less often, a Sponsor. This might be a nurse using GROW to support a group of day-care clients. Her primary role is to ensure that the meeting is run appropriately. Each GROW Group is supported by an area co-ordinator, who monitors the group's authenticity in using the GROW Program.

GROW provides access to leadership development for its members to ensure that its groups are both friendly and safe for them. All leadership is drawn from GROW's twelve Step Program of mental health. This program has been tried and tested over almost fifty years.

Aware

http://www.aware.ie/ (Republic of Ireland) *https://www.aware-ni.org/* (Northern Ireland)

The purpose of the group is to provide education, information, and support for people who experience depression or related mood disorders, as well as their concerned family members and friends. As well as the educational programs; Life Skills, Wellness@Work, and Beat the Blues, Aware offers three core support services: Support Mail, Support Line and Support Groups.

Samaritans UK and ROI

Phone number 116 123 *http://www.samaritans.org/ jo@samaritans.org*

The service helps through tough times, to explore the caller's options, understand his or her problems better or just be there to listen.

ADAA – Anxiety and Depression Association of America

http://www.adaa.org/ Your anxiety or anxiety-related disorder can make you isolated. Forty million adults in the United States have an anxiety disorder, and support is an important part of recovery. The association offers many various ways of recovery – coaching, counselling, books, and groups.

What Are Habits?

A habit is a reaction of the body, emotion or thought, which is 100% automatic if you don't decide to react differently at a given moment. In short, a habit is an automatic response to a given trigger. So, the cell of pattern has the following formula:

trigger + response

Some self-help gurus add a reward to this formula. However, the reward is not necessary when the habit is fully automated. You don't reward yourself for making a bed or brushing your teeth. The examples of triggers.

- A thought (positive or negative), e.g. I'm an idiot, I can't.
- Emotions – envy, jealousy, conceit, depression, fear
- Willingness or unwillingness to do something
- Sensations in the body (tiredness, tension)
- The need of assertiveness
- Situations
- A working alarm clock
- The proceeding activity
- A combination of may triggers mentioned above (thought, feeling, situation, the proceeding activity)
- The response may include:
- Thought (positive or negative)
- Action - things which you do
- The reaction of your body (e.g. Feeling tense)
- Emotion (sadness, joy, anger, etc.)

What can your reaction to the trigger be?

Let's look at some examples. The response for the trigger is underlined.

- Before going to bed, <u>I brush my teeth.</u>
- When I go to a busy restaurant, <u>I feel tense.</u>
- When I leave my house/flat, <u>I think of my goals</u>.

How to Create a New Habit

Habits cannot be changed, but they can be overwritten. Once created, they work as neuro associations. You can only make them weaker or stronger. Therefore, your task is not to fight with the old habit, like building a dam on the river, which will eventually break down, but to dig a new river bed and direct the water there. Then the more often you will use the new habit, the stronger it will become, and the old one will weaken, like an unused muscle. So how can you change, I mean reduce, the old habit? There are two ways of creating new habits:

1. Changing the environment or sudden changes in your life.
Habits work in each context – time, place, people. Imagine that you have changed your university and now study in a different location. Then you will need to learn how to study in the new dormitory, where is the library in the new university building, create a new group of friends.

Unfortunately, while changing the environment, both good and bad habits collapse. Suppose that you were going running with some friends at the old place. Now you have new running tracks and need to find new people to accompany you.

The sudden changes in your life may include: changing your material status, moving out, having a baby, starting a new job or studies, the death of your loved one. Again, as in the case of changing the environment, you need to create new habits. For example, when you become widowed you need to learn how to function on your own, how to cope with the negative emotions, how to find new friends.

You can artificially create changes in your life. Go to training and meet new people there, renovate your house or flat, move out, rearrange your place of work.

Now it's your turn. Think of one bad habit which you want to overwrite with the new one. Write it down. What is the trigger? How do you react?

…..

Now list three changes you could make in your environment to weaken the old habit.

1. …..
2. …..
3. …..

And finally define the new habit (you will change the response for your trigger)

…..

This method of changing habits (creating the new, better ones and weakening the old, bad ones) is quick, but you cannot use it for all habits and as you don't move out or have a baby every week. Then the second method is useful:

2. Training a new habit. As I wrote above, you need to weaken the old, bad habit and create a strong alternative habit. In short, you change the response, leaving the same trigger. Before you start forming a new habit, you need to learn about the old one as much as possible.

A. Learning about the old habit.

<u>Meet the old habit in detail.</u> Let's say that you have social anxiety. Write down all the triggers increasing your fear, like hearing people talking, laughing, passing by people. There probably will be places where you feel uncomfortable (e.g. restaurants full of people at lunch time or Sunday evening) or situations (like asking someone for help, public speaking). Now it's your turn. Describe the trigger to the habit you want to overwrite:

…..

…..

<u>Monitor the old habit</u> for a period of time, let's say a week, you are supposed to observe the old habit when it happens and what your response is. For example: when and where you become anxious during this week, how often you use the old habit, how high your reactions are. Now take your old habit and monitor when you use it for the next ten days. You can use your transformation diary for that.

My old habit …..

…..

Day 1	Day 2	Day 3	Day 4	Day 5	Day 6	Day 7	Day 8	Day 9	Day 10

Learn the earliest warning signs of the old habit. In other words – the aura. For example, when you have epilepsy, seizures are proceeded by such symptoms like feeling dizzy, blurred vision, etc. In the case of bad habits, it is often will be a feeling of discomfort or tension. While monitoring the old habit, mark which symptoms appear in your case.

My warning signs: …………………………………………………………………
………………………………………………………………………………………

Learn to recognise the trigger of your old habit. When you know the triggers, you will be more aware when to pay more attention to applying the new behaviour. In the meantime, note down all the triggers for the habit which you want to overwrite (i.e. change).

My triggers:

………………………………………………………………………………………
………………………………………………………………………………………
………………………………………………………………………………………

B. Creation and training of the new habit.

Now time has come to create a new habit, to overwrite the old reaction. You use the same trigger, but the reaction is new, more positive. What can your new response be?

Choose the competitive reaction. As I wrote above, you can only overwrite the old habit. You train your brain to react to the same trigger in a new, more desirable way. What can you do instead of your old, undesirable reaction? Here are some examples:

- Counting to 60
- Focusing on breath
- Imagining the consequences of the old bad habit
- Count your steps
- Put your hand on your buttocks
- Remind your goal connected with this habit
- Motivational quote
- Affirmations

- All desirable activities which you want to train (cleaning, tidying your house, getting up at x, going to bed at y etc.)

Choose the new response for your old trigger now and write down the new habit:

………………………………………………………………………………………

For example, in the case of social anxiety, you can write: When I go into a busy restaurant, I focus on my breath for 60 seconds, counting to sixty. Any time the fear comes back, I repeat the procedure.

Apply the new response and stop using the old one. Do it any time you face the trigger. And this is learning your new habit. Remember that the new trigger must last for 1 minute to be effective. Therefore, you can count to sixty or do sixty breaths to program the new habit. I have included the habit monitoring sheet at the end of that book. Print it and monitor the new behaviour which you want to train.

Find the people who will support your efforts. Social approval will dramatically increase your chances of creating the new behaviour. Think of one friend who can motivate you to work on your habits.

The Phases of Forming a New Habit

Some scientists base on the conception of conscious and unconscious doing a given thing. I will modify this a bit:

1. The phase of the initial reaction. You make the effort to create a new habit, so you write it down, both the trigger and your new response. And that's it. However, to succeed, you must believe that you will succeed in forming this new habit and be motivated enough to do it.

2.The phase of the continued reaction. You act the new habit correctly for the first time. It happens with the same trigger, but the behaviour is new. This phase is the most difficult and probably the longest as you need to train the new behaviour. To succeed, you still need to believe that you can perform the new behaviour and stick to the benefits of having the new habit. Therefore, now choose one habit that you want to train and list all the advantages of learning and all the costs of not training the new behaviour.

My new habit:

…..

Costs of not learning the   Benefits of learning the
new habit   new habit

You can also use the alternative scenario technique: "If, in case of facing the trigger, I acted in accordance with the new habit, today I would do/have...."

3. The phase of crystallising. You move to that step when you behave in the new way properly and for an extended period. You feel no internal fight performing the new habit. There is no fixed number of days after which you move to the phase of crystallising, and it depends on the behaviour which you are going to train. You need to experiment, like a scientist doing research. You also must make the decision that you want to keep the new habit and believe in the benefits listed above.

4. The phase of habit. At this stage, your new behaviour is automated, and you don't think if it's working for you. When you train the new behaviour, you still need to monitor how well you perform it.

How to Accelerate Creating a New Habit

You can speed up the formation of the new habit in some ways. Here they are:

1. Reward yourself. Dopamine is a neurotransmitter responsible for motivation. However, reward works only in the first two phases of automating a new habit. Your reward must be easy in use and without adverse side effects (like weight gain in case of eating sweets). Here are the examples of useful rewards:

- smiling to yourself
- gratitude
- satisfaction
- the pose of pride of doing something well
- applause
- compliment
- the dance of victory

To be efficient, you need to reward yourself within 10 seconds of the successful new behaviour. The reward should be random – randomly every second time. Let me explain it on the example of the sequence of 0s and 1s; where 1 means reward: 00101000100111010001.

2. Imagination training. In detail imagine yourself performing the new behaviour successfully when the old trigger occurs. Does it use all the senses – sight, hearing, and touch? What will you see? What can you hear? How are you feeling? Then imagine that your reward and the moment you obtain it. Do the visualisation for 5 to 10 seconds.

3. Repetition. You learn any activity, including habits, by repetition. Think of a new language, writing, calculating or reading. At the beginning of forming your new habit you also need to repeat your formula (if a trigger x occurs, I will behave in the y way) For example: "If I go to a restaurant full of people and start feeling anxious, I will count to sixty and focus on my breath." You can read your new habit formula aloud when marking your progress or write it on the adhesive notes, which you will hang in the visible place of your office, bathroom or kitchen.

Sometimes there might be obstacles for performing your new habit. You cannot count to sixty while speaking at the conference. Your new behaviour usually consists of some elements. You can choose the one which is the easiest or which you can stop doing easily.

Suppose that you are working on the habit of brushing your teeth. Before you start cleaning, you take the brush to your hand and put some toothpaste on it. In an emergency, you can just take the toothbrush and potentially put it away.

Define precisely your trigger and make it aware of some integrated elements. Like with the example of a busy restaurant, you can also add at what time of the day it happens and which restaurant it is. The previous activity can also be the trigger. In this case, you create a sequence of habits. Let me give you one example: "In the morning, when I wake up and look at the picture of the sea, I practice gratitude for one minute." The trigger is underlined here and consists of three elements.

Which Habits Are Desirable to Develop?

1. Regular monitoring of progress. Read the chapter about setting goals. Monitoring your progress is crucial to achieving success and be happy in general. Use HabitBull or Best You to this purpose.

2. The habits are saving the willpower. Generally speaking, all of the habits which automate your work are good for keeping your willpower. You can also do small activities to accelerate your willpower:

- Drinking one glass of water
- Tensing your muscles for a while
- Prayer (e.g. before starting your work – in the morning, after lunch and after each break)
- You can also renew your willpower by creating the following habits:
- Breaks – after each 50 minutes of work do 10-minutes break.
- Power nap (a short 15-minutes nap between blocks of work).
- Caffeine nap (the same as standard nap, but you add drinking a glass of coffee 30 minutes before the nap).
- Small talk about light topics, not requiring thinking, like the weather.
- Self-affirmation (think about your values, main goals, progress made lately).

If you want to accelerate the renewal of your willpower, train the following habits:
- Meditation
- Sitting straight
- Doing exercises

3. The habits improving the quality of your relationships. To be a happy person, you need to improve the quality of your relationships. Individuals who listen to you, like and help you are your greatest assets. Here are some habits which you can develop to improve your relationships:

- Making a conscious effort to smile.
- Listing three things you genuinely like about yourself. Read those three things out loud.
- Paying attention to how your lover is responding.
- Getting in touch with your playful side.
- Laugh, relax, have fun.
- Talking about common ground issues with your partner or friends.
- Repeating a mantra in your head.
- Asking open-ended questions about this new person's preferences.
- Asking for compliments from a trusted friend or relative.
- Finding a way to laugh together. Engage in an activity that makes you both laugh tell a joke, make a self-deprecating statement.
- Stand up straight. Let your hands hang naturally at your sides.
- Refuse to fidget.
- Make a list of things you like about yourself.
- Pay attention to the other person instead of your insecurity.

4. The habits increasing productivity. Time management is a must in today's reality. Being disorganised and unproductive decreases your level of happiness because then you can face negative reactions from other people. Here are some helpful habits which will increase your productivity:

- Completing the most challenging and ugly tasks as first. Morning is the best time as your willpower is at the highest level. Learn when your most productive times are and do the most work at them.
- Eliminating all distractions. This includes the phone, email notifications and having multiple web browsers open on the desktop.
- Finding a mentor.

- Stopping multitasking.
- Batching similar tasks.
- Setting up a system for your work and act on it.
- Telling other people about your goals.
- Prioritising your tasks.
- Auto paying your bills.
- Planning and reviewing your goals monthly, quarterly and yearly.

5. The habits helping you to stay healthy. Health is your biggest asset and without it, you cannot be happy. Just think of a toothache or joints pain, not to mention more serious ailments. Here are some useful habits which you can develop:

- Eating something live (fresh fruit or vegetables) every day.
- Going to sleep at the same time each night.
- Replacing something white (i.e. starch, processed foods) with something green, orange, red or brown (i.e. vegetables, protein, lentils) at every meal.
- Deliberately visualising something pleasant and calming as you relax in bed.
- Working out for a total of an hour a day, five days a week.
- Meditating, journaling or praying for ten minutes as part of your nightly bedtime routine.
- Drink a glass of (unsweetened) green tea three times a day.
- Keeping daily activities out of the bedroom.
- Flossing every night before bed.
- Tensing up all your muscles, and then relaxing them, repeatedly, until you feel completely relaxed.
- Moving your body for ten minutes or longer first thing in the morning.
- Drinking a glass of water before each meal.

- Waking up at the same time every morning (including weekends and holidays).
- Not drinking alcohol; instead, drink a cup of herbal tea in that hour before bed.
- Not drinking caffeine after 2 pm.
- Eating six small, healthful meals a day to keep satisfied and on track.
- Walk for a half hour every day.
- Eating that first meal within 30 minutes of waking up.
- Taking three to five milligrams of melatonin a half hour before bed.
- Hugging someone every day.

6. The habits reducing stress. They will help you to maintain happiness for longer, as you eliminate discomfort caused by stress. Here are some examples of habits to train:

- Breathing deeply for at least two minutes. Focus on your breaths.
- Detaching from the source of stress (e.g. take a break from a project, excusing yourself from a meeting, removing yourself from an argument) for a five-minute break.
- Stretching different body parts for ten minutes.
- Sniffing lavender or geranium essential oil (both lower blood pressure).
- Sitting in the sun (outside) for five minutes.
- Listening to something calming and distracting (news, music) unrelated to whatever is stressing you out.
- Painting a picture.
- Cuddling (with a lover, friend or even a pet – physical touch is comforting).
- Taking a nap.

- Taking a caffeine nap.

- Talking to a friend for ten minutes, even if just to hear about his or her life.

- Spending ten minutes grooming (nails, bath, hair).

7. Mindfulness. This technique is now very popular, and you will find many books describing how to be mindful, including audio recordings with meditation. The habits improving mindfulness skills include:

Paying attention to the details of now. What colour is that flower? How does that steak taste? How many shades of blue can you see right now?

Taking up meditation. For example: Find a quiet place, set a timer, close your eyes and focus on your breaths. Start with 15 minutes a day, then increase the time of the session to 45 minutes.

Focusing acutely on an immediate sensation, e.g. how invigorating that brisk wind is, or great it feels to be tucked into your comfortable bed.

Investing emotionally in a current interaction. How does your friend feel about her problem? What emotions are you feeling right now? What can you do rejoice with the person you are with right now?

Consciously letting go of worry or regret. Tell yourself "The past is the past" or "Future Me will take care of that."

8. Dealing with people. Building harmonious relationships is the base of happy life. Here are some simple habits which you can apply to get on better with people:

- Talking with a positive person.

- Writing down three good things that happened to you each day.

- Laughing – even if you must force it. The mere action of laughing releases endorphins.

- Genuinely listening to people.

- Asking for a hug from one person a day.
- Investing an extra thirty minutes a day in personal hygiene. Remember to leave home without being showered and groomed.
- Saying "Hello" to people met on the street, even if you don't know them.
- Calling an old friend or relative.

Chapter 9
Set and Achieve Awesome Goals

"The only real limitation on your abilities is the level of your desires. If you want it badly enough, there are no limits on what you can achieve." — Brian Tracy

Setting and achieving goals were real challenges for Tina. She has only done that for her business and at work, but she has never thought about what she wanted in her life. More than that, if she decided to set a goal, she abandoned it quickly, after the first obstacle. Tina has never monitored her goals, only those in her corporation because the boss ordered so. It took her some time to learn that only systematic work on the sown seed will bring her abundant crops to reap.

When you learn the tools described in this chapter, you will be able to manage your life more efficiently and in line with your rules. Thus, you will become happier and more fulfilled. You will learn:

- How to find life goals.
- How to recognise that the goal is yours.
- How to set smart goals.

- What other criteria must your goal meet to be achievable.
- How to set the difficulty of your goal.
- How to set emergency goals.
- How to measure the progress of your goals.
- How to achieve your goals.

How to Find Life Goals

It is a simple task to find your goals, easier than determining your beliefs. Just answer the questions below. Use your transformation diary for this exercise.

- What one great thing would you dare to dream if you knew you could not fail?
- What would you like to change in your life right now?
- What would you do now if you had only nine months of life to live?
- What do you most enjoy doing? What gives you the greatest feeling of personal satisfaction?

How to Recognise That This Is Your Goal

Have you ever wondered why some goals do not bring you pleasure and satisfaction? The answer is accurate; you are working on somebody else's agenda. They are using you to achieve their goals.

Who can it be? In most cases, there are your parents or your spouse. The first ones may have a plan for your life. For example, they may want the same career path for you as they have – just because they have not achieved their goals and hope that you will.

Your parents may plan your future regarding an ideal relationship, according to them. Let's say that your parents are very wealthy and expect someone will take care of the business when they become old and die. And if also you are a woman, they expect you to provide a suitable spouse for the job.

You may not be you because of the rat race. You buy a better house, a car, clothes – just to keep up with the Joneses. But are you truly happy doing that? Your goals may also be imposed by the community, e.g. the religious one.

So how can you distinguish your goal from the goal imposed by the other people? The first one will generate your passion. You will not see difficulties or hard work achieving this goal. If you are not sure, write down why you want to achieve this goal. Then check if the answers are truly yours or the opinions, beliefs of other people. If this is the case, eliminate the goal as you are working on other people's scenario at the cost of yours.

"Setting goals is the first step in turning invisible into the visible."
– Tony Robbins

How to Set SMART Goals

Use the six criteria which I will present below. A goal must be:

Specific In other words, your goal must be defined precisely. Doing so, you have much greater chance of accomplishment than a general goal. To set a specific goal, answer the five 'Wh' questions.

1. Who is involved?
2. What do I want to accomplish?
3. Where will you achieve your goal?
4. When will you pursue the goal?
5. Why do you want to achieve this goal?

Let's see it in an example. A general goal would be, "Leave my toxic partner." But a specific goal would say, "Prepare emotionally, mentally and financially for leaving my partner within two months." You could be even more specific: "Save up 200EUR and meet the counsellor four times to gain assertiveness and self-confidence within the next two months."

Measurable Establish concrete criteria for measuring progress towards the attainment of each goal you set. Measure your progress; when you reach your target dates, stay on track and experience the pride of achievement of your goal. How to determine if your goal is measurable? Ask questions and give answers to them:

• How much?

• How many?

• How will I know when my goal is achieved?

It is difficult to define the measures for mental and emotional goals. How can you measure assertiveness, for example? But you can say: "I will be assertive every second conflict and then stand up for myself confidently regardless of my partner's reaction within the next two months before leaving him for good." You can even specify what assertiveness means. Is it staying firm about your boundaries by speaking a certain way or is it ignoring your partner's nasty name calling, showing him that his abuse does not work anymore?

Attainable Goals that may have seemed out of reach eventually become achievable, because you grow and expand to match them, not because your goals shrink.

However, they cannot be too big. Brian Tracy suggests that your goals should not be larger than 10-30% of your current achievement. So, do not expect that you will learn assertiveness and become an expert in it. Assume that you will be able to stand up for yourself in some cases, gradually increasing the frequency of them.

Realistic A goal must have an objective towards which, you are both willing and able to work. In some cases, the goal can be both high and realistic. But you are the only one who can decide just how high your goal should be. Be sure that every goal represents significant progress, without overwhelming you.

Timely Your goals must have a deadline. With no time frame tied to them, there is no sense of urgency. If you want to leave your abusive partner, by when do you want to do it? 'Someday' will not work. Anchoring it within a time frame, 'by the end of October 2015,' you have set your unconscious mind into motion to be working on the goal. You will read more about setting deadlines in the next part of this sub-chapter.

T can also mean **Tangible**. Goals are tangible when you can experience them with one of the senses, that is, taste, touch, smell, sight or hearing. You have a better chance of making your goal specific and measurable and thus attainable when it is tangible.

Therefore, a goal "I am happy from tomorrow" is not the right goal – what does it mean to be happy? Even if you answer "I am in a happy relationship" - what does it mean? No arguments? Better sex? More quality time? Each of these questions marks a separate goal.

Some goals are more like resolutions, practicing a skill, you do not see tangible results at once or after at some specific time. If you set a goal like "I am assertive" or "I use the happiness language", you need to specify again, when you are assertive you use the happiness language. If you say: "I will stop using 'I have to' and replace it with 'I will'." then you know what exact goal to work on.

To set the deadline, just add some measures. For example: "I will stop using 'I have to' and replace it with 'I will' at least once per day, and I will practice this skill for 30 days." After a month, you evaluate your progress

What Are Other Criteria Essential for Achieving Goals?

Apart from SMART, there are seven more criteria which determine if your goal is achievable:

1. Write your goal in the positive language. "I won't smoke after the 1st of January 2016" is not the right goal because you still focus on your addiction. More than that, you will actually smoke as your subconscious mind does not recognise the word 'not'. "I am smoking-free since the 1st of January 2016" or "I stopped/gave up/ quit smoking since the 1st of January 2016." "Stop, leave or give up" suggest that you end the bad habit.

2. Make your goal congruent with your values. If you value honesty, manipulative games will repulse you, and you will sabotage any goal which involves some manipulation, using the others. Before you set a goal, check what your values are. It is why I have written so much about values at the beginning of this book.

3. Build it on strong points. Otherwise, you will struggle. Even if you can find help, it will not be very exciting, when you see only your limits. If you have epilepsy, you will not set a goal "I will get a driving license." Your health is not your personal excellence then; it is your limit. Then you need to solve the issue of transportation in a different way.

4. Let your goal be "the diamond right under your feet." I mean, a kind of a diamond which is not polished, but rough and therefore unseen. We tend to set big goals not basing them on what we already have. If you want to be a writer, take a notebook and a pen and just start writing. Your talent is just there.

5. Balance each field of your life. Therefore, you have set your life directions. You probably know some people who lost their relationships because of too much focus on their career. Choose some goals in each major area of life and focus equally on them.

According to Brian Tracy, set no more than three goals for one area of life and not more than fifteen in total.

6. Reconcile other goals you have. If you set a goal which will conflict with another goal, the chances are that you will achieve neither of them. Why? Because you will sabotage them. If you are going to save some money and at the same time to buy a new car, you will end up with either no money or no car. Your decision will depend on what is more important at a given moment, which is often impulsive behaviour.

7. Your goal must match to your principal purpose. You already know what your major goal is having done the exercises from Chapter 1. This is your life mission. Now you need to set the goals which will support your life mission. If you defined that helping others as a coach is your mission, then you need to learn how to be a coach, how to run a business and how to find customers. You also need the tools necessary for work – office or Skype connection, worksheets, etc. Now test your goals. Write down one set of this year's goals or any other goals that you have set lately:

My present yearly goal:

……………………………………………………………………………………

……………………………………………………………………………………

Then fill in the table, marking if your goal meets the criteria described above. Use 'x' when the standard is not fulfilled and 'v' when it is.

………… Specific
………… Measurable
………… Attainable
………… Realistic

....   Timely

....   Tangible

....   Positive statement

....   Congruent with values

....   Built on strong points

....   "diamonds under your feet"

....   Balanced in all areas of life

....   In harmony with other goals

....   In harmony with your major life purpose

If you noticed that your goal does not meet the criteria above, rewrite it.

....

....

How to Set Up the Difficulty of My Goal?

We usually set too difficult goals and do not appreciate their difficulty. According to Brian Tracy, a goal which is over 10% bigger than our present comfort zone will be overwhelming. Therefore, if you make €500 a month and want to earn more, do not set a goal of €5000 within a month. Planning yearly assumes that you will make 10 to 30 % more than now which means that your goal will be between €550 and 650. Then divide this goal into monthly and quarterly goals and even weekly ones. To plan your monthly amount, divide the €500 into 12 – this will be your extra monthly amount to earn. This option may work well if you have a job with steady income and want to start making more money selling something.

Let's look at another example. In the case of selling goods, e.g. in affiliate programs, you can also plan the monthly target gradually, e.g. €20 in the first month, then €30, €40 and so on. In the case of sales, you can also plan your weekly goals, e.g. €2.5 every week in the first month of €10 to earn. Eventually, you will end up with tiny amounts of money to earn weekly, which will not overwhelm you. The same rules will apply when you want to lose weight sell more items or find more customers.

In the case of intangible goals like assertiveness or stopping negative thoughts, make the goals tangible first. How to do it? Decide how many times you want to be assertive during a day or week. Now you can set the goal, ready for monitoring its progress. Let's say that the next month you are assertive at least once per day. You check if you met the goal or not on daily basis. If being assertive once per day is too difficult at the beginning, set an easier one. Remember that you need to think of your goal as ten times more complicated when it is while being set. It means that your goal can look like that "I behave in an assertive way at least once per week," even if you plan to work on assertiveness daily.

What Is an Emergency Goal and How to Set It?

While working on your goals, you are at risk of giving them up. It happens when you experience a failure. Suppose you decided to stop eating sweets. However, there will be the days when you face a temptation. And what happens when you do eat the sweets? You start feeling guilty, angry and your motivation plummets. Then you say: "What the hell! I cannot achieve that goal; I'll eat the sweets again." And in this way, you have abandoned your goal.

How to avoid that? Set a smaller goal, which when met means that you haven't totally collapsed your resolution. Suppose that in the case of sweets it can be: "I eat no more than one sweet per week since (add the date)."

Now choose one yearly goal on which you are working. Write it down below:

……...

Add an emergency goal:

……...

How to Measure Progress Made While Working on Goals

You have already defined where you are today and where you want to be in 5 years' time, reading Chapter One and doing the exercises described there. The simplest way to measure the progress is doing something which can be measured. In the case of making money – every cent means making progress. When you gain bigger sales figure than last week, month or even last year, you are making progress.

Goals can be separated according to their time frame. In each case, you plan and evaluate them over a given period. So, do not expect that your yearly goal will be achieved within a week, although it might happen rarely (e.g. while making money by product launch).

- Long-term goals where you check the progress even every five years.
- Medium-term goals which are yearly or last for 36 months
- Short-term goals which last for 90-days. You check their progress every 90 days and set another goal for that period.

The 90-days goals include three monthly (30 days) goals. In this case, you check their progress every month and set new ones for the next 30 days.

The shorter goals indicate the progress on the way to achieving your long-term and medium-term goals. Hence if you set a yearly goal, after a month or 90 days you can check how much of the annual goal you have already achieved.

You also set goals for each week and evaluate their progress every seven days. And plan for next week. Each week is planned by setting daily tasks.

Treat each of your goal like a mission, even if it is only one task of your weekly aim. Remember to set emergency goals for the short-term goals, too.

Now check how you and plan and evaluate your goals. Let's do this for your three yearly goals:

My Yearly Goal Today's State	My Achievements				
	Quarter 1	Quarter 2	Quarter 3	Quarter 4	360 Days Time

Do the same exercise for one of your 90-day-goals.

My Current 90 day goal The current state	My Achievements				
	Month 1	Month 2	Month 3	Month 4	My state in 90 days Time

Take one monthly goal and divide it into weekly goals.

My Monthly goal today	My Achievements				
	Week 1	Week 2	Week 3	Week 4	In 30 days time

Examples: The yearly goal is I will have published a 300-page book by Dec 31. Quarter 1: I will have done research about the topic of the book. Quarter 2: I will have written the book. Quarter 3: I will have promoted and edited the book. Quarter 4: I will have published the book and done the Christmas sales campaign.

How to Set Achievable Goals and Work on Them

"The more you seek security, the less of it you have. But the more you seek opportunity, the more likely it is that you will achieve the security that you desire." - Brian Tracy

Suppose that you want to learn a foreign language. You may plan to master the beginners level this year, the intermediate one next year and the advanced level in two years' time. So, during 2016 or for 365 days since the 1st of January 2016 you learn the beginners level regularly – let's say ten words daily and grammar three times a week. How can you set and achieve that goal?

"New Year = A New Life! Decide today who you will become, what you will give how you will live." - Tony Robbins

1. Do it all in writing. Everything which is not written is not a goal, but just a mere dream. When you write your goals, you program your subconscious mind to work on them, because the process of writing involves taking action and engages some of your senses, such as your sight and touch. It is like burning files on a CD. You engrave the goal and set your focus on it.

You can also use mobile applications like ColorNote, where you write your goals and even copy them to your calendar creating a recurring reminder, such as an alarm note which will display in the morning when you wake up.

You can write your goal on a computer, but I suggest to do it on paper, especially on small pieces, like flashcards or sticky notes. Then you can take the goals with you, to put them in your wallet, bag, etc. or hang in the bathroom. Doing so, you have more opportunities to look and read these goals, programming your mind even more.

2. Desire your goal. You need to want it desperately. Otherwise, your motivation will fade very soon, and your fears will flood your willingness to take action. As a result, you will quit. Since every decision to take any action is based on fear or greed, set your focus on greed, such as desire. You need to want the goal for yourself. That is why earlier I wrote about the importance of setting the goals which are your own.

In the case of learning a foreign language, you must have a big reason why you are doing so. Let's say that you want to emigrate and live in another country. Before you even start setting the goal, imagine your new life in vivid details. I will write more about visualisation later in this chapter. For now, just ignite your desire.

Now write down three goals which you have achieved and wanted to achieve during last five years. Describe what empowered your desire to work on them.

MY GOAL   **WHAT EMPOWERED MY DESIRE**

3. Develop a supporting belief. Be sure that you will achieve the goal. In other words, you need to believe that it is possible. Therefore, before setting goals you had to change your beliefs. Some of them manifest your faith in the achievement of your goals. Now you can be certain that with the help of others and your own determination you can attain your goals.

Napoleon Hill wrote, *"Whatever the mind of a man can conceive and believe, it can achieve."* However, completely unrealistic goals will demotivate you.

You will be working on big goals and take many months, or even years, to achieve them. Then be honest with yourself and accept that, if the goal is worth achieving, it is worth working patiently and persistently. Setting smaller goals, as the 90-day ones, will help you to see the progress and increase the faith in success.

If you want to believe in something, find your powerful 'why'. Then in times of disappointment and lack of progress, you will stay motivated and still work on your goals. Now look at one of your present ones. Define three reasons why you believe that you can achieve this aim.

I believe that I can achieve this

…………………………………………………………………………………………

because

…………………………………………………………………………………………

because

…………………………………………………………………………………………

because

…………………………………………………………………………………………

Example: "I can learn English and be fluent in this language because I am smart enough, because I will be happier living in another country, because I have enough helpful people to achieve it, because I want it badly."

4. Do the cost-benefit analysis. Before you start to work on any goal, you do have to want it. Otherwise, the goal will not give you pleasure; you will stop working on it soon, failing when facing the first obstacle.

Each goal bears consequences to you and other people. It is called the balance sheet of your goal. Some call it the ecology of your goals. After doing the cost-benefit analysis you will see if you will gain more or you have to pay the price which is not worth the trouble.

How can you define the benefits? Just write down what good things will happen if you achieve the goal. In a case of costs – what is the price – the things that you must resign from, the discomfort, the effort that you have to make. You define the costs and benefits for you and then for the environment as your goal could harm other people. Let's do it for one goal at this moment.

Apart from listing the costs and benefits for you and other people, you have to mark how important each item is as a cost or a benefit. You can use various symbols like stars, a '+' for benefits and a '−' for costs and then sum up all the scores for benefits and costs separately. Let's say you define the cost and benefit items on a scale from 1 to 5, where five means 'critical for me'. If the score for benefits is seven times higher than the score of costs, your goal is suitable for pursuing. You will be able to pay the price, and other people will not suffer.

My goal			
Benefits for me: What will I gain achieving this goal?	Score	My costs: What do I have to lose to achieve this goal?	Score
Benefits for other people. What positive consequences will be for other people acheiving this goal?	Score	Cost for other people. What negative consequences will be for other people by achieving this goal?	Score
Total score-benefits		Total score-costs	
The balance		Yes, I will work on that goal No, I will not work on that goal	

Do this analysis for each of your goals set for this year. You may notice that your goals may seem too difficult, and first, you must work on the issues from the 'cost' column.

5. Define your starting point. If you want to lose weight, write down the weight you have at the time of starting the diet or doing exercises. The same applies to goals connected with happiness. Determining your starting point gives you a baseline from which you can measure your progress, and this will motivate you to reach the target quicker.

Now define the starting point for your three goals for this year, each from a different area of your life. Let's say that your goals will concern your finances, your relationships and leisure. Write where you are currently in each of these fields of life. If it is hard for you, go back to Chapter One and do the exercise: "Where am I now?"

Goal one ………………………………………………………………………

………………………………………………………………………………

………………………………………………………………………………

Goal two ………………………………………………………………………

………………………………………………………………………………

………………………………………………………………………………

Goal three ……………………………………………………………………

………………………………………………………………………………

………………………………………………………………………………

6. Check if the goal is properly defined. Before you start your hard work, check if your goals are properly defined. Choose one area of your life now, where you want to become happier. Write down one goal on which you want to work for the next year.

………………………………………………………………………………

Now check if this goal is in accordance with the criteria which I have described at the beginning of this chapter.

....	Specific
....	Measurable
....	Attainable
....	Realistic
....	Timely
....	Tangible
....	Positive statement
....	Congruent with values
....	Built on strong points
....	"diamonds under your feet"
....	Balanced in all areas of life
....	In harmony with other goals
....	In harmony with your major life purpose

If you notice that not all the criteria are met, redefine the goal. Write it down below.

....

7. Set a deadline. It gives you a time frame. In the case of yearly or quarterly, and even monthly goals it is not enough to say: "in a year's time, in a quarter's time, in a month's time…" You will achieve more setting the deadline for the exact date, e.g. **by 31st of December 2016.**

You can also define the closing date of your goal in this way: **Within the next 30, 90, 365 days since (full date) I will achieve …......"**

Now practice setting the deadlines for your goal which you have defined in the previous step.

…..

Sometimes you must change your deadline. If you notice that you are not able to learn assertiveness within a week, do it within a month, but still work on that. You will achieve your goal by the deadline in 80 percent of cases. Just learn how to set the goals using the steps and criteria described in this chapter and take action.

You have already set the deadlines for your goals if you have done the exercises above (i.e. while defining your goals and checking them according to SMART and other criteria).

8. Define your resources. To achieve your goal, you must know what resources you can use. They may include your knowledge, skills, helpful people, and finance. Now take your goal and assess what resources you already have.

GOAL

PEOPLE   **SKILLS**   **RESOURCES**
                                            (E.G. MONEY)

9. Make the list of all obstacles. Do not deceive yourself that it will be easy to achieve your goal. You will certainly face obstacles. The play is to identify them and find the way to overcome them. Your obstacle can be external, like lack of skill, helpful people or internal, like low self-confidence, negative beliefs.

List three obstacles that you can face in the way of achieving your goals. If you notice that there are more challenges than you can write now, add then to your transformation dairy:

GOAL

OBSTACLES
1.
2.
3.

There will always be one obstacle that you will have to face, which is the biggest and the hardest to tackle. It might be your fear of abandonment, the aggression of your abusive partner, failure, lack of money. Identify that biggest obstacle by answering the question: "What is my biggest limiting step?" Write it down.

………………………………………………………………………………

In many cases, negative thinking or beliefs are your biggest obstacles. In other words, your attitude. Go back to Chapter Four and Five and set a goal which will help to change your thinking and beliefs. Sometimes before you start working on the goal of making more money, it is more important to change beliefs and the way you think.

10. Plan how to overcome the obstacles. Now you need to find the tools or help to overcome your challenges. Before you do so, remind yourself how you coped with your barriers in the past. Choose three obstacles and describe how you have handled it so far.

"Every minute you spend in planning saves 10 minutes in execution; this gives you a 1,000 percent Return on Energy!" - Brian Tracy

OBSTACLE

HOW I HAVE HANDLED IT BEFORE

OBSTACLE

HOW I HAVE HANDLED IT BEFORE

OBSTACLE

HOW I HAVE HANDLED IT BEFORE

Now you need to make a plan for overcoming your present obstacles and gaining the resources that you miss. To make things easier, choose only the biggest obstacle (e.g. negative thinking) and one missing resource that you may need the most (e.g. money). Do it for one goal. Define the first five steps, but you may need more to solve the problem. Use your transformation diary to make the whole plan.

The main obstacle

Steps to take to overcome the obstacle
1.

2.

3.

4.

5.

The main resource needed

Steps to take to obtain the missing resource
1.

2.

3.

4.

5.

Remember to make a plan containing the full list of steps for all your obstacles. If you lack a given skill, plan to learn it. For example, before leaving an abusive partner to become happy again, you need to learn to be more assertive and more self-confident to handle his anger and threats. It will be your sub-goal. Take the transformation diary with your goal and list all the skills necessary to achieve your goal and overcome the obstacles. Do not panic if you discover that there are lots to be learned. Eventually, you will achieve your goal.

11. Define what to give in return to the people who will help you. Be aware that people will not do things for free. Sometimes they may, but usually, you need to offer something in return. When you find the people, who may help you, ask them what they would like to obtain in exchange for helping you.

You have already defined your resources. Now determine how you will use them in order to give something in return to other people. Do it for three people now, but remember to make the full list in your transformation diary:

The Person	What I need from them	What I can offer in return

When you prepare a plan, organise all the items by time and priority. Use the 80/20 principle and the four quadrants defined by Stephen Covey (urgent and important – emergency tasks, not urgent, but important – long-term activity, urgent but unimportant – nasty phone calls, emails and neither urgent nor important – watching TV). You will find more tips how to use these two tools in Chapter Eleven.

"The future depends on what you do today" - *Ghandi*

12. Visualise your achieved goal. Visualisation is very powerful while setting goals and working on them. You activate your subconscious mind with pictures, tastes, smells, sounds and touch. So, every day, before going to bed and after waking up, imagine your goal as pursued.

I will share one technique with you now. It is called the mental contrast. Unlike the traditional visualisation, it also takes challenges into account. How does it work?

Define the two biggest benefits and two most major obstacles/ problems for your goal.

Take the first benefit and describe, in vivid details, how good you will have felt when your goal is achieved.

Then take the first obstacle. This time, you will not visualise the worst scenario. Instead, focus on solutions. Describe how you can overcome this obstacle and what resources you already have for doing that.

Take the second benefit and again describe the outcome in vivid details.

At the end take the second obstacle and define the solution.

Do all the four steps in one go. Remember to make the mental contrast for each of your yearly, 90-days and monthly goals. Do this exercise in writing in your transformation diary.

13. Take action. Once you have a detailed plan of action, get started. Accept that your plan will have flaws in it. However, the more detailed and better organised your plan, the more likely it is that you will achieve your goals on schedule and exactly as you defined them.

Nothing will change in your life if you don't take action. You can plan, visualise, awaken the burning desire, find helpful people... yet if you stay passive, your goal will not be pursued. So, take some massive action right now.

You will fail and fall sometimes. This is the usual process on the way to success. Stay positive then, because as Napoleon Hill said "Strength and growth come only through continuous effort and struggle."

14. Monitor your progress.

"Excellence/Perfection is not a destination;
it is a continuous journey that never ends."
- Brian Tracy

You monitor the progress of your goal by checking how much you have achieved every day. This method is the best in the case of resolutions such as: "I will stop eating sweets 24/7" or "I will stop negative thinking." They are resolutions which you work on regular basis.

However, monitoring daily progress is also important in the case of big goals, called missions. If you chipped away at your goals by doing smaller tasks, then it is easier to monitor and mark which task you have done. For example, if you want to lose weight and have planned to do exercises three times a week for 45 minutes, every day you check if the job was done and mark that.

Use the Android application HabitBull, which is free for monitoring five goals. It's an alarm app for your habits and is possibly more suited for developing a good habit than it is for beating out a bad one. You will find more information on the HabitBull website.

'Best You' is another impressive progress marker. It is an educational platform, so far in Polish, but the authors plan to launch the English version next year. 'Best You' enables you to monitor your progress on a goal board. There are four answers to the question: How well have I done today?

- When you succeed, you put a tick (√).
- A goal which you failed to achieve completely on a given day is marked with a cross (X).
- Sometimes you may achieve your goal halfway, which means that you have met your emergency goal (a goal which is a partial completion of the primary goal). Then you may use both tick and cross (√X).
- There are also goals which are not due every day. You mark them with a hyphen (-).

If you mark all your goals as achieved during a given day, this is your perfect day which gives you points which enable you to make progress in 'Best You'. If you reach all your mini-goals for more than one day, you can get an extra reward for a perfect week, or even a perfect month.

You can also monitor the progress of a goal which is not yet 'in action' but you are preparing for taking the challenge. Then you don't mark this aim as achieved or failed, but you can see if the goal is easy to work on or tough (when you fail for too many days in a row).

15. Never quit. Finally, all the steps above are meaningless when you give up at the first obstacle, like another argument with your abusive partner. There are no failures; there are only lessons. If you lost your temper again or become submissive hearing him yelling, think about what you could do better and what not to do the next time, but still work on your goal.

Remember, once you have set your goal and started working on it: **NEVER EVER GIVE UP.**

"A quitter never wins-and-a winner never quits."
— Napoleon Hill

Chapter 10
Win Challenges Powerfully

So far Tina has become more aware of her life. She has also learned to accept her limits using the happiness language. Now she is changing her beliefs. The journey is not easy. There are obstacles like lack of motivation or just the feelings of helplessness.

I have shown Tina that even in the case of challenges she can make progress. You will learn the same by reading this chapter and applying the tips described here. You will learn:

- The types of challenges you can meet in your life.
- The top ten questions you can use in case of any problem (more are in Chapter Six).
- What to do in case of the challenge.
- How to tackle the problem in fourteen steps.
- How to learn from challenges.

The Kind of Challenges You Meet in Your Life

Happy people have the natural ability to cope with two types of life challenges.

External. In other words, you feel are beyond your control. Think of all the disasters, the government decisions, the banks' regulations. How much influence do you have on them? Not much, although you can elect the members of parliament and choose the bank and, you can always choose how you will react in case of crisis.

Internal. You face challenges existing inside you. All your bad habits and addictions fall into this category of challenges. It may be hard to stop them at the first glimpse, but again, you have the power to transform them as every habit can be unlearned and substituted with a new one, every thought or belief turned into the positive one and every emotion can be managed.

Top 10 Powerful Questions When Facing Any Challenge

The asking of compelling questions can give you new perspective on your challenges. Now let's do a simple exercise. You will examine your current problem. While working on your goals when reading Chapter 1 and 9, you have probably faced some challenges, especially while working on the main obstacle to your goal. Choose this challenge and write it down.

……………………………………………………………………………………………

Now ask these questions, which may be difficult to answer at first.

1. What is good in this situation? Answering this question will help you to focus on positive side of your challenge and to find a solution. Write your answer down.

……………………………………………………………………………………………

……………………………………………………………………………………………

……………………………………………………………………………………………

2. What can I do to turn that the situation around? If you are still not sure what to do in the case of your challenge, the second question will ease the difficulty because you will start focusing on taking action instead of dwelling on how bad your situation is. In this way, you feel in control and gain more confidence. Think what action you can take to succeed. Having set your goals and defining an action plan, you probably have gotten your answers ready. List three of them below.

1. ....

2. ....

3. ....

3. What can I stop doing to turn that the situation around? Sometimes your action may cause the problems which you are just solving. For example, going to bed late while you are supposed to get up early will cause tiredness and poor concentration. When you stop going to bed late the problem will be solved. In this case, you may need to create a new habit. Read Chapter Eight again and start working on changing the time of going to bed for an earlier one.

....

....

....

4. What can I do differently to turn that situation around? In the above example, you must just go to bed earlier. If you go to sleep late because of still being busy, then think of changes in your time management. Chapter Eleven will help you to achieve this goal.

....

....

....

5. Have I missed considering any solution? Check once again all the options. You may notice that there is still at least one option which can be used to overcome your challenge. What is more, this option may be crucial for solving the problem. Now think for a while and brainstorm additional options which will help you resolving the problem. Write three of them down.

1. ....

2. ....

3. ....

6. What action was taken that could give the simplest and the fastest result? You already know what to do, what not to do and what to do differently for achieving the desirable effect. Now think which of actions you will make the most, achieving your goal faster and easier.

1. ....

2. ....

3. ....

7. Who can help me? In most cases, you will need someone to help you. List them while reading Chapter Nine; you have already defined your helpers. List three of them below.

1. ....

2. ....

3. ....

8. What kind of life lessons can I learn from this situation? Every challenge brings a lesson to learn. If you get up tired because of staying up all night, the lesson is 'go to bed earlier'. Define the experience from your current challenge. If it is difficult, think why you are facing the obstacles (especially the internal ones) while working on your goals. For example, negative thinking causes anxiety and stops you from taking opportunities in your life. Therefore, the lesson which you learn here is 'stop negative thinking'.

I am aware that you might not be ready to learn the lesson while discovering it. Then taking a small step will help you to start. It is up to you to learn the lesson or still face the same challenge. Assuming responsibility for your life will make learning your lessons easier and faster.

……………………………………………………………………………………

……………………………………………………………………………………

……………………………………………………………………………………

9. What will I gain solving this problem? This question is right in the case of procrastination, which I will discuss in the next chapter. Now look at your challenge and list the advantages of taking it. List the biggest benefit you will have while taking action. You can use the cost-benefits analysis from the previous chapter, where you have set your goals.

……………………………………………………………………………………

……………………………………………………………………………………

……………………………………………………………………………………

10. The last, but not the least question is: **What can I do right now to overcome the challenge?** Think of one small step which you will take immediately and take action. Remember that nothing will change if you stay passive and ruminate over your challenge.

……………………………………………………………………………………

……………………………………………………………………………………

……………………………………………………………………………………

What to Do in Case of Challenge

Apart from asking the compelling questions, you can use the tips described below to overcome your challenges.

1. Practice Gratitude. You already know how to do it after having read Chapter Two. Gratitude is a perfect tool to increase your self-acceptance and to get rid of shame. I know that it is easy to count your troubles rather than your blessings. However, such an attitude undermines your ability to draw from the good that you have been given and to see your life as a gift.

Notice that a change in perspective can make all the difference. Recognising the right and receiving it with gratitude enlarges the possibility of using of the asset which you have been given. Moreover, use it to cope with the difficulties that you inevitably have inherited. Practicing gratitude is good for your emotional health and well-being.

2. Stay close to your feelings, unless they are painful. You can often find your feelings scary, cumbersome, and confusing. Therefore, try to keep them at a distance. Remember that you need to know your beliefs to find satisfaction, meaning, and pleasure in life. Reading Chapter Seven and doing the exercises placed there, will enable you to cope with most of the negative states of your mind.

3. Turn towards reality. So often you turn away from life rather than towards it. What is more, you are the master of avoidance. If you want to be present, to enjoy life and to be more effective in it, focus on facing reality. Doing so, you develop a deeper capacity to deal with life more effectively. What once was difficult is now easier and what once frightened you now feels more familiar. You will notice that life becomes more manageable.

4. Take your time. Do you remember the story of the tortoise and the hare? It tells us that slow and steady wins the race. By being in a hurry, you can thwart your success. You often get ahead with yourself. And then you make more mistakes, cutting corners and paying for them later. You may learn the easy way but not necessarily the best way. The adage puts it like this: the slower you go, the sooner you get there. Slow, disciplined, incremental growth is the kind of approach that leads to lasting change.

However, the tortoise will also have to be smart. Being slow does not mean that you cannot manage the time or prioritise the tasks. Chapter Eleven will show you how to apply time management to achieve your goals smarter.

5. Accept your life as it is. Buddha taught that the secret to life is to want what you have and not to want what you don't have. This rule is also taught by the present self-help gurus, and I agree with that. While writing about acceptance, I insisted on following this rule because if you are ill and constantly ruminating on it, you miss seeing all the opportunities which emerge for you.

There is freedom in taking life as it comes to you, the good with the bad, life with death, the excellent with the tragic and the love with the loss. When you embrace it all, then you have a real chance to enjoy life, to value your experiences and to savour the treasures that are there for the taking. Surrendering to the reality of who you are, you give yourself a chance to do what you can do.

Tackle the Problem In 15 Steps

1. Accept that this challenge is happening. Many people will dismiss challenges that come before them. Thinking in the same way, you convince yourself that the challenge is smaller than it is or that it doesn't exist in the first place. Recognise when you start thinking this way and start noticing the real size of the challenge. Remember what some sages say: "The first step in overcoming a problem is admitting that you have one."

Accepting that this challenge is real and that you are going to have to deal with it can be scary. While fearing what this problem can mean for you, remember that so far in life, you had met every other challenge and made it out okay. There's no reason to think that this problem is any different.

Define the challenge. In many cases, just doing so will decrease the harmful impact of your problems on your attitude. As an exercise, write down your biggest problem which bothers you now.

……………………………………………………………………………………………

2. Brainstorm solutions. Brian Tracy suggests 'The 20 Ideas Method'. Take a piece of paper and write your problem at the top. Then write down 20 answers, without assessing them. Do it now.

Problem _____

1 ……………………………………………………………………………………
2 ……………………………………………………………………………………
3 ……………………………………………………………………………………
4 ……………………………………………………………………………………
5 ……………………………………………………………………………………
6 ……………………………………………………………………………………
7 ……………………………………………………………………………………
8 ……………………………………………………………………………………
9 ……………………………………………………………………………………
10 …………………………………………………………………………………
11 …………………………………………………………………………………
12 …………………………………………………………………………………
13 …………………………………………………………………………………

14 ....

15 ....

16 ....

17 ....

18 ....

19 ....

20 ....

<u>You must find 20 or more ideas of solving your problem</u>. Otherwise, this method will not work. The last plans will be the hardest to guess, but they are usually the best solutions to your problem. Focusing on solutions will increase your confidence.

3. Take action. It's important to start doing something about the problem as soon as you possibly can for the challenge that you end up facing. Each moment of inaction also means taking action. By doing nothing, you're still doing something. Having the twenty solutions, pick out the one which you want to apply and follow the next steps described below.

....

4. Evaluate the facts. Are you ready to start tackling this challenge? Great! Now start evaluating the effects. Ask the questions and answer them in writing.

What do you know about what's going on? (How well do you know your problem?)

Are you sure you understand the situation?

Stop dealing with what you think the problem is. Take some time to make sure that you understand the situation as fully as possible. For example, in the case of having social anxiety, your problem may lie in your beliefs and negative thinking. It is your real challenge.

5. Define who would help you. Here are some ideas: Talk to people, although who will depend on your situation. Are you having problems with your health? Speak to your doctor. Problems at work? Speak to your boss or a co-worker. Problems in your relationship? Talk to your partner or a counsellor. Again, choose one challenge you are facing right now. Write down the three people who can help you.

1. ....
2. ....
3. ....

6. Make a list. Your challenge is rarely one single task or problem. In most cases, it is instead made up of lots of different parts. Now define the smaller, sub-challenges. List three of them now.

1. ....
2. ....
3. ....

7. Take stock of what you have. Now that you know what you are dealing with think about what skills and resources are available for you facing this challenge. I have given you plenty in this book. Some of them you will learn in the next chapter. Apart from those described in this book, you have your resources, many skills and life wisdom.

Make a short list of your assets. Write down five things which you already have or can use which will help you to solve your problem.

1. ....
2. ....
3. ....
4. ....
5. ....

Examples: your strengths, the people that can help you and any physical resources you might have (like money, fitness). Also, remember about your mental assets, like creativity, persistence or staying focused on your goals

Now think about the areas in which you are weak. It will let you plan ahead so that you can compensate or at least prepare in areas where something might go wrong. Make a list of five things which need compensation in order to solve your current problem. However, never dwell on them.

1. ....
2. ....
3. ....
4. ....
5. ....

8. Find more information. Now that you know about what the facts of the situation are and what you have available to you, start finding information that can help you. Find out more about the challenge you're facing. List the three sources of information which you can use right now.

1. ....
2. ....
3. ....

Examples: Google, the library, your friend, your co-worker, your counsellor.

Talk to the people who have faced the same challenge. The easier time you'll have making smart decisions about facing your own challenge the more you know about similar situations, the facts and the experiences of others.

9. Look at all possibilities. When you are worried, you tend to see only a few paths out of a challenge. You might see the situation as 'either I do this or I do that'. However, this is rarely an accurate view of the situation, and such thinking can often be harmful to your decision-making process. Check the list of twenty solutions once again. Which of them shows you alternative ways of solving the problem? Write it down.

…..

10. Communicate. If the challenge that you are facing in any way involves other people, then you will deal with it by talking to other people. Most of our problems come up in the first place because you fail to communicate in the way that you should. Now define your problem which requires many interactions with people, then determine who you need to talk to.

…..

…..

Example: relationship problems. You will need to talk to your partner, your counsellor and maybe also your best friend.

11. Look for a mentor. While facing a challenge, one thing you can do to tackle it is to find a mentor. It does not necessary have to be a person; it may be a book, a website – just anything giving you advice on your situation and inspiring you to take it like a champ. Having a mentor can make your experience more positive and help you change how you experience what is happening to you. Now define who or what can be the mentor for you.

....

12. Keep trying until you find a solution. The final key to dealing with challenges in your life is to just try it again. Be persistent. Otherwise, you will frequently find yourself unsuccessful in the things you do.

Sometimes the solution to a challenge is accepting the inevitable, like a chronic illness. Fighting to get rid of the illness will not help you. The reality is probably that you are stuck with it. However, finding a sense of community and identity with others who share your challenge would be the solution for this problem. Also, learn how to embrace better and appreciate the good things that you do have in your life. Chapter Two contains the tools that will help you to accept your limits.

13. Remind yourself of the positive things in your life. You tend to forget about all the beautiful things that exist in your life when bad things happen to you, or when you are stressed. The world is a wonderful place no matter how bad things seem. Acknowledge the good things in your life. Spend more time enjoying them and tell the people that love you how much you love them in return. Now write three good things in your life.

1. ....
2. ....
3. ....

14. Be flexible. When you face your challenge, being flexible will make a huge difference in helping you face the problem. Imagine yourself as a tree that has fallen in a river. You can try to go with the flow, yet you'll end up struggling and you'll bang against every rock on the way. While going with the flow, change the direction in which the river wants to take you. In this way, you will glide smoothly until it carries you to a resting place.

The only thing you will need is a steering wheel to navigate where you are going. Chapter One and Four have helped you to define your steering wheel.

15. Find meaning in your life. Having a goal or finding some greater meaning in your life, you will find it is easier to face any challenge because it gives you something to work towards, or will simply inspire you and make you happy.

Learn from Challenges

Each challenge which you are facing has a lesson to learn. Sometimes these lessons may be painful, and you will do all you can to avoid hearing them. Even the painful lessons will help you to grow and become stronger eventually. So how do you learn from challenges?

1. Admit that you need to change. Challenges give you an opportunity to learn when things go wrong in your life. Most people escape it. You may also deny the truth life presents to you because of discomfort and pain that the challenge brings, but by doing so you will not face and overcome the challenge.

Problems occur because something is not right. For example, you become irritated because of not having slept at all last night, and this happened because you drank five coffees. Then you need to admit that drinking too much coffee and lack of sleep are your real challenges which you need to overcome.

2. Take control of yourself. I have written about it in Chapter Three. There are circumstances in life that you cannot control. For example, you may have been born into a dysfunctional family, have lost your family member at a young age, have become a victim of an unforeseeable accident or have cancer. You become weak and vulnerable surrendering to life.

Then you become easily influenced especially by drugs and alcohol which in your opinion could help you heal pain. Your friends are dangerous strangers, and eventually you become sad, emotionally unstable, which leads to depression and beyond.

However, you will not ignore the unfortunate circumstances but use them as springboards for the better you, if you realise that you are in control of yourself no matter what happens, bringing yourself to a healthy environment and building yourself a support system. Surround yourself with good influences. In this way, you build yourself skills and never stop improving yourself. And this means taking responsibility for your life.

3. Change the way you look at things. Brian Tracy describes it in the quote:

"You cannot control what happens to you, but you can control your attitude toward what happens to you, and in that, you will be mastering change rather than allowing it to master you."

Going through life's challenges requires strength, both mental and physical because they go hand in hand. You need to stay strong. But you also need support from family and friends. Most importantly, you need to change your outlook on life. Understand that you cannot change the way things are, but you can change the way you look at them.

Tony Robbins says:

"The secret of success is learning how to use pain and pleasure instead of having pain and pleasure use you. If you do that, you're in control of your life. If you don't, life controls you."

You have already learned how to change your focus on your limits and challenges, by creating new beliefs and habits. If you are not sure how to modify the way you look at things, go back to Chapter Four, Five, Six and Seven and do the exercises described there. Remember to start small and tackle one thing at the time (e.g. only your thoughts) at first.

4. Use pain to motivate you. Pain is the greatest motivator. It is the biggest thing which you want to avoid. If you want to change a belief, thought or behaviour the first thing you must do is to associate the negativity with massive pain. Read Chapter Eight again to see how it works.

5. Use your strengths. Oliver Wendell Holmes describes it in the quote below:

"A mind that is stretched by a new experience can never go back to its old dimensions."

Increasing your self-confidence and knowing your life path, you become a stronger person who is not afraid of anything in life, even if you need to face your limits and challenging challenges. You know that no matter what happens, you will be just fine, because of using your strengths or with the help of other people. The strength which you have built up over the years has become one of the most valuable assets you have. You know that you have the willpower to combat anything in life. Now write the three things that have made you stronger within your life.

1. …..
2. …..
3. …..

6. Tame your internal enemy and forgive yourself. Remember that you are both your worst enemy and your best friend. Learn how to tame the enemy and how to obtain support from your friend. Buddha describes it in this way:

"Your worst enemy cannot harm you as much as your unguarded thoughts."

How does your enemy work in your life? He appears when life hits you with a brick. Then you hate yourself for not being more disciplined, for letting people who have done you wrong into your life, for not doing the right thing and so on. Self-hate for what you did in the past which caused your life to go sideways is also very common. It may be challenging for you to forgive yourself. As the result, you feel upset, sad and angry. You just keep thinking about this over and over. You also listen to your inner critic who undermines your achievements, blaming yourself for what's gone wrong.

However, you can always change this attitude by forgiving yourself past mistakes, getting rid of guilt and resentment, practicing mindfulness will help you to find peace of mind. You have already learned how to forgive yourself in Chapter Two.

At this moment ask yourself: What would you say to your best friend if your best friend was in the situation? Will you put them down, blame them even more for what went wrong? No. Instead, you would rather cheer your best friend up and try every way you can to make them feel better. So why do you treat yourself worse, stricter? Choose to be your own best friend, not the enemy.

7. Realise what does matter and what does not. Being in a good financial situation, you go to events, shopping and travel. However, when life gets tough, you cannot afford to do those things. If you spend time feeling sad about the situation and missing the things you used to get to do, then you'd be unhappy. Do you want to be a happy person?

Start enjoying the simple things in life little by little, and appreciate what you have. You will realise then that instead of dining out, you will start cooking, that you can invite your friends over or go to their house and enjoy their company instead going clubbing. Instead of going shopping, you can learn to be happy with what you already have. These are only a few examples. Think of one thing that frustrates you right now and list it.

…..

Now think of an alternative which you could use to enjoy the thing which you don't have at this moment.

…..

How can you implement the alternative solution?

…..

Make a plan – when and with whom you will enjoy the alternative thing.

…..

…..

…..

Chapter 11
Become a Time Wizard

Tina was a perfectionist. Therefore, she procrastinated being involved in projects in her corporation and postponed asking the boss for promotion. It took her some time to learn how to manage time. Yet by doing the exercises which ware described in this chapter she has dramatically changed her life.

It also applies to your life. To be a happier person, you need to learn how to manage your time. This chapter will teach you:

- How to find more time for yourself.
- How to use the Pareto Principle for maximising your happiness.
- How to apply the first things first principle.
- Why people procrastinate.
- How to overcome procrastination.
- How to stop being a perfectionist.
- How to kill your inner critic.
- How to focus on a given task at hand.
- What are time management skills.

Reasons for Procrastination

There are nine reasons of procrastination. Usually, more than one is present in every case. Check why you might procrastinate.

1. Lack of motivation. It is a common reason for not tackling an unpleasant task. You might believe that something is wrong with you if you do not feel motivated to begin work. This simply is not true. Dr. Burns writes that the 'doing' comes first, then the motivation follows. Therefore, starting a task is the real motivator and motivation does need to be present before beginning the task.

2. Tedious tasks. Lack of interest is a crucial reason for procrastination. Who wants to do a tedious task? From time to time, all students lack interest in a course. However, not all of them delay in studying or completing assignments because of developed self-discipline.

3. Fear of success. This reason can be the other side of 'fear of failure'. You procrastinate because you are afraid of the consequences of your achievements. You may fear that if you do well, then next time, other people will expect more of you. Succeeding may also place you in the spotlight while you prefer the background. And you will face jealousy from your neighbours or family, especially when you become richer.

4. You don't know how to tackle the task. Skill deficits are one of the most fundamental reasons for procrastination. It is only natural to avoid doing the job if you lack skills. For example, English is not your first language. If you have several lengthy articles in English to read before you can write a blog post, you may postpone the reading because it is difficult. You may even have trouble admitting your poor language skills because you do not want to seem dumb. In this case procrastinating, may seem better than facing your need to improve your English.

5. Fear of failure. It is another reason people procrastinate. It goes something like this: It is worse if I try hard and fail than if I don't try and end up failing. For example, you may postpone writing a report for your boss and then pull an all-nighter. You can face the criticism from your boss, or even be threatened with losing your job, but you can say, "I could have done better if I had had more time to prepare the report." The pay-off for procrastinating is protecting yourself from the possibility of perceived 'real' failure. Until you do not commit 100% to your work, you will not find out what your actual capabilities are.

6. Perfectionism. The fear of failure is often underlined by perfectionism. In this case, life is an endless report card on accomplishments or looks, which is a fast track to unhappiness. When you learn how to deal with perfectionism, procrastination will not be your problem, and you will become a happier person.

7. Rebellion and resistance. You may rebel against imposed schedules, standards and expectations because the expectations are often those of a power struggle, usually not on a conscious level.

You can also rebel and procrastinate because of external evaluation. For example, if your boss has offended or angered you in some way, you may retaliate by turning something in late or procrastinating indefinitely – even if you risk losing your job.

8. Being overwhelmed. This feeling can stifle you. When there's just too much to do, you can freeze because there are so many urgent things to do, that it seems impossible to handle. So, you go off on a tangent and do something entirely different instead of getting on with the task.

9. You are tired and need a break. This is normal to procrastinate at certain times of the day. There are cycles of productivity; you can't work for eight hours straight flat-out. Otherwise, you would be exhausted. Therefore, you will find your mind starts to wander, or you'll get distracted when your body needs a break, let's say from concentrating intently. This happens after 90 minutes of focused activity, and then you need a short break. What you're doing here is giving yourself a break that you need. In this case, procrastination is normal and can be useful as a productivity tactic.

Now think of one task which you are currently procrastinating about. Think of the reasons why you are doing so and write them down. Choose two now, but if there are more, use your transformation diary.

1. ………………………………………………………………

2. ………………………………………………………………

How to Stop Procrastination

Now when you know why you procrastinate, the time has come to stop it. Here are some tools which you can use:

1. Use the 2-minute rule. This method overcomes procrastination and laziness by making it very easy to start taking action that you can't say no to. The idea was introduced by David Allen in his bestselling book, *Getting Things Done.* The 2-minute rule consists of two parts: "If it takes less than two minutes, then do it now." and "When you start a new habit, it should take less than two minutes to do."

It's surprising how many things you put off that you could get done in two minutes or less. For example, brushing your teeth, making your bed, sending an email. Therefore, if a task takes less than two minutes to complete, then follow the rule and do this task right now.

In the case of things that take up more time and you procrastinate about them, set the two-minute time span during which you will work on this task. For example, if you are learning a new language and delay using Super Memo to rehearse your vocabulary, set a timer for two minutes and repeat only ten words. You can even choose to repeat one word first. The idea is to start doing the task which is procrastinated.

In the case of habits, you can also use the 2-minute rule. For example, you can read your goals, do some exercises for 2 minutes daily. Check which of your habits that you are currently working on can be done within two minutes.

Now think which big task you could do, using the two-minute technique. Write it down.

…………………………………………………………………………………………

2. Break your work into little steps. You can procrastinate because subconsciously, you find the work too overwhelming. Break it down into small parts, then focus on one part at the time. In case you still procrastinate about the task after breaking it down, then break it down even further. The task will be so simple that you will be eager to do it.

Try this tool for your current challenge. Look at the goals you have set for the next week and the tasks which you have assigned to these aims. Choose the task which you procrastinate the most often. Write it down.

…………………………………………………………………………………………

Now think of the steps which you could take to make the task easier. List three of them.

1.   …………………………………………………………………………………

2.   …………………………………………………………………………………

3.   …………………………………………………………………………………

Start working on the first step immediately. You will notice that the task is so easy that it is worth it to continue doing it.

3. Create a detailed timeline with specific deadlines. When you have just one deadline for your work, it is like an invitation to procrastinate. You might get the impression of having plenty of time and therefore, keep pushing everything back until it's too late. However, when you break down your project, you can create an overall timeline with specific deadlines for each small task. Then you know you should finish each task by a certain date. For example, when you are learning a foreign language, you need to decide how many words you will hear within a week, month, quarter and then plan the deadlines for each of the four weeks of each month.

I do it when writing my articles. Every week I am supposed to write four articles, which gives sixteen per month and forty-eight within 90 days.

Now think of the goal you are supposed to achieve this year. Write it down:

……...

Then set the deadlines for your sub-goals for each week and the goal for the next month:

My monthly goal   **Deadline**

My sub-goal for week one

My sub-goal for week two

My sub-goal for week three   **Deadline**

My sub-goal for week four

4. Change your environment. Look at your work desk and your room. Do they make you want to work or rather tempt you to have a rest and procrastinate? If it's the latter, see how can you change your workspace. An environment that made you feel inspired before may become annoying and demotivate you after a period. If that's the case, modify the environment again.

Eliminate your procrastination pit-stops. Too much procrastination may happen because you make it too easy to procrastinate. For example, while surfing the Internet instead of working, identify your browser bookmarks to the time-consuming websites and shift them into a separate folder. Then it will be harder for you to use these sites, as we are usually lazy and don't like the extra work of opening an additional folder. Disable the automatic use of these bookmarks. Get rid of the distractions around you. For example, you can delete/deactivate your Facebook accounts. Also, uninstall computer games.

Think of the website which is time-consuming that you use while procrastination. Write down what you could do to make it harder to use this site.

....

This also works in the other way. How many times have you procrastinated about the task because you could not find the file or had to open ten folders before finding it? Then create desktop shortcuts or a folder which will be on your toolbar. It is also possible to have the toolbar at the top of your screen.

Now think about what you could do to make it easier to start to do your work. What could you change while using your computer or another device? Write it down.

....

5. Hang out with people who inspire you to take action. The people you are with influence your behaviours. Think of the five people you spend the most time. Do they motivate you to take action? If not, try to change the environment and the circle of friends. Join productivity groups. Soon you will absorb their drive and spirit too. Now make an action plan. First, write down the names of five people with whom you spend the most of the time.

1. ....

2. ....

3. ....

4. ....

5. ....

Now think what impact they have on your life. Which of them motivates you to be more productive (e.g. you go for training with this person) and who consumes your time (e.g. you are watching lots of TV with this person, you listen his/her victim talk). Write your conclusions down.

....

....

The next step is to define what measures you will take to find the people who will inspire you to be more productive or to end the relationship with those who consume your time unproductively.

....

....

6. Get a friend. Having a companion makes the whole process much more fun. Let's say that you have decided to run three times a week. If you do it with a friend, the chances are that you will be more committed to running regularly so as not to disappoint your friend. Ideally, your buddy could be someone who has similar goals to yours. Both of you will hold each other more committed to your goals and plans. Even if your friend does not have the same goals, you can learn from each other. Now decide what you could do together with your friend and write it down.

Activity: ....

Your friend's name: ....

7. Stop perfectionism. Do you always have to be perfect? No, you don't. Bill Gates releases new editions of Windows regularly, workable but which may contain mistakes. Then Microsoft updates the system. Every writer started with a pen and a piece of paper. Learn to create beta versions of your projects – you can always improve them. And remember, there will never be the perfect time to do something, you can even lose your opportunity waiting for too long. Now think of one thing that you might start doing, but procrastinate about because of perfectionism. Write it down and commit to start working on that thing immediately.

....

8. Tell others about your goals. When you publicly announce your goals, then you have no choice – you must achieve this aim. The pressure to keep your good reputation will motivate you to take action, because people will ask you about your status on those projects. It's a great way to keep yourself accountable to your plans. Now think of your goals for this year. Choose one of them and decide who you will announce it to.

My goal: …..

People I'll inform about my goal: ....

9. Find someone who has already achieved your goal. Then it will be easier for you to model their system and accomplish your aim. Seek them out and create the relationship; the business or the personal one. When you see living proof that your goals are achievable if you take action, it will trigger you to take that action. Now think of people who have already achieved your goal. Define this connection when you contact him/her.

…..

10. Re-clarify your goals. If you have been procrastinating for a length of the time, it might mean that your goals are misaligned with your values or your life path. For example, it happens that you may outgrow your goals discovering more about yourself. However, the goals stay the same. Go on holiday to refresh your mind and reflect on your life. Answer these questions in writing.

• Does your current work align with your goal?

• If not, what can you do about it?

• What exactly do you want to achieve?

• What should you do to get there?

• What are the steps to take?

11. Do the cost-benefits analysis. List all the things which you procrastinate. List five of them now.

1. …..

2. …..

3. …..

4. …..

5. …..

Then choose one task which the hardest to start. Make the cost-benefit analysis for one of it:

TASK

COSTS OF **DOING**
THE TASK

BENEFITS OF
DOING THE TASK

COSTS OF **NOT DOING**
THE TASK

BENEFITS OF **NOT**
DOING THE TASK

After having listed all the costs and benefits, mark each item from 1 to 10, where one means totally unimportant and 10 means critical. I am sure that the costs of not doing the task and benefits of doing it will motivate you to take action, in most cases. However, pay attention to the bottom right quarter of the table. These are your pay-offs which must be eliminated if you want to stop procrastination.

Use the leverage and associate these pay-offs with as much pain as possible. Define how you will suffer by NOT doing the task. Choose one, biggest pay-off now.

Pay-off: ……...

What pain I will experience NOT doing the task (list three items).

1.   …...

2.   …...

3.   …...

12. Analyse the underlying problem. You may procrastinate because of something that happened in your past; therefore, your beliefs and thoughts sabotage your productivity. In this case, read Chapter Four and Five again and start transforming your negative thoughts and beliefs. You may also need to reset your goals as they may not be SMART or have adverse consequences for the environment. For example, if you set the goal that requires more work and therefore, you will have less time for your spouse, the chances are that in the long run, your goal will have an adverse impact on your life (let's say that there will be more conflicts in your relationship).

13. Just do it. The hardest part is to start. Imagine that you need to wash up. It is always the hardest to take the first dish and remove it. The next ones are easier to handle. The same rule applies to any task you need to do. If you, therefore have applied the 2-minute rule and used other tips described in this chapter, I believe that starting any work may be easy for you.

Perfectionism

According to Wikipedia: "Perfectionism, in psychology, is a personality trait characterised by a person's striving for flawlessness and setting excessively high-performance standards, accompanied by overly critical self-evaluations and concerns regarding others' evaluations."

Check if you are the victim of perfectionism. Mark the following statements as true or false.

STATEMENT	TRUE	FALSE
You have a hard time opening up to other people.		
You take pleasure in someone else's failure, even though it has nothing to do with you.		
You know your drive to perfection is hurting you, but you consider it the price you pay for success.		
You get defensive when criticised.		
You are a big procrastinator.		
You are never quite 'there yet'.		
You are always eager to please.		
You know there's no use crying over spilled milk... but you do anyway.		
You are highly critical of others.		
You take everything personally.		

If you agree with more than three of the statements above, time has come to unlearn perfectionism. The next section of this book will help you.

How to Stop Being a Perfectionist?

1. Define a goal. This will enable you to set standards – the deadline, the measures and the level of progress you want to make. Setting these three things will set you free from perfectionism as you will not have to do the job ideally. Also, monitoring your progress will inspire you to work even more, as you will be encouraged by your achievements.

2. Define emergency goals. As I wrote in the chapter about goals, you need to set emergency ones. These are the goals with a lower standard, which will satisfy the minimum requirements applied to your goals. Read Chapter Nine once again to practice setting emergency goals.

3. Focus on what is needed. When you buy software, you focus on functionality, not a perfect design. The same applies to your goals. Think of your tasks, like creating a website or writing a blog post, or even cooking the dinner and answer this question, any time when you are tempted to be perfect:

What is needed, necessary for the customers, my family?

No, think of the task that you are avoiding doing. Answer the question above.

………..

4. Separate results from judgement. The result is always neutral, but you can interpret it in many ways. For some people a 3-course dinner served on the most modern crockery is perfect, while you might think about how healthy the meal is, even if served on traditional crockery and it is only a two-course meal. Strive for the results that are best for you, instead of being paralysed by the fear of others' judgement. Eat and exercise for health and fitness, not for simple weight targets.

5. Set a time limit. Some things are never really finished. Let's say that you are cleaning the floor; no matter how well you do it today, it will get just as muddy tomorrow when people forget to wipe their feet. Therefore, set a timer for a reasonable amount of time and clean for just that long instead of spending hours scrubbing. The place will still become cleaner, you will work faster and without obsessing over details. In the case of a longer or more detailed project, set a deadline, which can get you started and keep you moving instead of worrying over details.

6. Use the 80/20 principle. Pareto discovered that we spend only 20% of time or energy on the things which give us 80% of the outcome. Therefore, you must find the tasks which are more important, as they will bring you more benefits than others in any project to finish or goal to achieve. Look at the task or goal which you are supposed to pursue and decide what is crucial, giving you 80% of the outcome and start doing this task. As an exercise, take one of your weekly goals now and define what will bring you 80%.

………………………………………………………………………………………………

7. Forgive yourself for your shortcomings. Nobody is perfect – we are human. Remember that apart from deficiencies, you have strengths which you can always use to improve your performance. Think of your latest goal and list all the skills which may help you to achieve it even better than your have-to date. Choose three of them and write them down.

1.   ………………………………………………………………………………………

2.   ………………………………………………………………………………………

3. …...

8. Remember that there is no right way or right answer. If you are evaluated, it is always done subjectively. For example, you cannot possibly please everybody who reads your writing. Never forget to follow your individual preferences to be original, even if keeping an audience in mind can help give your work direction.

9. Learn from criticism. Even destructive criticism can teach you something. The next time you show your work there will be more people liking it, when you learn the lesson. Achieving acceptance is often only a step towards the desired results. Think of the last time you have been criticised. What could you learn from this criticism? Write it down.

…...

10. Create a training environment. You will be able to make mistakes there, sharpening your saw. Rehearse. Experiment. Practice. Do a survey before the real test. When writing, prepare a rough draft.

11. Get started. Even if you are not sure what you are doing, give it a try. Your first attempt may not get you anywhere, yet you may know what or who to ask to get going, and discover what not to do.

12. Try a new approach to the task. The method which you are using to work on your goals is not always the best. It might also not always work so you might have some false starts which might discourage you. The more unusual and newer an activity you undertake, the more you will have to learn by trial and error. Therefore, instead of blaming yourself for mistakes, try a new approach to work on your goal. Ask other people or learn about what you want to improve on. If you are stuck at any of your goals, think who you could ask for advice and what to improve. Write this information down.

....

....

13. Reflect on your failures. Failure is relative. Maybe your article had some semantic mistakes and the linguists have noticed them, but most of the readers have not noticed anything at all and what is even more, have given you some positive comments. You probably know more about what went in than other people. Remember that whoever benefited from your work, cares more about the result than the process.

14. Treat failure as an opportunity to be a better person. We often live with the feeling of "I am not good enough." However, there is no such thing as you are good at or excellent in something. Just listen to your heart's desire and do the job which you enjoy. You are 'enough' just as you are.

15. Reflect on your success. Think about something you have done or made which was successful. It may not have been perfect, but you have achieved an objective. Which of the successful methods that you have used, could you apply to your next projects? List them down below.

....

....

....

....

How to Cope with Your Inner Critic – More Tips

Self-criticism is very common in our society. Can you recognise the statements which are just blaming yourself – like "I'm stupid!", "I'm an idiot!", "I can't get anything right!", "I'm not good enough to..." Here are some tips which you can apply to overcome self-criticism.

1. Identify what your critical inner voice is saying. Be aware that this thought process is separate from your real point of view, and that your critical inner voice is not a reflection of reality. Instead, it is a viewpoint you adopted based on negative early life experiences and attitudes directed towards you, and then internalised as your point of view. When you make a mistake, you will probably notice your inner critic. Write down some of your critic voices. Pay attention to them while doing this task. Choose five critical statements.

1. ………………………………………………………………………………

2. ………………………………………………………………………………

3. ………………………………………………………………………………

4. ………………………………………………………………………………

5. ………………………………………………………………………………

2. Write the statements in the second person. For example: "You are an idiot.", "You are stupid." Then you see that these thoughts are an alien point of view and not true statements. Remember to notice how hostile this internal enemy can be. Take the examples of self-criticism which you have written above and change them into 'you' statements.

………………………………………………………………………………………

………………………………………………………………………………………

………………………………………………………………………………………

………………………………………………………………………………………

....

3. Question the self-critical statements. Make an effort to keep yourself in check when your inner critic gets into a shouting match with reason, and self-doubt begins to bubble over reality. Here is how you can question your critical statements.

- What's the worst thing that could happen?
- How likely is that to happen?
- Will this matter in five years' time?
- Is this situation as bad as I'm making it out to be?
- What is the evidence for that critical statement?
- What distortion is it (read the Chapter Four and Five for examples)?

Choose one of the critical statements which you have written down a minute ago and answer the questions listed above.

....
....
....
....
....

4. Write down the most realistic and compassionate evaluation of yourself. This time use the 'I' statements. Let's say that your critical statement is "You're such an idiot!", one of the empowering statements may be: "I may struggle at times, but I am smart and competent in many ways...." (you can mention when exactly). Now write down the empowering statements for your self-critical ones.

………...

………...

………...

………...

………...

5. Never act on the directives of your inner critic. Instead, manifest the empowering statements in your life. For example, in the case of "I might not be good at Maths, but I am excellent as a writer" – become a journalist, write a book or start a blog. Your critical inner voice may become louder, telling you not to take chances or stay in line. You will grow stronger by identifying, separating from and acting against this destructive thought process.

Time Management

According to Wikipedia: "**Time management** is the act or process of planning and exercising conscious control over the amount of time spent on specific activities, especially to increase effectiveness, efficiency or productivity."

What Are Time Management Skills?

The time management skills include:

The ability to focus on a given task. It is a critical skill at the times of high level distraction, like incoming emails, unexpected phone calls and social media.

The ability to prioritise. The Pareto rule and Stephen Covey's matrix will help you to define which task is the most important. You will read about these tools later in this chapter.

The ability to resign from doing things which are not important. Self-discipline is a huge part of time management. You can practice it by setting and monitoring the progress of your goals.

<u>The ability to say 'no' when necessary.</u> Assertiveness is the essential skill both in communication and in time management. Practice saying 'no' any time when you need to prioritise.

<u>The ability to plan and monitor the progress of these tasks.</u> You do it on a daily, weekly and monthly basis. You have already mastered this skill, by reading Chapter Nine and doing all the exercises described there.

How to Focus on the Task at Hand

1. Eliminate distractions. Reducing or eliminating distractions is the first step to become a focused person. Do you often use Facebook while working? If so, the time has come to cut it off. You can log out and change your password or block Facebook on your browser for the time you are working.

Eliminate as many auditory or visual distractions around you as possible. If you're on your computer, minimise the applications which you are not using now and turn off all other distractions, like email messengers. That's the first way to get focused. Clearing your workstation is also necessary.

It is proven that every single time you face a distraction, it can take you up to 21 minutes to regain your focus. Never waste your time. Eliminate, or at least reduce distractions, as much as possible. If you find a new task while working on something, write this work down and come back to it when your current job is finished. Plan the new task according to these rules:

I can do it immediately => do it

I can't do it immediately => plan it or delegate it (after completing the current task.)

Think of the most frequent distractions that you have during your work. List three below and decide how to tackle them.

1. …..
2. …...
3. …...

2. Train your focus skills. Being able to concentrate is like a muscle. The more you practice, the better you will be at focusing on the task at hand. Start with small steps, perhaps for 5 minutes, then increase the time to 10, then 20 minutes, until you reach 50 minutes. Then add 10 minute breaks and learn how to focus during the break. It is an excellent opportunity to create a new habit. Read Chapter Eight again and plan how you will work on improving your concentration skills.

3. Have a plan. If you do not have a plan, your mind is going to keep wandering around. Instead of focusing on the task, you start thinking about what to do and waste your precious time, energy and willpower. Without a plan, you choose one job which seems the most important one; you start doing it, without checking its priority. Then, something else pops into your mind, which appears to be more important. You don't finish the first task but you start another one.

On the contrary, if you have a plan your mindset changes; you know you are supposed to be doing this one thing. Always have a plan. At the end of each day write down what you need to do, when do you need to do it, what you need to achieve with it.

4. Do the first thing in the morning. You have the highest level of concentration in the morning, like your energy or your willpower. Therefore, put the work requiring focus as close to the morning as possible. For example, instead of checking your mailbox, write the report or prepare training.

Think what activities you could do in the morning. Look at your plan and decide what you will do first. Get up earlier so you will have an opportunity to do more in the morning.

5. Take Regular Breaks. You are living in a society where taking breaks and relaxation is not 'cool'. However, taking breaks renews your focus. Your energy follows a very predictable pattern every single day; it takes about 90 minutes to go down. And your concentration, your focus and your willpower plummet after this period if you don't take a break.

Work to the 50/10 pattern: 50-minutes of work and 10-minutes for a break. Concentrate your attention on the task at hand for 50-minutes, stick to the plan which you have made earlier. Then take a 10-minute break and focus on something else. You can get up and do some exercises, eat something or look outside. Follow it up with another 50-minutes of work, then take another 10-minute break.

How to Have More Time

We often complain that there is too little time available. But few people look at the quality of activities during their day, at work and home. To have more time, you don't need to work longer; you can work smarter.

1. Stop being a perfectionist. When you are a perfectionist, lots of time is wasted on tiny details or even doing the same job again, because you are not satisfied with the result. Perfectionists often procrastinate because of fears and being overwhelmed. Scientists confirm this theory. For example, Dr. Sherry found a robust correlation between increased perfectionism and decreased productivity.

2. Stop overworking and take breaks. Have you ever wondered where the 40-hour work week came from? In 1926, Henry Ford conducted experiments on the length of the working day and hours per day. He noticed that the workers were more productive when Ford decreased the daily hours from 10 to 8 and the working week from 6 to 5 days. Also, as I wrote above, even within the 8 hours of the working day, you need to have breaks to stay focused and motivated. Getting enough sleep to maintain a high level of productivity is also important. Being short of sleep drastically decreases your productivity and concentration.

3. Learn to be assertive and say 'no' more often. Instead of working harder, focus primarily on those efforts that produce most of the results and delegate or abandon the rest. Then you will have more time to concentrate on the most important tasks. Stop saying 'yes' to tasks that bring small or almost no result. In many cases, you have to say 'no' to so-called urgent telephone calls, to the jobs that suddenly appear but do not contribute to your goals, doing things for other people including for your family.

4. Stop doing everything yourself and delegate tasks. We are unable to be experts at everything. Hence, when you know that someone can do the task faster and better, don't hesitate to delegate it. Make your tasks measurable because if you cannot measure them, they are not manageable. Explain to the person who you delegate the task to: what is to be done, how it should be done, the reasons for doing this job in the first place.

5. Stop doing repetitive tasks and start automating it. Repetitive tasks use up much of your willpower and concentration. It is easy to lose focus when you do the same single works. You become less motivated than before.

Let's say that you are working on your computer. Some of the tasks are mundane and repetitive. Unfortunately, they are also often the most important. However, you can turn many of these annoying processes into one-click (or tap) affairs by using an application or system tools. For example, you can set automatic updates of the system or disk checking.

Categories of Tasks in Time Management

Dr. Stephen Covey, in his book *The 7 Habits of Highly Effective People*, proves that every activity can be put in one of the four quadrants, and this can be used for prioritising tasks. Each of them belongs to one of these categories: urgent and important, not urgent and important, urgent but not important, neither important nor urgent. Remember that if you want to be happier, then you need to feel comfortable with the amount of time you have. Moreover, avoiding stressful tasks will give you peace of mind. Here are some examples of tasks belonging to each of the four categories:

1. Important and Urgent. The first category contains the tasks which you must do or else you will face negative consequences. Usually, these are deadlines and emergency actions. This category involves lots of pressure and stress.

Examples:

- Medical emergencies
- Last minute changes
- Writing a report which is due today, although you have had a week to do so, you have procrastinated.

Write down the five things which you have to do urgently this week.

1. ....
2. ....
3. ....
4. ....
5. ....

2. Important and Not Urgent. It is the category of tasks where you should invest most of your time because it contains the tasks which are in direct alignment with your goals and things you want to achieve in the long run. Because these duties and things are not important, we often procrastinate about them. By doing so, they will jump into the first quadrant. Here are the examples of the tasks which are 'important, but not urgent':

- Writing a report immediately, not waiting until it is due.
- Learning for the exam one month in advance.
- Working on your business while you are holding your current job.
- Spending time with your friends and family.
- Doing exercises.
- Designing and implementing systems.

Remember that everyone's goals and dreams are different. What might be a Quadrant II task for me, might not be for you. Within a specified timeline, anything that benefits you in the long run and you are not under the pressure of urgency, belongs to Quadrant II.

Look at your goals for this year. Choose one goal and write down five activities which are not urgent, but beneficial for your goal in the long run.

My goal is…

…..

The tasks that are not important now, but are beneficial for the goal.

…..

…..

…..

....

....

3. Not Important and Urgent. All the tasks belonging to this category are urgent, and you may think that they are also important. However, the task is important only when it directly helps to achieve your goal or current project. In the case of this category of tasks, the criterion of importance does not work. Most of the tasks will not help you to grow.

The tasks of Quadrant III are also called distractions, as they seem urgent while they are not. For example, while writing a report you can suddenly receive a text message and answer it, before finishing your primary task. Here are the examples of tasks which are 'urgent, but not important':

- Reading emails which have just come.
- Helping your co-worker while you are doing your project and need focus.
- Checking Facebook updates.
- Checking your phone for text messages.

Now it is your turn. Write down your five tasks belonging to Quadrant III.

....

....

....

....

....

4. Not Important and Not Urgent. Avoid tasks belonging to this category much as you can if you want to increase your productivity. You don't want to deal with time wasters. The tasks belonging to the category 'not urgent and not important' will never help you to achieve your goals, but might give you lots of pleasure. When you identify tasks from this quadrant and eliminate them, you will notice how much more time you have for yourself. Examples of 'neither urgent nor important' are:

- Playing computer and video games.
- Watching too much TV.
- Following the news and political debates.
- Watching videos on YouTube, or another live stream online.
- Personal grooming.
- Reading junk books and magazines.

Choose your five-time wasters and write them down.

....
....
....
....
....

It does not mean that you should totally resign from the activities listed above, as we also need some fun after the long day or week of work. Limit the amount of time for them and let these activities be a reward for hard work on the 'important but not urgent tasks'. For example, you can watch TV for one hour after having worked for five hours (according to the 50/10 minute system).

Apply the First Things First Principle

Before you apply the First Things First Principle, check how much time you are spending now doing the tasks in each category. List all the activities – let's say 10, below. Then classify them to one of the four categories and write down the amount of time spend on these tasks.

TASK	CATEGORY	AMOUNT OF TIME (HOURS)

Now think for a while and answer the questions in writing using your transformation diary.

What one thing from Quadrant IV, could I eliminate or cut the time spent on this task next week?

What thing belonging to Quadrant II, can I add to the list of my activities, using the extra time?

....

....

My productivity goal for the next month is ....

....

In short, every day do your best to do the tasks belonging to the category 'not urgent but important' and if necessary 'both urgent and important'. However, pay attention to eliminating the jobs from the category 'urgent, but not important' and limit the amount of time spent on the last category (i.e. 'neither urgent nor important'). Every day use HabitBull or other application for monitoring your progress.

After one month, make the list of top ten activities during the day again and check if there is a difference in the time spent on the tasks belonging to each quadrant.

Using the matrix of four categories of tasks will increase your happiness as you will achieve more in life and avoid negativity often presented on TV, in magazines or on the Internet. You will be more satisfied with the achievement of your goals.

How to Use the Pareto Principle to Be Happier

According to Wikipedia: *"The Pareto Principle (also known as the 80–20 rule, the law of the vital few, the principle of factor sparsity) states that for many events, roughly 80% of the effects come from 20% of the causes."* The Italian economist Vilfredo Pareto showed that "approximately 80% of the land in Italy was owned by 20% of the population." (Wikipedia) This principle can be used for anything, even to learn how to be a happy person.

Choose one goal for this year. You have defined it in Chapter Nine.

…..

Look at your list of activities which you have made while implementing the four quadrants of Covey's matrix. List them again and mark which activity contributes 80% and which 20% to the achievement of your goals. Add the amount of time spent on a given activity.

ACTIVITY	TIME	IMPORTANCE	
	(HOURS)	80%	20%

Now look at your log. Answer these questions:

Which of the activities contribute the most to the achievement of my goal?

How could I manage my time better to focus on the activities which contribute 80% to my goal?

Does this goal make me happy? If not, how can I adjust it?

....

....

....

....

....

Now list five things (activities) that make you happy, regardless of your goals. Define their real value, such as: How much do they contribute to your happiness? To which quadrant do they belong? How much time do you spend on them?

ACTIVITY

**CONTRIBUTION
TO HAPPINESS (%)**

Examples: reading a book, going for a walk, doing exercise, dinner with my partner, listening to the music, meeting friends.

However, here are some activities which when done, will contribute 80% to your happiness:

- Listening to positive affirmations.
- Changing your language for an uplifting one.
- Transforming your beliefs by questioning the self-limiting ones.
- Thinking more positive thoughts.
- Asking better questions.
- Reading uplifting books.
- Writing down your achievements.
- Meditation.
- Yoga.

Some of them are like doing exercises, which means regular training is necessary for forming new habits. At first, you might not see the results, but within time your language, thinking and beliefs will change to being more positive and you will become a happier person. Think which of the activities contributing 80% to your happiness, you can add this to your daily routine. Write one activity now.

Decide how much time you are going to spend on this activity.

daily   .... hours/minutes

weekly   .... days per week

monthly   .... days per month

For example, listening to empowering affirmations daily for 40 minutes for at least 90 days, to form a new habit. On the other hand, you can go to yoga twice per week, also increasing your happiness level.

Conclusion

When you follow the guidelines in this book, you can efficiently and permanently become a happier person. Now you can take control over your beliefs, thoughts, language, behaviour and emotions, using them to your advantage.

The changing of your life will not happen overnight. However, if you use at least one technique described in this book and work on just one element of your life – for example your thoughts, beliefs, language or emotions, if you set compelling goals, improve your time management skills, face the challenges with courage and persistence, you will increase the level of your overall happiness.

Another important point: you do have choices. You are no longer a victim and no longer have to suffer in silence. If you are around toxic people, you can always choose to work on your reactions and attitude instead of trying to change them. If you are not happy with your job or your relationship make changes, starting from within yourself. If you are not happy with your achievements, learn new skills and find people who will help you to pursue your goals. The only thing you have to do is to take responsibility for your life, and particularly your happiness.

You can probably find many tools which I have not described here. You might question some of them. You are right. Self-help is similar to medicine and some techniques may be more efficient in your case, while others may not. However all the tools are tested, not only by me but by the people who have inspired me to share my experience with you.

Remember to read this book at least twice, and I strongly advise you to have your own copy, so that you can do the exercises at your own pace and in the order which is convenient for you. Good luck becoming a happier person. I am looking forward to sharing more tips with you in my next book or perhaps even meeting you at one of my workshops.

Victoria Herocten

About the Author

Victoria Herocten is the owner of websites in two languages. She has studied, researched and published for 14 years on the subject of Personal Development, helping many people to become happier and more fulfilled.

Her mission is to help people living in toxic relationships, coming from abusive families or dealing with a long-term illness to change their lives and start a new, happy life. Her mission can be described by the motto: **"I help you to live a happy and fulfilled life, despite your past and your personal limits."**

Victoria has written: ***The 23 Questions About Domestic Abuse and The Ultimate End of Domestic Abuse*** and produced some videos. She has cooperated with Donna Kozik, a famous coach in the field of writing books, to write ***The Gratitude Book*** which was a bestseller on Amazon. She is the member of Wexford Toastmasters, where she has delivered twelve speeches and is the member of the committee for the 2016/17 term.

If you want to find more about Victoria Herocten, go to her website: http://success-achiever.com.

To order your complimentary coaching session:
http://awakenhappiness365.com/coaching

Follow her on Twitter:
http://twitter.com/VickyHerocten

Join her community on Facebook:
https://www.facebook.com/say.no.to.emotional.abuse/

Connect on LinkedIn:
https://www.linkedin.com/in/victoria-herocten-24001235

Follow Victoria Herocten on Google Plus:
https://plus.google.com/107179131389200553970

Subscribe to her channel on YouTube:
https://www.youtube.com/channel/UCiAOx58qII_-OZ2_8DBDPnw

You can also send her an email to:
info@victoriaherocten.com

Appendices

Appendix 1: My Activities During the Last 2 Days

List the activities from the last three days and the reasons for doing them.

Activity   **Why I did it**

....

....

....

....

....

....

Appendix 2. My Values

© Copyright by Victoria Herocten

List your move-to and move-away-from values.

My Move-To Values   **My Move-Away-From Values**

List the values and number from the most to the least important one. Then, in the next table, define your values:

The moving towards values

Value   **Definition**

The moving-away-from values

Value   **Definition**

Transform the moving-away-from values to the happiness values. Then number them from the most to the least important one:

The moving-away-from value   **New happiness value**

Appendix 3. The Roles in My Life

© Copyright by Victoria Herocten

List all the roles that you act in your life

Family	Career	Others
....	....	....
....	....	....
....	....	....
....	....	....
....	....	....
....	....	....
....	....	....

Appendix 4 My Ideal Life, Day and Self

© Copyright by Victoria Herocten

Describe your ideal life, day and self.

My Ideal Life

....
....
....
....
....
....
....
....
....
....
....
....
....
....
....

My Ideal Day

....
....
....
....
....
....
....
....
....
....
....

....
....
....

My Ideal Self

....
....
....
....
....
....
....
....
....
....
....
....
....

Appendix 5. My Life 5 Years Ago, Today and in 5 Years' Time

© Copyright by Victoria Herocten

Describe your achievements in the life categories listed below and define how happy you are. (1 – totally unsatisfied and 10 – excellent)

5 Years ago

The Area of Life	Satisfaction 1-10	Comments
Physical health (weight, fitness)		
Mental health (mood, fears)		
Relationships (family, networks)		
Career (job/ business)		
Finance (living conditions, assets, salary/profit)		
Spiritual life		
Personal development (goals, thinking, beliefs)		

Fun

Today

The Area of Life	**Satisfaction 1-10**	**Comments**
Physical health (weight, fitness)		
Mental health (mood, fears)		
Relationships (family, networks)		
Career (job/ business)		
Finance (living conditions, assets, salary/profit)		
Spiritual life		
Personal development (goals, thinking, beliefs)		
Fun		

In five years' time

The Area of Life	**Satisfaction 1-10**	**Comments**
Physical health (weight, fitness)		
Mental health (mood, fears)		
Relationships (family, networks)		
Career (job/ business)		
Finance (living conditions, assets, salary/profit)		
Spiritual life		
Personal development (goals, thinking, beliefs)		
Fun		

Victoria Herocten

Appendix 6. My Major Goals in the Past, Today and in the Future

© Copyright by Victoria Herocten

MY GOALS 5 YEARS AGO	SATISFACTION 1-10	COMMENTS
Goal 1		
Goal 2		
Goal 3		
Goal 4		
Goal 5		

MY GOALS FOR THIS YEAR	SATISFACTION 1-10	COMMENTS
Goal 1		
Goal 2		
Goal 3		
Goal 4		
Goal 5		

MY GOALS IN 5 YEARS' TIME	SATISFACTION 1-10	COMMENTS
Goal 1		
Goal 2		
Goal 3		
Goal 4		
Goal 5		

Appendix 7: Examples of My Beliefs

Finish the beginning of each sentence, without long thinking. Each line means one answer.

I believe that ....
....
....
....
....

Love is ....
....
....
....
....

Life is ....
....
....
....
....

Money is ....
....
....
....
....

Awaken Mega Happiness

I feel happy when ....

....

....

....

....

I can   ....

....

....

....

....

I can't   ....

....

....

....

....

Appendix 8: Mental Contrast

Goal …..
…...

Benefit 1....................................	My vision of obtaining the benefit. How great it is. Describe.
Obstacle 1....................................	When does it exist? How can I overcome it?

Benefit 2..	My vision of obtaining the benefit. How great it is. Describe.
Obstacle 2..................................	When does it exist? How can I overcome it?

Appendix 9: Costs-Benefit Analysis of Goals

© Copyright by Victoria Herocten

List the costs and benefits of your goals. Then evaluate how important each item of costs and benefits where 1 – little importance and 5 – extremely important.

Goal 1 ....
....

Benefits for me: What will I gain achieving this goal?	My costs: What do I have to lose to achieve this goal?
Benefits for other people: What positive consequences will be for other people by achieving this goal?	Costs for other people: What negative consequences will be for other people by achieving this goal?
Score for benefits	Score for costs
Final decision	Yes/No

Goal 2 …………………………………………………………………………………
………………………………………………………………………………………………

Benefits for me: What will I gain achieving this goal?	My costs: What do I have to lose to achieve this goal?
Benefits for other people: What positive consequences will be for other people by achieving this goal?	Costs for other people: What negative consequences will be for other people by achieving this goal?
Score for benefits	Score for costs
Final decision	Yes/No

Appendix 10. Habits Log

© Copyright by Victoria Herocten

Print or photocopy this sheet and fill in regularly. If you need a longer time of working on your habits, print more copies.

My new habit

trigger …...

….................................

response (behaviour) …...

Phase of automation (highlight the current one). Read the chapter about habits again.

1	2	3	4

Monitoring start date: …......................

Write down the dates and mark your progress (performance) every day:

v – done successfully, x – fail, xv – partial success, 0 – the habit is not due to use

Date							
Performance							
Date							
Performance							
Date							
Performance							
Date							
Performance							
Date							
Performance							

Date							
Performance							
Date							
Performance							
Date							
Performance							
Date							
Performance							
Date							
Performance							
Date							
Performance							

Appendix 11. Addiction Test

Fill in the test.

Statement	True	Somewhat true	False
I cannot function without alcohol, drugs, benzodiazepines etc.			
I cannot stop taking the substance.			
I have withdrawal symptoms (e.g. insomnia, dizziness, seizures and delirium tremens).			
I give up some activities because of addiction.			
I buy the addictive substances in bulk to have enough supply of them even if I am short of money.			
I take the substances alone.			
I deny that I am addicted.			
I drop hobbies and activities in favour of taking the addictive substances, compulsory behaviour.			

Statement	True	Somewhat true	False
I lost control over the frequency and amount of taking a drug, drinking, doing something, spending money.			
I have problems with the law (theft, aggression etc.)			
I have problems with my relationships.			
I take too much risks after using some substances.			
I have to do some things many times, even if it is not necessary (checking if the doors are locked, wash my hands etc.).			

Calculate your score: true – 3 points, somewhat true – 1 point, false – 0 points.

0-7 points You are at low risk of being addicted. However, pay attention at the statements with which you agreed, even partially and talk to someone to prevent the development of addiction.

8-15 points You are at high risk of addiction. If you answered most of the questions 'somewhat true' and at least one as 'true,' chances are that you are unaware of your addiction. It is still not too late to start treatment and prevent from more serious adverse effects of your life.

16-26 points You are seriously addicted and totally lost control over your life. You need immediate help of professionals, like medical staff or a psychologist. The earlier you take action, the better for you.

Appendix 12: Time Management

© Copyright by Victoria Herocten

Fill in all the boxes listing your everyday activities:

	Urgent	Not Urgent
Important		
Not Important		

Appendix 13: Happiness Management – Applying the 80/20 principle

List all the activities done daily, how long they last and how much they contribute to your happiness.

Activity	Time (hours)	Importance	
		80.00%	20.00%

Appendix 14: My Identity Card

Fill in the identity card and print it.

My name's definition (e.g. in the dictionary, on the media, by religion)

....

....

Who I am, according to my own judgement?

....

....

....

....

....

....

....

....

....

....

....

Appendix 15: My Mission Statement

© Copyright by Victoria Herocten

Write down your mission statement.

....

....

....

....

....

....

....

....

....

....

....

....

....

....

Appendix 16: The Cognitive Log
© Copyright by Victoria Herocten

Fill in the cognitive log

Situation	Automatic thoughts	Twisted thinking types	Consequences	New alternative thoughts	New behaviour. Risk of the Day

Appendix 17: The Cost-Benefit of Beliefs Analysis

© Copyright by Victoria Herocten

Fill in the table below.

My negative belief is...

Costs of holding this belief	Benefits of holding this belief (pay-offs)
Score	
Benefits of changing this belief	Costa of changing this belief
Score	

Appendix 18: The Declaration of Commitment ©

Copyright by Victoria Herocten

I (your name) _____, declare here that I am making the decision to commit to creating a happy and fulfilled life.

I commit to: change my negative thoughts, beliefs and language into happiness ones and to manage my emotions wisely.

I also commit to create happiness habits and become a productive person.

I declare that I will set my goals and evaluate their progress regularly.

I commit to working on my goals 100%.

I also commit to eliminating all excuses on the way to working on my fulfilment in life.

_____   _____

Place of residence   Date

(Town/city)

_____

Signature

References

Robbins, Anthony, Awaken the Giant Within, Simon and Husters Paperbooks, 1992

Tracy, Brian, Maximum Achievement, Simon and Husters Paperbacks, 1993

Hill, Napoleon, Think and Grow Rich, Hawthworn Books Inc, 1968

Jeffers, Susan, Feel the Fear and Beyond, Brandom House, 2000

Branden, Nathaniel, The Six Pillars of High Self-Esteem, Bantan Books, 1995

Burns, David MD, Feeling Good Handbook, Plume 1989

McKay Mathew, Fanning Partick, Self-Esteem, Raincoast Books, 2000

Allen David, Getting Things Done, Piatkus, 2015

72327516R10224

Made in the USA
Columbia, SC
16 June 2017